the Biosphere

the Biosphere

W. H. FREEMAN AND COMPANY
San Francisco

The eleven chapters in this book originally appeared
as articles in the September 1970 issue of *Scientific
American*. Each is available as a separate Offprint
(Numbers 1188–1198) from W. H. Freeman and
Company, 660 Market Street, San Francisco,
California 94104.

Library of Congress Catalogue Card Number:
78–140849

Standard Book Number: 0-7167-0946-5 (cloth)
0-7167-0945-7 (paper)

Printed in the United States of America

9 8 7 6 5 4 3 2 1

Contents

Foreword

Photographs of the earth show that it has a green-blue color. The planet acquired this pleasant distinction, it appears, after turning in the sunlight for about three billion years. Solar energy, arriving at its surface at the rate of two calories per square centimeter per minute, ignited the processes of life in the primordial waters. The earth, in consequence, soon became endowed with an atmosphere of approximately its present composition. For about a billion and a half years the mixtures and compounds of the principal constituents of the air and water—the light elements carbon, hydrogen, oxygen and nitrogen—have been maintained in steady state by cyclic passage through the tissues of plants, the animals that eat them, and the decomposers of both. The biosphere—this thin film of air and water and soil and life no deeper than ten miles, or one four-hundredth of the earth's radius—is now the setting of the uncertain history of man.

The biosphere provides the context and perspective for consideration, in this book, of the questions that are clustered in public discussion in the United States today under the horizon-sweeping title of "Environment." The very word has become a term of reproach, and a millenial anxiety pervades the discussion. The classical Malthusian equation (in which production increases arithmetically in the numerator and human reproduction increases geometrically in the denominator) shows once again that population growth must outrun the means of subsistence. The same logic argues that industrial technology only hastens the despoliation of the earth's finite resources and makes survival meanwhile a dubious privilege.

It is not enough to note the irony in the fact that such despair is characteristically to be found among the most fortunate members of the few national populations for whom the iron law of scarcity has been annulled. The mood requires examination from a bigger set of premises supplied by enlargement of the context. Man must learn to see himself in his true place and proportion in the biosphere.

The rate and scale of the life-mediated processes in the earth's outer green-blue depth of air and water continue to dwarf human appetite and capacity. The great cycles go on turning unperturbed. While increase in production now proceeds geometrically—and at arbitrary multiples of population growth—in industrial societies, the despoliation of resources remains local and as yet not irreparable. Heedless use of technology has so far created no problems that wise use cannot resolve. On the other hand, the worldwide, accelerating spread of industrial civilization requires the coordinate spread of a world view that embraces the needs and rights of every man in the common destiny of mankind and within the finite dimensions of the planet. If the outcry against pollution, still largely aesthetic, among the well-off peoples of the world promotes such longer-range, considerate and conserving attitudes, it will serve a constructive purpose.

A reordering of values is already evident in the United States and other industrial societies. The spread of material well-being is accompanied by a trend toward stabilization of populations. In the transaction between buyer and seller that starts up new technologies, the public is finding representation as a third party. The pollution of air and water and land is tolerated less and less as an external diseconomy of "progress." Responding to pressures and inducements of the market and of politics, industries are internalizing these diseconomies with all the goodwill their public relations departments can muster. This is no time for the young or the old to despair that the rational process and the technologies it fosters will fail to serve human purpose more rationally chosen and defined.

The chapters in this book were first published as articles in the September, 1970, issue of *Scientific American*. This was the twenty-first in the series of single-topic issues published annually by the magazine. The editors herewith express appreciation to their colleagues at W. H. Freeman and Company, the book-publishing affiliate of *Scientific American,* for the enterprise that has made the contents of this issue so speedily available in book form.

THE EDITORS°

September, 1970

°BOARD OF EDITORS: Gerard Piel (Publisher), Dennis Flanagan (Editor), Francis Bello (Associate Editor), Philip Morrison (Book Editor), Jonathan B. Piel, John Purcell, James T. Rogers, Armand Schwab, Jr., C. L. Stong, Joseph Wisnovsky.

I

The Biosphere

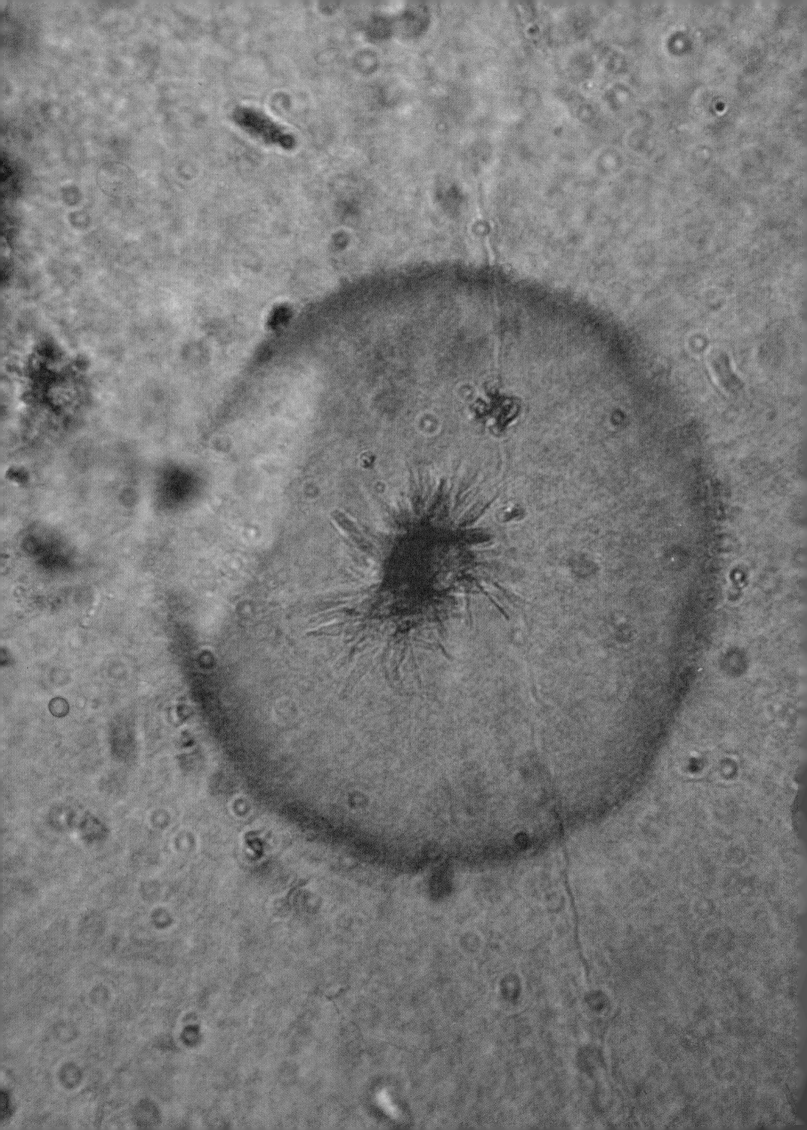

The Biosphere

by G. EVELYN HUTCHINSON

The earth's thin film of living matter is sustained by grand-scale cycles of energy and chemical elements. All of these cycles are presently affected by the activities of man

The idea of the biosphere was introduced into science rather casually almost a century ago by the Austrian geologist Eduard Suess, who first used the term in a discussion of the various envelopes of the earth in the last and most general chapter of a short book on the genesis of the Alps published in 1875. The concept played little part in scientific thought, however, until the publication, first in Russian in 1926 and later in French in 1929 (under the title *La Biosphère*), of two lectures by the Russian mineralogist Vladimir Ivanovitch Vernadsky. It is essentially Vernadsky's concept of the biosphere, developed about 50 years after Suess wrote, that we accept today. Vernadsky considered that the idea ultimately was derived from the French naturalist Jean Baptiste Lamarck, whose geochemistry, although archaically expressed, was often quite penetrating.

The biosphere is defined as that part of the earth in which life exists, but this definition immediately raises some problems and demands some qualifications. At considerable altitudes above the earth's surface the spores of bacteria and fungi can be obtained by passing air through filters. In general, however, such "aeroplankton" do not appear to be engaged in active metabolism. Even on the surface of the earth there are areas too dry, too cold or too hot to support metabolizing organisms (except technically equipped human explorers), but in such places also spores are commonly found. Thus as a terrestrial envelope the biosphere obviously has a somewhat irregular shape, inasmuch as it is surrounded by an indefinite "parabiospheric" region in which some dormant forms of life are present. Today, of course, life can exist in a space capsule or a space suit far outside the natural biosphere. Such artificial environments may best be regarded as small volumes of the biosphere nipped off and projected temporarily into space.

What is it that is so special about the biosphere as a terrestrial envelope? The answer seems to have three parts. First, it is a region in which liquid water can exist in substantial quantities. Second, it receives an ample supply of energy from an external source, ultimately from the sun. And third, within it there are interfaces between the liquid, the solid and the gaseous states of matter. All three of these apparent conditions for the existence of a biosphere need more detailed study and discussion.

All actively metabolizing organisms consist largely of elaborate systems of organic macromolecules dispersed in an aqueous medium. The adaptability of organisms is so great that even in some deserts or in the peripheral parts of the antarctic ice sheet there may be living beings that contain within themselves the only liquid water in the immediate neighborhood. Although such xerophytic (literally "dry plant") organisms may be able to conserve internal supplies of water for a long time, however, they still need some occasional dew or rain. (The hottest deserts appear to be formally outside the biosphere, although they may be parabiospheric in the sense explained above.) In the immediate past this kind of situation had a certain intellectual interest, since it seemed for a time that organisms might exist on Mars, in an almost waterless environment, by retaining water in their tissues. The most recent studies, however, seem to make any kind of biosphere on Mars quite unlikely.

The energy source on which all terrestrial life depends is the sun. At present the energy of solar radiation can enter the biological cycle only through the photosynthetic production of organic matter by chlorophyll-bearing orga-

REVOLUTION IN THE BIOSPHERE is symbolized by the fossilized blue-green alga in the photomicrograph on the opposite page. The cell, which is one of a variety of similar fossils found in the Gunflint geological formation in southern Ontario by Stanley A. Tyler and Elso S. Barghoorn of Harvard University, is estimated to be approximately two billion years old. The Gunflint algae are the oldest known photosynthetic and nitrogen-fixing organisms. As such they contributed to the original oxygenation of the earth's atmosphere and so prepared the way for all higher forms of plant and animal life in the biosphere.

YEARS BEFORE PRESENT	EVENT	GEOLOGICAL FORMATION	FOSSIL
0	OLDEST HOMINID	SIWALIK HILLS (INDIA)	RAMAPITHECUS
	OLDEST LAND PLANT	LUDLOVIAN SERIES, UPPER SILURIAN (BRITAIN)	COOKSONIA
	OLDEST METAZOAN ANIMAL	EDIACARA HILLS (AUSTRALIA)	SPRIGGINA
1 BILLION			
	OLDEST EUCARYOTIC CELLS	UPPER BECK SPRING DOLOMITE (CALIFORNIA)	UNNAMED
	FORMATION OF OXIDIZING ATMOSPHERE		
2 BILLION	OLDEST PHOTOSYNTHETIC AND NITROGEN-FIXING ORGANISM	GUNFLINT FORMATION (ONTARIO)	GUNFLINTIA
3 BILLION	OLDEST KNOWN ORGANISM	FIGTREE FORMATION (SOUTH AFRICA)	EOBACTERIUM
	FIRST ROCKS IN EARTH'S CRUST; FORMATION OF OCEAN		
4 BILLION	DIFFERENTIATION OF EARTH'S CRUST, MANTLE AND CORE; CRUST MELTED BY RADIOACTIVE HEATING		
4.5 BILLION	FORMATION OF EARTH		

ROUGH CHRONOLOGY OF THE BIOSPHERE as represented in the fossil record is given on this page, along with the geological formations in which the fossils were found and some other major events in the history of the earth. Data are from various sources.

nisms, namely green and purple bacteria, blue-green algae, phytoplankton and the vast population of higher plants. Such organisms are of course confined to the part of the biosphere that receives solar radiation by day. That includes the atmosphere, the surface of the land, the top few millimeters of soil and the upper waters of oceans, lakes and rivers. The euphotic, or illuminated, zone may be only a few centimeters deep in a very turbid river, or well over 100 meters deep in the clearest parts of the ocean. The biosphere does not end where the light gives out; gravity continues the energy flow downward, since fecal pellets, cast skins and organisms dead and alive are always falling from the illuminated regions into the depths.

The plant life of the open ocean, on which most of the animals of the sea depend for food, is planktonic, or drifting, in a special sense that is often misunderstood. Most of the cells composing a planktonic association are slightly denser than seawater, and under absolutely quiet conditions they would slowly sink to the bottom. That the upper layers are not depleted of plant cells and so of the capacity to generate food and oxygen is attributable entirely to turbulence. The plant cells sink at a speed determined by their size, shape and excess density; as they sink they divide and the population in the upper waters is continually replenished from below by turbulent upwelling water.

The sinking of the phytoplankton cells is in itself the simplest way by which a cell can move from a small parcel of water it has depleted of the available nutrients into a parcel still containing these substances. The mechanism can of course only operate when there is an adequate chance of a lift back to the surface for the cell and some of its descendants. The cellular properties that determine sinking rates, interacting with turbulence, are doubtless as important in the purely liquid part of the biosphere as skeletal and muscular structures, interacting with gravity, are to us as we walk about on the solid-gaseous interface we inhabit. Although this point of view was worked out some 20 years ago, largely through the efforts of the oceanographer Gordon A. Riley, it still seems hardly recognized by many biologists.

In addition to the extension of the biosphere downward, there is a more limited extension upward. On very high mountains the limit above which chlorophyll-bearing plants cannot live appears to be about 6,200 meters (in the Himalayas); it is partly set by a lack of liquid water, but a low carbon dioxide pressure, less than half the pressure at sea level, may also be involved. At still higher altitudes a few animals such as spiders may be found. These probably feed on springtails and perhaps mites that in turn subsist on pollen grains and other organic particles, blown up into what the high-altitude ecologist Lawrence W. Swan calls the aeolian zone.

The rather special circumstances that have just been recognized as needed for the life of simple organisms in the free liquid part of the biosphere emphasize how much easier it is to live at an interface, preferably when one side of the interface is solid, although quite a lot of microorganisms do well at the air-water interface in quiet pools and swamps. It is quite possible, as J. D. Bernal suggested many years ago, that the surface properties of solid materials in contact with water were of great importance in the origin and early development of life.

Studies of photosynthetic productivity show that often the plants that can produce the greatest organic yield under conditions of natural illumination are those that make the best of all three possible states, with their roots in sediments under water and their leaves in the air. Sugarcane and the ubiquitous reed *Phragmites communis* provide striking examples. The substances needed by such plants are (1) water, which is taken up by the roots but is maintained at a fairly constant pressure by the liquid layer over the sediments; (2) carbon dioxide, which is most easily taken up from the gaseous phase where the diffusion rate at the absorptive surface is maximal; (3) oxygen (by night), which is also more easily obtained from the air than from the water, and (4) a great number of other elements, which are most likely to be available in solution in the pore water of the sediment.

The present energetics of the biosphere depend on the photosynthetic reduction of carbon dioxide to form organic compounds and molecular oxygen. It is well known, however, that this process is only one of several of the form: $nCO_2 + 2nH_2A + \text{energy} \rightarrow (CH_2O)_n + nA_2 + nH_2O$. In this reaction the hydrogen donor H_2A may be hydrogen sulfide (H_2S), as in the case of the photosynthetic sulfur bacteria, water (H_2O), as in the case of the blue-green algae and higher green plants, or various other organic compounds, as in the case of the nonsulfur purple bacteria. (The last-mentioned case presents a paradox: Why be photosynthetic when there is plenty of metabolizable organic matter in the immediate neighborhood of the photosynthesizing cell?) The actual patterns of the possible reactions are extremely complicated, with several alternative routes in some parts of the process. For the purposes of this discussion, however, the important fact is probably that any set of coupled reactions so complex would take a good deal of mutation and selection to evolve.

The overall geochemical result of photosynthesis is to produce a more oxidized part of the biosphere, namely the atmosphere and most of the free water in which oxygen is dissolved, and a more reduced part, namely the bodies of organisms and their organic decomposition products in litter, soils and aquatic sediments. Some sediments become buried, producing dispersed organic carbon and fossil fuels, and there is a similar loss of oxygen by the oxidation of eroding primary rock. The quantitative relation of the fossilization of the organic (or reduced) carbon and the inorganic (or oxidized) carbon clearly bears on the history of the earth but so far involves too many uncertainties to produce unambiguous answers. From the standpoint of the day-to-day running of the biosphere what is important is the continual oxidation of the reduced part, living or dead, by atmospheric oxygen to produce carbon dioxide (which can be employed again in photosynthesis) and a certain amount of energy (which can be used for physical activity, growth and reproduction). The production of utilizable fossil fuels is essentially an accidental imperfection in this overall reversible cycle, one on which we have come to depend too confidently.

It is necessary to maintain a balance in our attitude by stressing the fragility and inefficiency of the entire process. If one considers a fairly productive lake, for example, it is usual to find about 2.5 milligrams of particulate organic matter under an average square centimeter of lake surface. Assuming that this organic matter is all phytoplankton, with a water content of 90 percent, there are about 25 cubic millimeters of photosynthetic organisms per 100 square millimeters of lake surface. If this were all brought to the surface, it would form a green film a quarter of a millimeter thick. Both assumptions undoubtedly exaggerate the thickness, which may well be no more than a tenth of a millimeter, or the thickness of a sheet of paper.

The total photosynthetic material of the open ocean can hardly be greater and

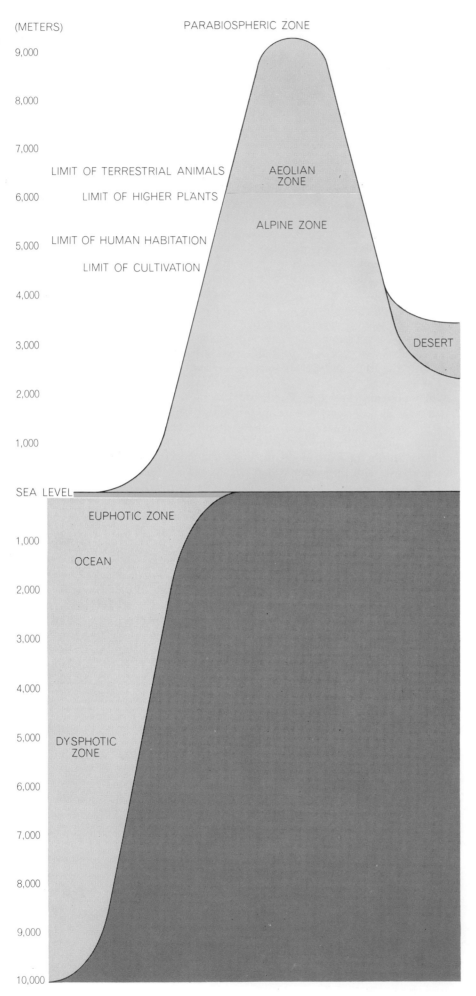

(METERS)

9,000

8,000

7,000

6,000

5,000

4,000

3,000

2,000

1,000

PARABIOSPHERIC ZONE

AEOLIAN ZONE

LIMIT OF TERRESTRIAL ANIMALS

LIMIT OF HIGHER PLANTS

ALPINE ZONE

LIMIT OF HUMAN HABITATION

LIMIT OF CULTIVATION

DESERT

SEA LEVEL

EUPHOTIC ZONE

OCEAN

1,000

2,000

3,000

4,000

5,000

DYSPHOTIC ZONE

6,000

7,000

8,000

9,000

10,000

may well be much less. Similarly, when one looks up from the floor of a broad-leaved forest, there is obviously some overlap of leaves, but five leaves, one above the other, would usually remove almost all the available energy. Moreover, in this case much of the organic material is in the form of skeletal cellulose, which provides support and control of evaporation; as a result there is an even less economical use of the volume of the plant than in the case of the phytoplankton. The machinery by which energy enters the living world is clearly quite tenuous.

Estimates of the efficiency of the photosynthetic process are quite variable and depend greatly on the circumstances. Under conditions of optimum cultivation an annual utilization of several percent of the incoming visible radiation is easily achieved on land, the limit probably being set by the carbon dioxide content of the air, but the overall efficiency of land surfaces as a whole seems to lie between .1 and .3 percent. In water, under special circumstances aimed at maximum yield, very high levels of production, apparently approaching the theoretical quantum efficiency of the photosynthetic process, seem possible, but again in nature as a whole efficiencies of the order of a few tenths of a percent are usual. On land much of the radiant energy falling on a tall plant is not wasted but is needed to maintain the stream of water being transpired from the leaves.

The movement of material through living organisms involves many more elements than those contained in water and carbon dioxide. In addition to carbon, oxygen and hydrogen, all organisms use nitrogen, phosphorus, sulfur, sodium, potassium, calcium, magnesium, iron, manganese, cobalt, copper, zinc and probably chlorine, and some certainly use for special functions aluminum, boron, bromine, iodine, selenium, chromium, molybdenum, vanadium, silicon,

VERTICAL EXTENT of the biosphere is depicted schematically in the illustration at the left. As a terrestrial envelope the biosphere has a somewhat irregular shape inasmuch as it is surrounded by an indefinite "parabiospheric" region in which some dormant forms of life, such as the spores of bacteria and fungi, are present. The euphotic, or illuminated, zone of aqueous bodies may be only a few centimeters deep in a very turbid river or well over 100 meters deep in the clearest parts of the ocean.

strontium, barium and possibly nickel. A few elements that occur fairly regularly in specific compounds or situations, such as cadmium in the vertebrate kidney or rare earths in the hickory leaf, are obviously of interest even if they are not functional. Some of the elements now known to be significant only in a particular group of organisms, such as boron in plants, iodine in many animals, chromium in verebrates or selenium in some plants, birds and mammals, may ultimately prove to be universally essential. A few more functional elements, germanium perhaps being a good candidate, may remain to be discovered. Even the rarer trace elements, when they are unquestionably functional, are present in metabolically versatile tissues, such as those of the liver, in quantities on the order of a million atoms per cell. Very little substitution of one element by another is possible, although some bacteria and algae can use rubidium in place of potassium with no adverse effects other than a slowed growth rate. We all know that certain elements are highly toxic (lead, arsenic and mercury are obvious examples), whereas many of the functional elements are poisonous when high levels of intake are induced by local concentrations in the environment. This means that the detailed geochemistry of each element, particularly in the process of crossing the solid-liquid interface, is of enormous biological importance.

Often the possibility of an element's migrating from the solid state to an ionic form in an aqueous phase (from which an organism can obtain a supply of the element) depends on the state of oxidation at the solid-liquid boundary. Under reducing conditions iron and manganese are freely mobile as divalent (doubly ionized) ions, whereas under oxidizing conditions iron, except when it is complexed organically, is essentially insoluble, and manganese usually precipitates as manganese dioxide. Chromium, selenium and vanadium, all of which are required in minute quantities by some organisms, migrate most easily in an oxidized state as chromate, selenate and vanadate, and so behave in a way opposite from iron. The extreme insolubility of the sulfides of iron, copper, zinc and some other heavy metals may limit the availability of these elements when reduction is great enough to allow hydrogen sulfide to be formed in the decomposition of proteins or by other kinds of bacterial action. Phenomena of this kind mean that under different chemical conditions different materials determine how much living matter can be present.

Expanding this 19th-century agriculturist's idea of limiting factors a little, it is evident that in a terrestrial desert hydrogen and oxygen in the form of water determine the amount of life. In the blue waters of the open ocean the best results indicate that a deficiency of iron is usually limiting, the element probably being present only as dispersed ferric hydroxide, which can be used by phytoplankton cells if it becomes attached to their cell wall. In an intermediate situation, as in a natural terrestrial soil in a fairly humid region, or in a lake or coastal sea, phosphorus is probably the most usual limiting element.

The significance of phosphorus in controlling the quantity of living organisms in nature is due not only to its great biological importance but also to the fact that among the light elements it is relatively scarce. As an element of odd atomic number it is almost two orders of magnitude rarer in the universe than its neighbors in the periodic table, silicon and sulfur. Moreover, in iron meteorites

LIFE AT THE FRINGE of the biosphere is represented by this strange-looking creature photographed recently by an automatic camera lowered to a depth of 15,900 feet from the U.S. Naval oceanographic vessel *Kane,* which at the time was situated in the South Atlantic some 350 miles off the coast of Africa. The plantlike organism is actually an animal: a polyp of the family Umbellulidae. The stem on which its food-gathering tentacles are mounted is approximately three feet long and is leaning toward the camera at an angle of 30 degrees.

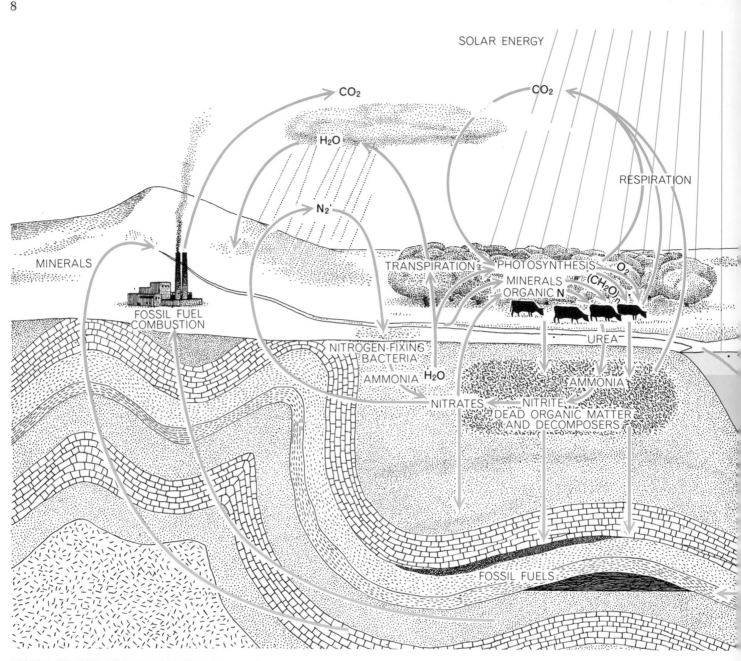

SOLAR ENERGY

CO_2

CO_2

H_2O

RESPIRATION

N_2

MINERALS

TRANSPIRATION · PHOTOSYNTHESIS · O_2

MINERALS
ORGANIC **N** · $(CH_2O)_n$

FOSSIL FUEL
COMBUSTION

UREA

NITROGEN-FIXING
BACTERIA

AMMONIA · H_2O

AMMONIA

NITRATES · NITRITE

DEAD ORGANIC MATTER
AND DECOMPOSERS

FOSSIL FUELS

MAJOR CYCLES OF THE BIOSPHERE are indicated in a general way in the illustration on these two pages; more detailed versions of specific cycles accompany the succeeding articles in this issue. In brief, the operation of the biosphere depends on the utili-

phosphorus is found to be enriched in the form of the iron-nickel phosphide schreibersite, so that it is not unlikely that a good part of the earth's initial supply of the element is locked up in the metallic core of our planet. The amount of phosphorus available is thus initially limited by cosmogenic and planetogenic processes. In the biosphere the element is freely mobile under reducing but not too alkaline conditions; since the supply of reduced iron is nearly always much in excess of the phosphorus, oxidation precipitates not only the iron but also the phosphorus as the very insoluble ferric phosphate.

In many richly productive localities where phosphorus is reasonably accessible the quantity of combined nitrogen evidently builds up by biological fixa-

tion, so that the ratio of the two elements in water or soil will tend to be about the same as it is in living organisms. In such circumstances both the phosphorus and the nitrogen are limiting; the addition of either one alone produces little or no increase in living matter in a bottle of water or in any other system isolated from the environment, whereas the addition of both often leads to a great increase. Where nitrogen alone is limiting it may be the result of a disturbance of the ecological balance between the nitrogen-fixing organisms (mainly blue-green algae in water and bacteria in soil) and the other members of the biological association. Limitation by nitrogen is never due to a dearth of the element as such, since it is the commonest gas in the atmosphere, but rather

depends on the level of activity of the special biological mechanisms, chemically related to photosynthesis but retained only by primitive organisms, for dissociating the two atoms of molecular nitrogen (N_2) and forming from them the amino ($-NH_2$) groups of proteins and other organic compounds.

If the biosphere is to continue in running order, the biologically important materials must undergo cyclical changes so that after utilization they are put back, at the expense of some solar energy, into a form in which they can be reused. The rate at which this happens is quite variable. The rate of circulation of the organic matter of terrestrial organisms, derived from the carbon dioxide of the atmosphere, is measured in decades. In

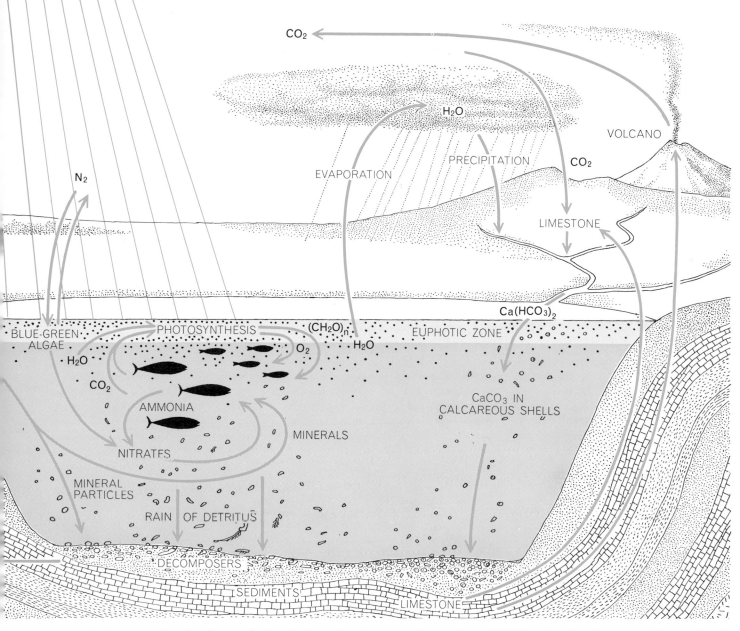

CO₂

H₂O

VOLCANO

EVAPORATION   PRECIPITATION   CO₂

N₂

LIMESTONE

Ca(HCO₃)₂

BLUE-GREEN
ALGAE · · PHOTOSYNTHESIS · · · (CH₂O)ₙ · · EUPHOTIC ZONE
· H₂O · · · · O₂ · H₂O

· CO₂

AMMONIA

CaCO₃ IN
CALCAREOUS SHELLS

NITRATES   MINERALS

MINERAL
PARTICLES

RAIN OF DETRITUS

DECOMPOSERS

SEDIMENTS

LIMESTONE

zation of solar energy for the photosynthetic reduction of carbon dioxide (CO₂) from the atmosphere to form organic compounds on the one hand (CH₂O)ₙ and molecular oxygen (O₂) on the other. The cycling of certain other vital elements is also indicated.

the case of calcium, which is carried from continental rocks in rivers as calcium bicarbonate (Ca(HCO₃)₂) and precipitated as calcium carbonate (CaCO₃) in the open ocean largely in the form of the tiny shells of foraminifera, most of the replacement must be due to the movement of the ocean floors toward coastal mountain-building belts; presumably the rate of cyclical replacement would be measured in hundreds of millions of years. Phosphorus would behave rather like calcium, nitrogen more like carbon, although the atmospheric reservoir of nitrogen is of course much larger and the biological fixation of the element is less widespread and energetically more expensive.

At present the artificial injection of some elements in a mobile form into

the ocean and atmosphere is occurring much faster than it did in preindustrial days; new cycles have come into being that may distribute very widely and in toxic quantities elements such as lead and mercury, as well as fairly stable new compounds such as insecticides and defoliants. It should be obvious that the possible action of all such substances on the tenuous and geochemically inefficient green mantle of the earth demands intense study if life is to continue in the biosphere.

How did the system we have been examining come into being? There are now a few facts that seem clear and a few inferences that are reasonable. We know that the present supply of atmospheric oxygen is continually replenished

by photosynthesis, and that if it were not, it would slowly be used up in the process of oxidation of ferrous to ferric iron and sulfides to sulfates in weathering. All the evidence points to the atmosphere of the earth's being secondary. The extreme rarity of the cosmically abundant but chemically inert gas neon compared with water vapor, which has almost the same molecular weight, shows (as Harrison Brown pointed out 25 years ago) that only gases that could be held in combination in the solid earth were available for the formation of the secondary atmosphere. The slow production of oxygen by the photolysis (literally "splitting by light") of water and by the thermal dissociation of water with the loss of hydrogen into space is possible even in the early atmosphere, but nearly everyone agrees that this would merely lead to a little local oxidation of material at or near the earth's crust.

Some mixture of water vapor, methane, carbon monoxide, carbon dioxide, ammonia and nitrogen presumably initiated the secondary atmosphere. We know from laboratory experiments that when an adequate energy source (such as ultraviolet light or an electric discharge) is available, many organic compounds, including practically all the building blocks of biological macromolecules, can be formed in such an atmosphere. We also know from studies of meteorites that such syntheses have occurred under extraterrestrial conditions, but that a good many substances not of biological significance were also formed. It is just possible that ultimately exploration of the asteroids may produce evidence of the kind of environment on a disrupted planet in which these kinds of prebiological organic syntheses took place.

However that may be, we can be reasonably confident that a great deal of prebiological organic synthesis occurred on the earth under reducing conditions at an early stage in our planet's history. The most reasonable energy source

would be solar ultraviolet radiation. Since some of the most important compounds are not only produced but also destroyed by the wavelengths available in the absence of an oxygen screen, it is probable that the processes leading to production of the first living matter took place under specific structural conditions. Syntheses may have occurred in the water vapor and gases above a primitive system of pools or a shallow ocean, while at the bottom of the latter, somewhat shielded by liquid water, polymerization of some of the products on clay particles or by other processes may have taken place.

The first hint that organisms had been produced is the presence of bacterialike structures in the Figtree geological formation of South Africa; these fossils are believed to be a little more than three billion years old. Carbon-containing cherts from Swaziland that are older than that have been examined by Preston Cloud of the University of California at Santa Barbara, who did not find any indication of biological objects. The oldest really dramatic microflora are those described by Stanley A. Tyler and

Elso S. Barghoorn of Harvard University from the Gunflint formation of Ontario, which is about two billion years old [*see illustration on page 2*]. Sedimentary rocks from that formation seem to contain genuine filamentous bluegreen algae that were doubtless both photosynthetic and nitrogen-fixing. Cellular structures that were probably components of blue-green algal reefs certainly occurred a little earlier than two billion years ago. The most reasonable conclusion that can be drawn from the work of Barghoorn, Cloud and others, who are at last giving us a real Precambrian paleobiological record, is that somewhere around three billion years ago biochemical evolution had proceeded far enough for discrete heterotrophic organisms to appear.

These organisms (which, as their name implies, draw their nourishment from externally formed organic molecules) could utilize the downward-diffusing organic compounds in fermentative metabolism, but they lived at sufficient depths of water or sediment to be shielded from the destructive effect of the solar ultraviolet radiation. After somewhat less than another billion years procaryotic

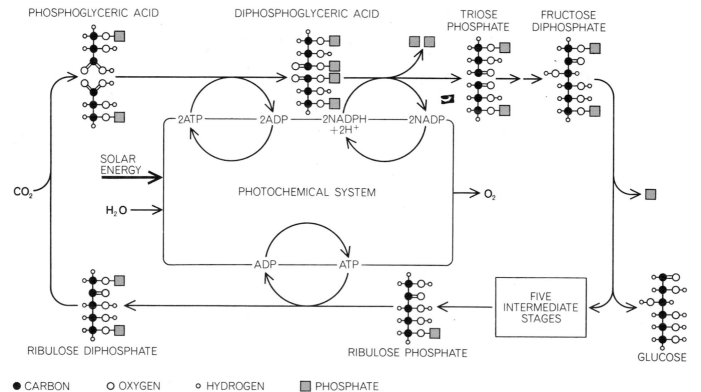

●CARBON   ○OXYGEN   ₀HYDROGEN   ▨PHOSPHATE

PHOTOSYNTHESIS, the fundamental process for sustaining life on the earth, is accomplished by plants on land, by freshwater algae and by phytoplankton in the sea. Utilizing the energy contained in sunlight, they convert carbon dioxide and water into some form of carbohydrate (for example glucose), releasing oxygen as a waste product. This simplified diagram shows the cyclical process by which a molecule of carbon dioxide is attached to a five-carbon molecule, ribulose-1,5-diphosphate, previously assembled from five molecules of carbon dioxide. The photochemical system packages part of the incoming solar energy by converting adenosine diphosphate (ADP) to adenosine triphosphate (ATP) and by converting nicotinamide adenine dinucleotide phosphate (NADP) to its reduced form (NADPH). Two molecules of NADPH and three of ATP are required to fix one molecule of carbon dioxide. Carbon atoms from CO_2 can be incorporated into a variety of compounds and removed at various points in the cycle.

cells—cells without a fully developed mitotic mechanism for cell division and without mitochondria—had already started photosynthesis. The result of these developments would have ultimately been the complete transformation of the biosphere from the old heterotrophic fermentative regime to the new autotrophic (self-nourishing), respiratory and largely oxidized condition. How fast the change took place we do not know, but it was certainly the greatest biological revolution that has occurred on the earth. The net result of this revolution was no doubt the extermination of a great number of inefficient and primitive organisms that could not tolerate free oxygen and their replacement by more efficient respiring forms.

Cloud and his associates have recently found evidence of eucaryotic cells—cells with a fully developed mitotic mechanism and with mitochondria—some 1.2 to 1.4 billion years old. It is reasonable to regard the rise of the modern eucaryotic cell as a major consequence of the new conditions imposed by an oxygen-containing atmosphere. Moreover, Lynn Margulis of Boston University has assembled most convincingly the scattered but extensive evidence that this response was of a very special kind, involving a multiple symbiosis between a variety of procaryotic cells and so constituting an evolutionary advance quite unlike any other known to have occurred.

If the first eucaryotes arose 1.2 to 1.4 billion years ago, there would be about half of this time available for the evolution of soft-bodied multicellular organisms, since the first fossil animal skeletons were deposited around 600 million years ago at the beginning of the Cambrian period. Although most of the detailed history consists of a series of blanks, we do have a time scale that seems sensible.

Without taking too seriously any of the estimates that have been made of the expectation of the life of the sun and the solar system, it is evident that the biosphere could remain habitable for a very long time, many times the estimated length of the history of the genus *Homo*, which might be two million years old. As inhabitants of the biosphere, we should regard ourselves as being in our infancy, particularly when we throw destructive temper tantrums. Many people, however, are concluding on the basis of mounting and reasonably objective evidence that the length of life of the biosphere as an inhabitable region for organisms is to be measured in decades rather than in hundreds of mil-

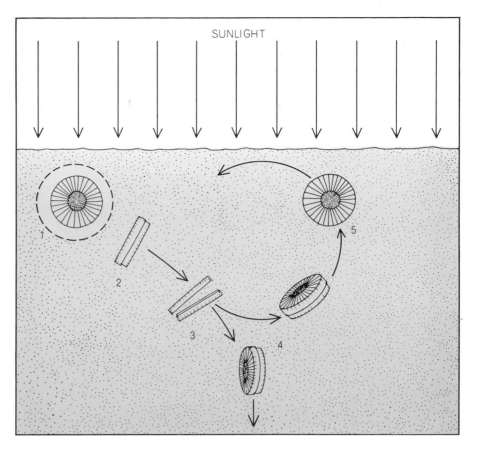

PHYTOPLANKTON CELL is slightly denser than seawater and under absolutely quiet conditions would slowly sink to the bottom. In this way the cell can move from a small parcel of water (*broken circle*) from which it has removed all the available nutrients (*black dots*) into a parcel still containing these substances. As the cell sinks it divides, and losses from the population in the surface waters that constitute the euphotic zone are continually made good by upward turbulence, which returns some of the products of cell division to the surface layer. The particular phytoplankton shown is a diatom of the genus *Coscinodiscus*.

lions of years. This is entirely the fault of our own species. It would seem not unlikely that we are approaching a crisis that is comparable to the one that occurred when free oxygen began to accumulate in the atmosphere.

Admittedly there are differences. The first photosynthetic organisms that produced oxygen were probably already immune to the lethal effects of the new poison gas we now breathe. On the other hand, our machines may be immune to carbon monoxide, lead and DDT, but we are not. Apart from a slight rise in agricultural productivity caused by an increase in the amount of carbon dioxide in the atmosphere, it is difficult to see how the various contaminants with which we are polluting the biosphere could form the basis for a revolutionary step forward. Nonetheless, it is worth noting that when the eucaryotic cell evolved in the middle Precambrian period, the process very likely involved an unprecedented new kind of evolutionary development. Presumably if we want to continue living in the biosphere we must also introduce unprecedented processes.

Vernadsky, the founder of modern biogeochemistry, was a Russian liberal who grew up in the 19th century. Accepting the Russian Revolution, he did much of his work after 1917, although his numerous philosophic references were far from Marxist. Just before his death on January 6, 1945, he wrote his friend and former student Alexander Petrunkevitch: "I look forward with great optimism. I think that we undergo not only a historical, but a planetary change as well. We live in a transition to the noosphere." By noosphere Vernadsky meant the envelope of mind that was to supersede the biosphere, the envelope of life. Unfortunately the quarter-century since those words were written has shown how mindless most of the changes wrought by man on the biosphere have been. Nonetheless, Vernadsky's transition in its deepest sense is the only alternative to man's cutting his lifetime short by millions of years. The succeeding chapters of this study of the biosphere contain many useful suggestions about how this alternative may be brought to fruition.

II

The Energy Cycle
of the Earth

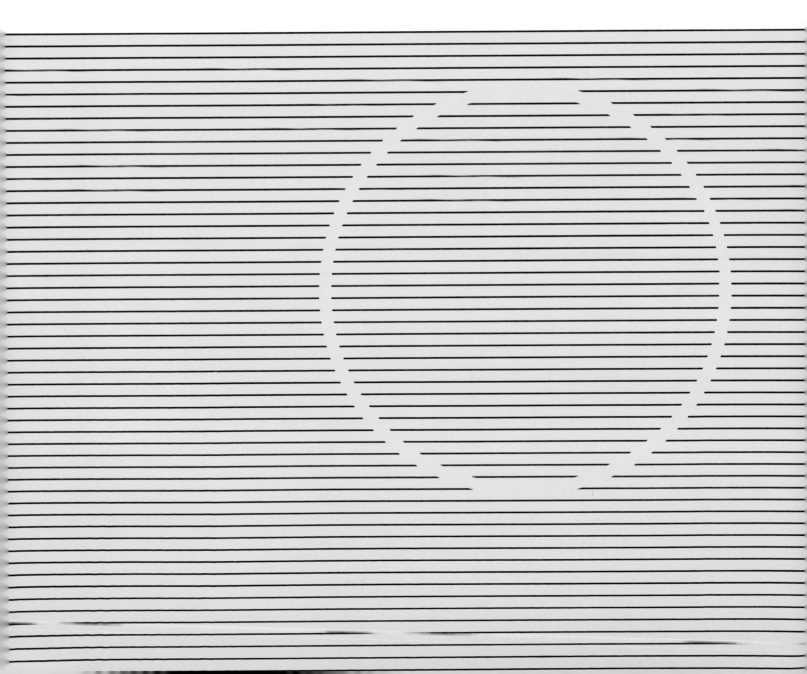

The Energy Cycle of the Earth

by ABRAHAM H. OORT

The solar energy absorbed by the earth is eventually reradiated into space as heat. Meanwhile it is distributed over the surface of the earth by the circulation of the atmosphere and the oceans

All life on the earth is of course ultimately powered by the sun, and accordingly it is strongly affected by variations of the incoming solar radiation over the globe. The distribution of sunlight with latitude determines to a great extent the location of the major climatic zones—tropical, temperate and polar—and these zones in turn set broad geographic limits to the different forms of terrestrial life.

What is less familiar is the central function of the atmosphere and the oceans in redistributing the incoming solar energy and hence in determining the "macroclimate" of the earth. The importance of the circulation of the atmosphere and the oceans to the operation of the biosphere becomes apparent when one considers that present forms of life could not endure the harsh climate that would exist if conditions of radiative equilibrium were to prevail at all latitudes (that is, if the incoming solar radiation to a zone were exactly balanced by the outgoing terrestrial radiation from that zone). This chapter is devoted not only to an examination of the character of the incoming short-wave radiation and the outgoing long-wave radiation but also to an attempt to trace the cycle of the solar energy from the time it enters the atmosphere as sunlight until it finally finds its way back into space as heat. At the end of the chapter I shall take up the question of the possible effects of man's intervention in these vast energy processes.

When the sun is over the Equator on March 21 and September 23 (the equinoxes), a maximum amount of solar radiation is received at the Equator [*see illustration on page 18*]. On the same dates the radiation received at the north and south poles is practically zero. This symmetrical decrease of radiation with

latitude toward both poles only occurs, however, during the transition seasons, spring and fall. In the summer hemisphere, for example, there is almost no meridional (north-south) heating gradient. Even more surprising is the fact that the 24-hour average sunshine has a maximum value at the summer pole, not at the subsolar point in the Tropics! This of course is owing to the permanent daylight at the summer pole. From a consideration of these factors alone one would expect significant differences in the large-scale circulation between the summer and the winter hemispheres. In addition one would expect climatic effects related to the variation of incoming radiation with local time in each hemisphere [*see illustration on page 19*]. Diurnal changes (that is, changes with a period of 24 hours) in the wind, temperature and humidity are only important, however, close to the ground and at high levels in the atmosphere. Locally the interaction of land and sea breeze effects may also play a role, but the overall atmospheric circulation cannot respond well to such short-period phenomena.

This is even truer of the oceanic circulation. In addition to the imposed diurnal and annual periodicities in the incoming solar radiation, one finds a slight semi-annual variation of insolation in the Tropics, where the sun passes overhead twice during the year.

How is the solar energy transmitted and transformed once it enters the top of the atmosphere? Averaged over the globe about 30 percent of the radiation is either scattered back by the constituents of the atmosphere or directly reflected by clouds or the earth's surface. This portion of the solar energy is lost into space and cannot be used to generate atmospheric motions. About 50 percent of the incoming radiation finally reaches the ground or ocean, where it is absorbed as heat. The properties of the surface determine the thickness of the layer over which the available heat is distributed. In the case of an ocean surface wave motions are quite effective in distributing the heat through a thick layer, sometimes extending down to a depth of 100 meters. The diurnal variation in temperature of the ocean surface itself

MOSAIC OF COLORED SQUARES on the opposite page is actually a "map" showing the relative infrared reflectance of various land and water surfaces in a region of the Middle East. The data used to construct the map were obtained at noon on May 4, 1969, by means of a high-resolution scanning infrared radiometer on board the unmanned artificial earth satellite *Nimbus 3*. The data were digitized, adjusted for differences in sun angle and displayed in a format in which the color of each square represents a range of relative reflectance. In assigning different colors to each range an attempt was made to render the scene in "natural" colors. Thus the lowest ranges of relative reflectance, which correspond generally to water surfaces, are represented by different shades of blue. Areas of intermediate reflectance, corresponding roughly to vegetated regions, are green. Highly reflective desert areas are beige. The large body of water at lower right is the Red Sea. At its northern end the reflectance is modified by haze, obscuring much of the gulfs of Suez and Aqaba, which flank the Sinai Peninsula. The blue area at top left is the Mediterranean Sea. The triangular green area adjacent to it is the Nile delta. The string of green squares at bottom left represents the lake forming in the Nile River valley as a result of the construction of the Aswan Dam. The map was produced as part of a study conducted by Norman H. Mac-Leod of the National Aeronautics and Space Administration in an effort to develop a quantitative technique for observing the earth in terms of the relative reflectance of its parts.

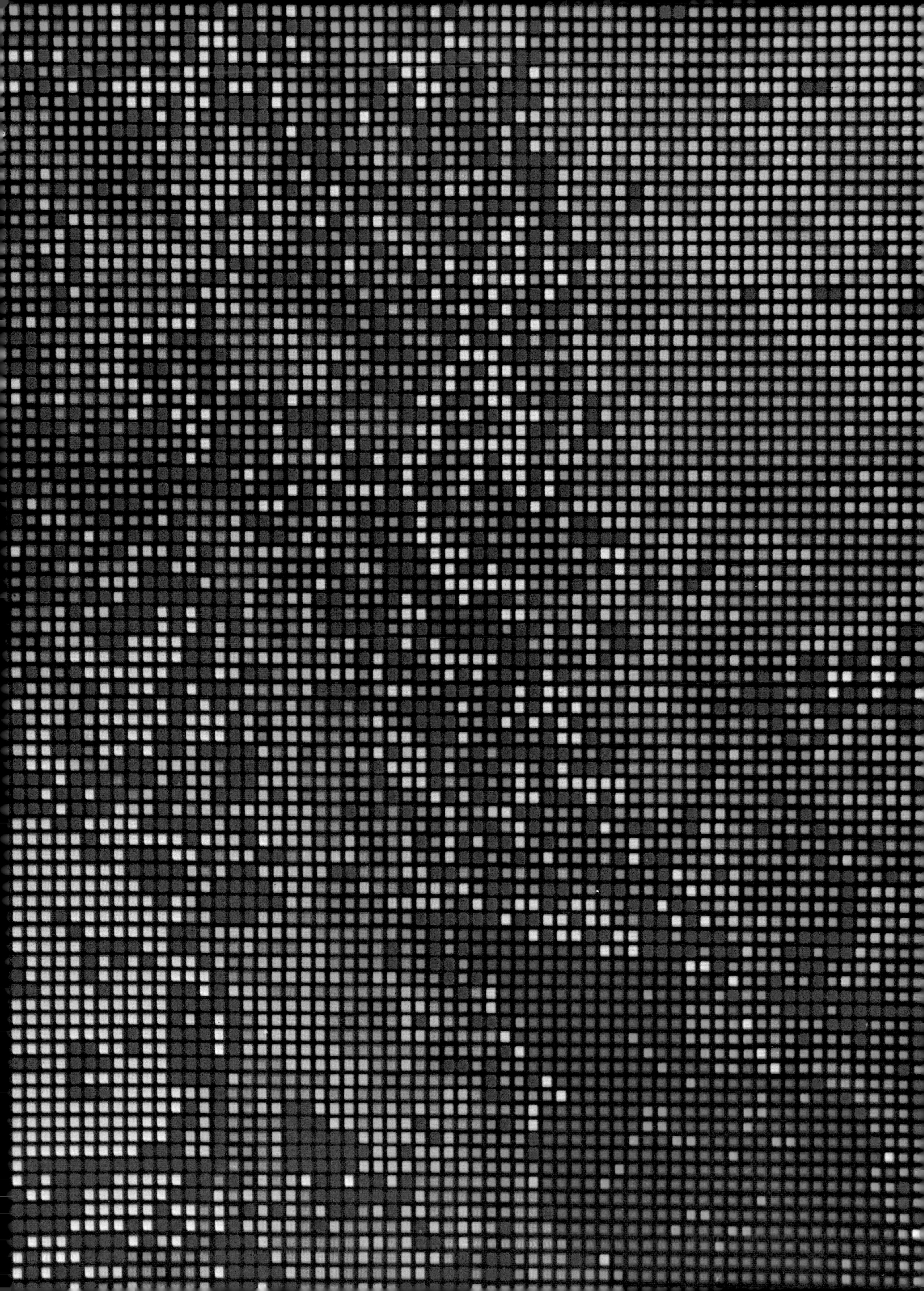

HURRICANE GLADYS was photographed by the *Apollo* 7 astronauts as it approached the west coast of Florida on the morning of October 17, 1968. The view is toward the southeast with Cuba in the distant background. The lack of the usual high cloud cover made it possible to view the spiral lower cloud structure of this cyclonic storm in considerable detail. Traveling cyclones (of which hurricanes are a particularly violent form) contribute to the net poleward transport of heat in the middle latitudes and thus help to moderate the harsh climate that would exist on the earth if conditions of radiative equilibrium were to prevail at all latitudes.

is thus generally less than 1 degree Celsius. The situation on land depends not only on the diurnal amplitude of the incoming radiation but also on the properties of the soil (for example its wetness) and the presence or absence of vegetation. The energy transfer down into the ground occurs through the slow process of molecular heat conduction. Over bare ground the diurnal temperature range at the surface can amount to several tens of degrees Celsius, but the temperature change is hardly noticeable below a depth of half a meter.

What happens to the remaining 20 percent of the incoming solar radiation that is apparently absorbed on its path through the atmosphere? Here it is necessary to consider the spectrum of the incoming and outgoing radiation [*see top illustration on page 20*]. The emission spectrum of the sun roughly resembles that of a "black body" radiating at a temperature of 6,000 degrees Kelvin. (A black body is defined as one that absorbs all the radiation falling on it.) In the visible portion of the spectrum (wavelengths between .4 and .7 micron), where the maximum influx of solar energy takes place, the radiation can penetrate almost without loss down to the earth's surface except where clouds are present. High in the atmosphere ordinary oxygen (O_2) and ozone (O_3) molecules absorb an estimated 1 to 3 percent of the incoming radiation. This absorption occurs in the ultraviolet portion of the spectrum and effectively limits the penetrating radiation to wavelengths longer than .3 micron. Although this effect is relatively small, it is important because it is the main source of energy for the circulation above 30 kilometers [see "The Circulation of the Upper Atmosphere," by Reginald E. Newell; SCIENTIFIC AMERICAN, March, 1964]. Moreover, the absorption at these levels shields the biosphere from the damaging effects of ultraviolet radiation. At wavelengths longer than one micron most of the atmospheric absorption is due to water vapor, dust and water droplets in clouds. This process operates in the lower troposphere and involves most of the remaining 20 percent of the total incoming radiation.

In spite of certain long-term climatic changes climatological records do not show an appreciable net heating or cooling of the earth and its atmosphere. Therefore the earth must emit an amount of radiation equal to the radiation absorbed. A characteristic shift to longer wavelengths does take place, however, since the earth radiates at an effective

black-body temperature of about 255 degrees K., a very low value compared with the sun's black-body temperature of 6,000 degrees. The earth's emission occurs throughout a broad range of wavelengths with a flat maximum at about 12 microns. In this range of the spectrum the atmosphere is not transparent. Water vapor, ozone and carbon dioxide absorb significant amounts of long-wave radiation.

If one now calculates the vertical transfer of solar and terrestrial radiation using the observed temperature and humidity structure, one finds that the atmosphere is not in local radiative equilibrium. The net effect due to solar and terrestrial radiation alone would be an intense heating of the earth's surface and a cooling of the atmosphere at the rate of up to two degrees C. per day, depending on the height. In reality the air is prevented from cooling by the vertical transfer of heat directly from the earth's surface and by the release of heat through the condensation of water va-

por. It is at this point that the dynamics of the atmosphere begin to play an important role.

The transport of energy upward into the atmosphere forms the major energy supply for the atmospheric heat engine. A large portion of this energy, however, is "latent" (that is, in the form of water vapor), and it is used to raise the atmospheric temperature only when condensation takes place. Close to the surface the energy transport occurs through evaporation of water, through heat conduction and through the transfer of long-wave radiation. At a certain height above the surface turbulent eddies mix the water vapor and heat further upward. The scale of the effective eddies increases with distance from the surface, finally growing to convective clouds of the cumulus type in the free atmosphere. This upward transfer of energy from the surface compensates for the radiative cooling of the atmosphere. A schematic diagram of the average energy cycle in the atmosphere reveals the important

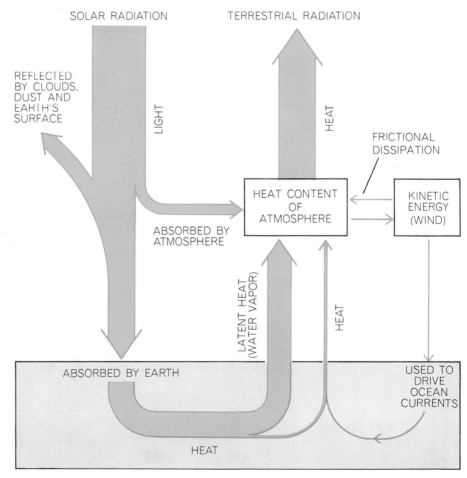

ATMOSPHERIC HEAT ENGINE is averaged over the entire atmosphere in this diagram. The thickness of the arrows indicates approximately the strength of the various energy flows and conversion rates. As the diagram shows, the earth's surface acts as an indirect source of energy for the circulation in the atmosphere. Estimates of the efficiency of the atmospheric heat engine differ widely, depending on the energy inputs and outputs used to define efficiency. By one definition (the amount of energy used to generate ocean currents divided by the incoming solar energy) the efficiency of the system is less than 1 percent.

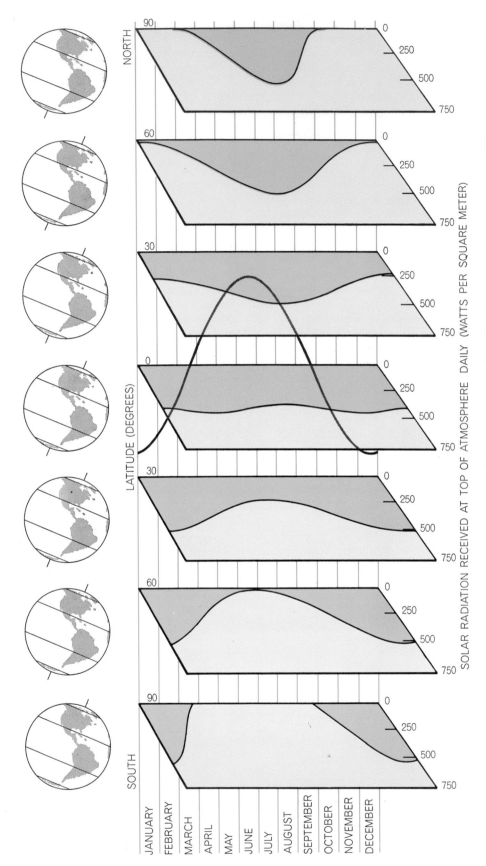

INCOMING SOLAR RADIATION (*dark color*) is shown in this three-dimensional chart at seven different latitudes as a function of month of the year. A large difference in the meridional (north-south) heating gradient exists between the winter and the summer hemispheres. In winter the gradient is very large, whereas in summer it practically disappears. The annual cycle in declination of the sun between 23 degrees north latitude (the Tropic of Cancer) and 23 degrees south latitude (the Tropic of Capricorn) is indicated by the solid black curve in the latitude plane (*background*). The radiation is averaged over all hours of the day. Data are from the Smithsonian Meteorological Tables, compiled by Robert J. List.

role of the earth's surface as the source of latent heat and sensible heat [*see illustration on preceding page*].

There is a significant difference in the character of the heating for the ocean and for the atmosphere. In the ocean the heating is applied at the top, which leads to stable conditions, whereas in the atmosphere the heating is applied at the bottom, giving rise to vigorous convection. The ocean currents, which are driven mainly by the winds, redistribute the absorbed solar heat horizontally and thereby influence in turn the pattern of the heat supply to the atmosphere that finally closes the cycle. The oceans and the atmosphere are strongly coupled systems and cannot very well be treated separately. The final circulation pattern is determined by the interaction of the two systems, each system influencing the other in a complicated cycle of events.

The effects of radiation and convection alone tend to maintain the proper energy balance for the earth as a whole, but the atmospheric and oceanic circulation must be considered if one wishes to explain the observed north-south temperature distribution [*see bottom illustration on page 20*]. The fact that the incoming solar radiation drops off more rapidly toward the winter pole than the outgoing terrestrial radiation does means that there is an excess in radiational heating in the summer hemisphere and a deficit near the winter pole. The storage of heat in the ocean during summer and the release of a large portion of this heat during winter has a moderating effect on the climate. Without an efficient north-south transfer of heat, however, the earth would still become very hot in the summer hemisphere and extremely cold at high latitudes in the winter hemisphere. The heating gradient constitutes the major driving force for the large-scale atmospheric currents and ultimately also for the oceanic currents. Judging from the existing temperature gradient, these circulations must be quite effective agents for transporting energy toward the winter pole.

What type of atmospheric and oceanic circulation patterns would develop as a consequence of such an imposed heating gradient? Let us limit the discussion for the time being to the winter situation. It is in this season that the north-south gradient in the solar heating is strongest and that the differences between the radiative equilibrium temperature and the observed temperature are at a maximum. What simple mechanism would suffice to transport heat poleward?

Let us first consider a model atmo-

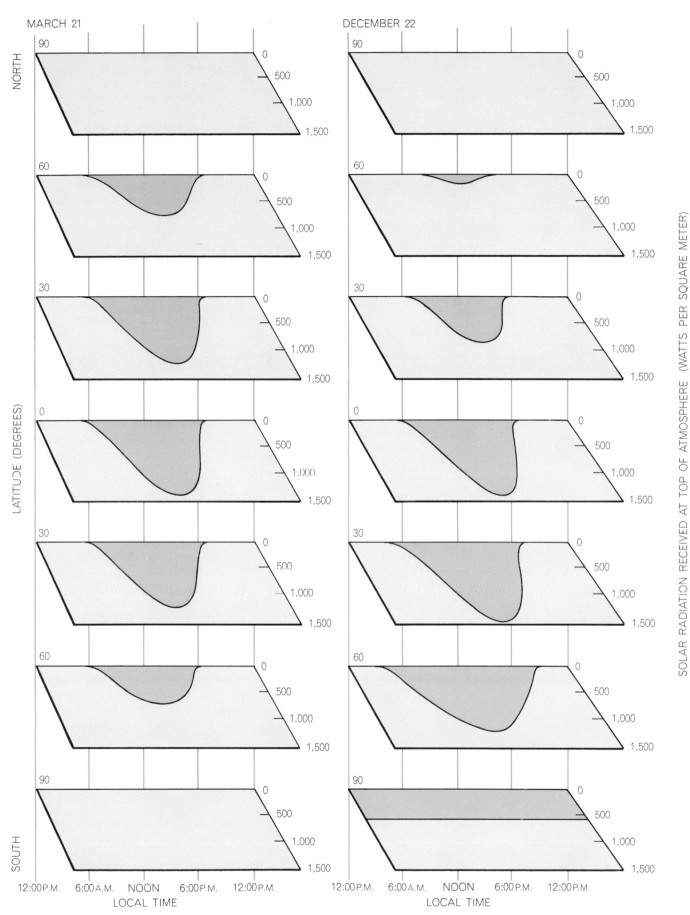

MARCH 21

DECEMBER 22

NORTH

90

60

30

0

30

60

90

SOUTH

LATITUDE (DEGREES)

SOLAR RADIATION RECEIVED AT TOP OF ATMOSPHERE (WATTS PER SQUARE METER)

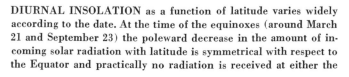

12:00 P.M. 6:00 A.M. NOON 6:00 P.M. 12:00 P.M.
LOCAL TIME

12:00 P.M. 6:00 A.M. NOON 6:00 P.M. 12:00 P.M.
LOCAL TIME

DIURNAL INSOLATION as a function of latitude varies widely according to the date. At the time of the equinoxes (around March 21 and September 23) the poleward decrease in the amount of incoming solar radiation with latitude is symmetrical with respect to the Equator and practically no radiation is received at either the North Pole or the South Pole (*chart at left*). At the solstices (around June 21 and December 22) the latitudinal differences in diurnal insolation between the two hemispheres are extreme (*chart at right*); the summer pole (*bottom*) receives sunlight 24 hours a day, whereas the winter pole (*top*) receives no sunlight at all.

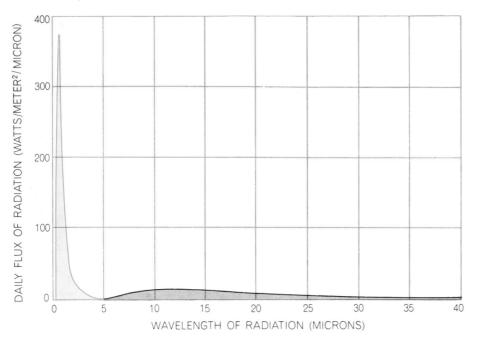

APPROXIMATE EMISSION SPECTRA of the sun (*colored curve*) and the earth (*black curve*) are represented in this graph under the assumption that they radiate as "black bodies" with temperatures of 6,000 degrees and 250 degrees Kelvin respectively. The solar curve is corrected for the distance between the sun and the earth, for the fact that only one side of the earth is illuminated by the sun at any instant and finally for the mean albedo (reflectance) of 30 percent for the earth. The areas under the two curves are equal; in other words, the earth emits as much radiation as it absorbs. The important change in the character of this radiation from the short-wave to the long-wave part of the spectrum is evident.

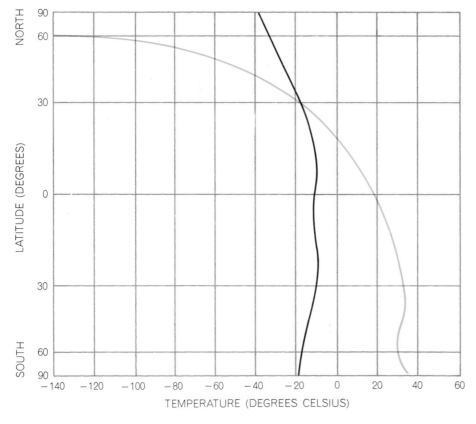

IMPORTANCE OF ATMOSPHERIC DYNAMICS in moderating the earth's climate is demonstrated by this graph, which compares the calculated radiative-equilibrium temperature for a "black" earth (*colored curve*) with the observed vertical mean temperature (*black curve*) as a function of latitude during January. At this time no sunshine reaches the earth north of the Arctic Circle; neglecting any lag effects due to the storage of heat, the radiative-equilibrium temperature in the polar cap would go down to absolute zero (−273.2 degrees Celsius), while the summer hemisphere would tend to become extremely hot.

sphere that has a uniform temperature and rotates at the same rate as the earth. If one starts to heat the air at low levels on the summer side of the Equator, the local temperature will rise and the air column will expand mainly in the vertical direction. This process will create at the upper levels a relatively high-pressure belt located over the "thermal" Equator. Next the north-south pressure gradient will force the equatorial air at all longitudes to move toward the low-pressure zone, mainly into the winter hemisphere, where initially vertical contraction occurred as a result of radiational cooling. The air will then slowly start to sink over a wide region in the winter hemisphere and will return to the Equator at low levels. The cycle will be closed finally through a rise of the air after it has arrived in the vicinity of the thermal Equator.

A simple cellular circulation of this kind, called a mean meridional circulation, would be completely symmetrical with respect to the earth's axis of rotation. The existence of one such cell in each hemisphere with rising warm air near the Equator and sinking cold air near the poles was originally postulated by the English meteorologist George Hadley in 1735. Such a cell is called a direct cell since it releases potential energy and converts it into kinetic energy. Later investigators, notably the 19th-century American meteorologist William Ferrel, showed that one actually needs three cells in each hemisphere to explain the important climatological features at the earth's surface [*see illustration on opposite page*]. This picture has been confirmed by many observational and theoretical studies and seems to represent rather well the annual mean conditions in the atmosphere. Recent and more detailed observations, however, have shown that only during the transition months in fall and spring is such an idealized circulation symmetrical with respect to the Equator realized. The asymmetry in heating during most of the year appears to favor the development of only one strong cell in the Tropics: the one in the winter hemisphere. This cell circulates on the average about 2×10^8 metric tons of air per second. At the same time the "summer" Hadley cell has shrunk to an insignificant size [*see illustration on pages 22 and 23*].

Let us consider in somewhat greater detail what energy transformations take place in the tropical Hadley cell. In its lower branch subtropical air flows close to the earth's surface toward the summer hemisphere with an average velocity of one or two meters per second. During the long journey equatorward heat and moisture are absorbed from the warm underlying ocean. This is the region of the trade winds. Near the Equator the air starts to rise in a fairly narrow region called the intertropical convergence zone, where intense precipitation occurs. In that zone a powerful conversion from sensible and latent heat into potential energy occurs as the air expands and the water vapor condenses, the net effect being a cooling of the equatorial atmosphere.

The upper branch of the Hadley cell now transports the air, which has become relatively cold but which has a high potential energy, into the winter hemisphere. In the rather wide downward branch in the subtropics the subsiding cold air is strongly heated by compression, and the potential energy supplied to the air in the equatorial convergence zone is converted back into heat. One would expect that the sinking air in the subtropics would be dry, since almost all the moisture was rained out in the upward branch of the Hadley cell. That expectation is confirmed by the location of the continental deserts and the small amount of rainfall over the oceans in this latitude.

The large overturning in each hemisphere of the kind Hadley envisioned is not adequate to transport enough energy poleward to counteract the externally imposed heating gradient. In such a situation temperatures near the Equator would start to rise above the observed values, and near the Pole they would start to drop. This would continue until a critical value of the north-south temperature gradient was reached, at which point zonal (east-west) asymmetries would start to develop (this process is called baroclinic instability). Theoretical models indicate that the maximum instability would tend to develop with atmospheric waves a few thousand kilometers long. In the middle latitudes, where the strong meridional temperature gradients are found, these waves can grow very fast and can take over the task of transporting energy poleward from the Hadley cell.

The familiar traveling cyclones and anticyclones, which can be found on every weather map in the middle latitudes, are a manifestation of this instability process. They form an extension of the large waves in the middle and upper troposphere. These systems mix heat in an efficient way through horizontal processes. At the same level one finds warm, humid air flowing poleward and cold, dry air flowing equatorward. On the

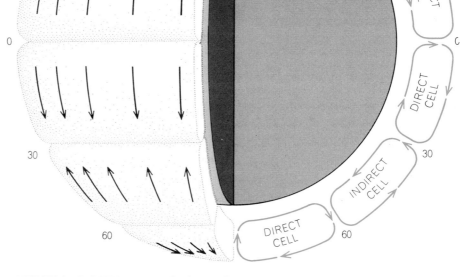

CELLULAR MODEL of atmospheric circulation was first proposed by the English meteorologist George Hadley in 1735 and was modified by the American meteorologist William Ferrel in the 19th century. The pattern has a rotational symmetry around the earth's axis. The two tropical cells are called Hadley cells; two mid-latitude cells are called Ferrel cells.

average these flows are equivalent to a net poleward transport of sensible and latent heat. Waves with lengths of a few thousand kilometers and with time scales of a few days to a week appear to be mainly responsible for the transfers. The typical "variable" climate of middle latitudes is determined to a great extent by such large-scale waves. These waves are more intense and frequent in winter than they are in summer, since they generally develop in regions of strong horizontal temperature contrasts.

In middle and high latitudes the mean meridional circulation is weak. One can probably interpret the reverse, mid-latitude Ferrel cell as a circulation that is being driven, or forced, by the atmospheric waves. The net effect of this "indirect" cell is the sinking of relatively warm air and the rising of cold air! At high latitudes near the Pole there is some suggestion of a direct polar cell; in the Northern Hemisphere this cell is very weak. The slow rising motion between roughly 50 and 60 degrees north latitude is connected with the upward branches of the Ferrel and polar cells, and its effects are evident in the climatological records. In this belt one finds a second

maximum in rainfall. The precipitation, however, occurs at irregular intervals and is mainly determined by the frequency of the weather systems passing by.

In summer the mean meridional circulation appears to be disorganized and weak at all latitudes. Asymmetries connected with the distribution of continents and oceans dominate the circulation. The land generally acts as a heat source and the colder water at middle and high latitudes as a heat sink. One apparent asymmetry is the Asian monsoon, which carries warm and humid air far north into the Asian continent. At most other longitudes in the northern part of the Tropics the air still moves equatorward. In this season studying the asymmetries in the circulation is probably more relevant than studying the mean meridional circulation, which has rotational symmetry around the earth's axis.

Up to this point I have discussed only some mean features of the climate as they have been derived from the observations of the past 20 to 30 years. Paleontological and even meteorological records show that the climate has changed slowly but significantly in the past and probably is changing now. On the other hand, it appears unlikely that either the total influx of solar energy or the rotation rate of the earth have changed drastically during the period in which life developed on the earth. Therefore it is probably safe to assume that the basic circulation regime has not changed. However, relatively minor changes in the strength of the north-south energy exchange, through either the mean meridional circulations at low latitudes or the large-scale horizontal waves at middle latitudes, can cause deviations from the present climate. Needless to say, any such deviations could be very significant as far as the living organisms are concerned.

The most likely way the climate could be influenced by either natural or artificial means seems to be through a trigger mechanism that ultimately changes the radiation balance. For example, if the cloud cover or dust content of the air were changed at high latitudes, the amount of reflected radiation would increase and consequently less solar radiation would be available to heat the atmosphere and the earth's surface at these latitudes. The resulting increase in the north-south heating gradient would presumably lead to more violent and more

frequent disturbances in the middle latitudes. These circulations would in turn affect the original cloud cover. From that point on it seems hopeless to predict with any degree of certainty what the additional effects on the climate would be.

Changes in the reflectivity or absorptivity of the earth's surface can also alter the climate. It has been suggested that if the snow and ice fields near the North Pole were to be covered with black carbon, the Arctic Ocean might become ice-free through the increased absorption of solar radiation in summer. Again the present radiation balance and the climate over the earth would be affected. Still another possibility would be a change in the relative proportion of the atmospheric gases. For example, the measured slow increase in the carbon dioxide content of the air due to the burning of fossil fuels would presumably lead to more absorption of long-wave terrestrial radiation in the atmosphere and consequently to extra heating. One can think of many other ways in which changes in the earth's macroclimate might occur.

One must also consider the possibility of external influences such as natural variations in the amount and the spectral distribution of the incident solar radiation itself associated with variations in the level of solar activity. For instance,

during periods of high solar activity the solar output mainly increases in the ultraviolet portion of the spectrum. Since most of that radiation is absorbed above 30 kilometers, one would expect to find the largest dynamic response at those levels. It is still an open question whether or not such variations in solar emission—either in the form of increased ultraviolet radiation or possibly also in the form of showers of energetic particles—affect the weather deep down in the atmosphere. The meteorological evidence for direct climatic variations caused by such changes in solar output is inconclusive, but variations of this kind certainly cannot be ruled out.

As an example one can imagine that through a change in the radiation balance the general regime of atmospheric and oceanic circulation could be brought to settle in a new quasi-equilibrium state that would be slightly different from the state it is in now. According to some recent studies conducted by M. I. Budyko in the U.S.S.R. and William D. Sellers in the U.S., even the present state of the atmosphere might not be as stable as one would like to think; these authors suggest that comparatively small changes in the present state can lead to a new ice age. Another consideration is that an initial disturbance of the circulation might, if maintained for a long enough time, ex-

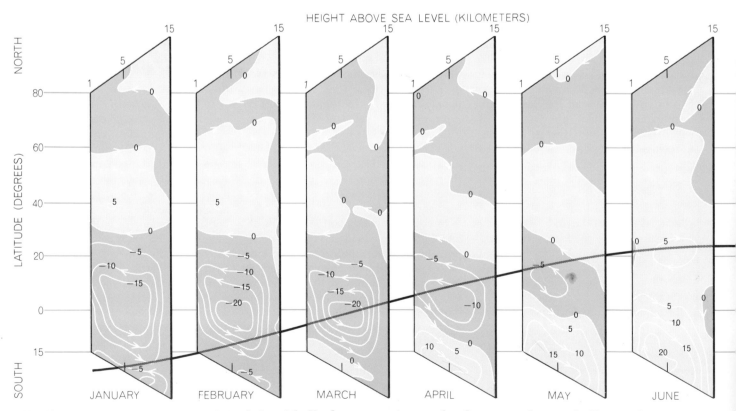

ANNUAL CYCLE in the mean meridional circulation of the Northern Hemisphere was investigated by the author and Eugene M. Rasmusson using data from an extensive radiosonde network. They found that while the Hadley cell on the winter side of the Equator grows in strength and even expands across the Equator, the summer Hadley cell tends to weaken and finally almost disappears. Thus in contrast to the Hadley-Ferrel model there appears to be little symmetry in the tropical circulation with respect to the Equator, except

cite a long-term climatic fluctuation. The period of this fluctuation would probably be related to the natural turnover time of the oceans (of the order of a century or more) because of their capacity to store large amounts of heat.

Some reassurance that our present climate is not too unstable may be gained from the fact that during the past few centuries the climate has not fluctuated widely. An important complicating factor is the highly interactive nature of the different processes that operate in the ocean and the atmosphere. This makes it practically impossible to deduce through simple reasoning or even by using a simple model what would happen if one could bring about a slight, but more or less permanent, change in the radiation budget.

A high-priority task in the examination of these problems is to establish from observations how the present general circulation in both the ocean and the atmosphere is maintained. Here important contributions have been made in the past 20 years by three groups, one led by Victor P. Starr of the Massachusetts Institute of Technology, the second by Jacob Bjerknes of the University of California at Los Angeles and the third by Erik H. Palmén of the University of Helsinki. The next tasks are to determine whether or not slow changes in the general circulation are taking place, and to try to establish possible cause-and-effect relations. The limited records and the tremendous job of reducing the observations to meaningful parameters, however, severely restrict this direct approach.

With the arrival of large electronic computers a powerful new method for studying the climate has been developed. The thermal structure and the dynamics of the atmosphere are simulated through numerical integration in time of the equations that govern the behavior of the atmosphere. The basic equations are the equations of radiative energy transfer, the equations of motion and the thermodynamic equation. Starting from certain initial conditions (for example a uniform-temperature atmosphere at rest), the integration is carried out in time steps of the order of 10 minutes, and new values for the meteorological parameters (wind components, temperature, pressure and humidity) are calculated at each point in a three-dimensional grid covering the global atmosphere. The most realistic numerical experiments to date have been conducted at the Geophysical Fluid Dynamics Laboratory of the Environmental Science Services Administration by Joseph Smagorinsky, Syukuro Manabe and Kirk Bryan, Jr. In their experiments the number of grid points in space is of the order of 50,000 (about 10 vertical levels and a horizontal grid distance of about 300 kilometers). After the atmosphere has settled down and recovered from the unrealistic initial conditions, the relevant general circulation statistics are calculated in the same way they would be for the real atmosphere. With the present grid the large-scale weather systems seem to be rather well resolved.

On the other hand, the smaller-scale phenomena such as cumulus convection cannot be simulated explicitly. They have to be incorporated in a different way. In spite of these uncertainties and others (such as the lack of knowledge of how to properly incorporate the exchange processes near the earth's surface), the results so far are encouraging. Although the ability to forecast the exact location and intensity of the important weather systems degrades rather quickly in the course of a week, the predicted statistics of the average behavior taken over a much longer period appear to reproduce the observed statistics rather well. The numerical experiments seem to be the most promising road to a better understanding of the present climate. In addition they provide a powerful tool for evaluating the effects on the climate of natural or man-made disturbances.

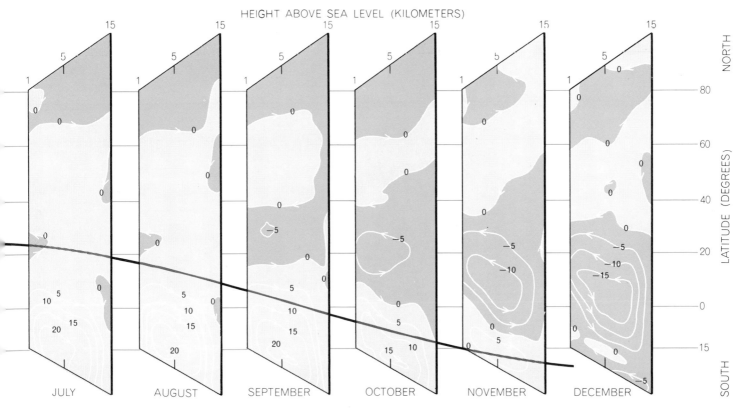

possibly in the spring and fall. Outside the Tropics they found only a weak, indirect circulation in middle latitudes and a very weak, direct circulation near the Pole. In both middle and high latitudes asymmetric "weather" systems dominate the circulation and the mean meridional circulation is almost negligible. Contour units indicate the total mass transport of air (times 10^7 tons per second) integrated both horizontally along the latitude circle and vertically from the earth's surface up to the height of the contour.

III

The Energy Cycle
of the Biosphere

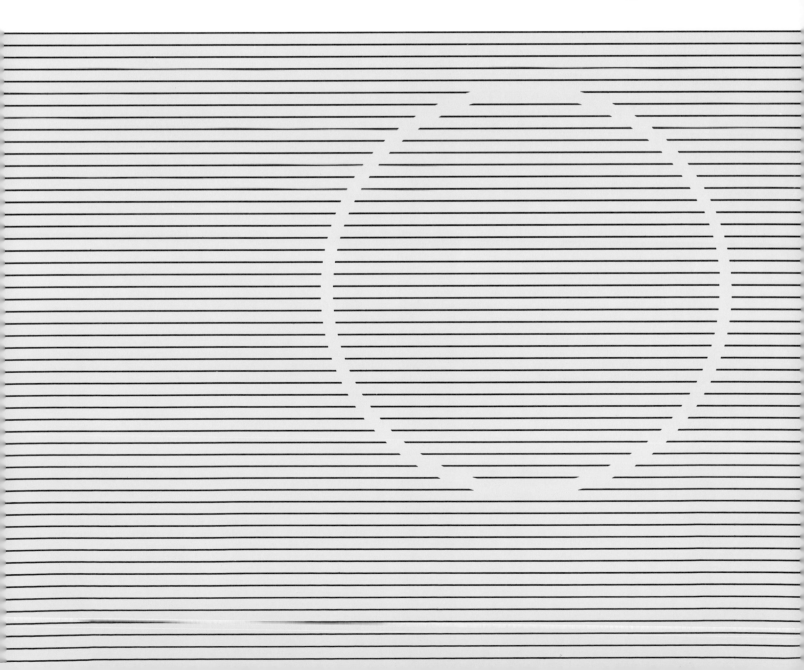

The Energy Cycle of the Biosphere

by GEORGE M. WOODWELL

Life is maintained by the finite amount of solar energy that is fixed by green plants. An increasing fraction of that energy is being diverted to the direct support of one living species: man

The energy that sustains all living systems is solar energy, fixed in photosynthesis and held briefly in the biosphere before it is reradiated into space as heat. It is solar energy that moves the rabbit, the deer, the whale, the boy on the bicycle outside my window, my pencil as I write these words. The total amount of solar energy fixed on the earth sets one limit on the total amount of life; the patterns of flow of this energy through the earth's ecosystems set additional limits on the kinds of life on the earth. Expanding human activities are requiring a larger fraction of the total and are paradoxically making large segments of it less useful in support of man.

Solar energy has been fixed in one form or another on the earth throughout much of the earth's 4.5-billion-year history. The modern biosphere probably had its beginning about two billion years ago with the evolution of marine organisms that not only could fix solar energy in organic compounds but also did it by splitting the water molecule and releasing free oxygen.

The beginning was slow. Molecular oxygen released by marine plant cells accumulated for hundreds of millions of years, gradually building an atmosphere that screened out the most destructive of the sun's rays and opened the land to exploitation by living systems [see "The Oxygen Cycle," by Preston Cloud and Aharon Gibor, page 57]. The colonization of the land began perhaps 400 million years ago. New species evolved that derived more energy from a more efficient respiration in air, accelerating the trend.

Evolution fitted the new species together in ways that not only conserved energy and the mineral nutrients utilized in life processes but also conserved the nutrients by recycling them, releasing more oxygen and making possible the fixation of more energy and the support of still more life. Gradually each landscape developed a flora and fauna particularly adapted to that place. These new arrays of plants and animals used solar energy, mineral nutrients, water and the resources of other living things to stabilize the environment, building the biosphere we know today.

The actual amount of solar energy diverted into living systems is small in relation to the earth's total energy budget [see "The Energy Cycle of the Earth," by Abraham H. Oort, page 14]. Only about a tenth of 1 percent of the energy received from the sun by the earth is fixed in photosynthesis. This fraction, small as it is, may be represented locally by the manufacture of several thousand grams of dry organic matter per square meter per year. Worldwide it is equivalent to the annual production of between 150 and 200 billion tons of dry organic matter and includes both food for man and the energy that runs the life-support systems of the biosphere, namely the earth's major ecosystems: the forests, grasslands, oceans, marshes, estuaries, lakes, rivers, tundras and deserts.

The complexity of ecosystems is so great as to preclude any simple, single-factor analysis that is both accurate and satisfying. Because of the central role of energy in life, however, an examination of the fixation of energy and its flow through ecosystems yields understanding of the ecosystems themselves. It also reveals starkly some of the obscure but vital details of the crisis of environment.

More than half of the energy fixed in photosynthesis is used immediately in the plant's own respiration. Some of it is stored. In land plants it may be transferred from tissues where it is fixed, such as leaves, to other tissues where it is used immediately or stored. At any point it may enter consumer food chains.

There are two kinds of chain: the grazing, or browsing, food chains and the food chains of decay. Energy may be stored for considerable periods in both kinds of chain, building animal populations in the one case and accumulations of undecomposed dead organic matter and populations of decay organisms in the other. The fraction of the total energy fixed that flows into each of these chains is of considerable importance to the biosphere and to man. The worldwide increase in human numbers not only is shifting the distribution of energy within ecosystems but also requires that a growing fraction of the total energy fixed be diverted to the direct support of man. The implications of such diversions are still far from clear.

Before examining the fixation and flow of energy in ecosystems it is important to consider the broad pattern of their development throughout evolution. If one were to ascribe a single objective to evolution, it would be the perpetuation of life. The entire strategy of evolution is focused on that single end. In realizing it evolution divides the resources of any

GREEN PLANTS are the "primary producers" of the biosphere, converting solar energy into organic compounds that maintain the plants and other living things. Forests, which cover about a tenth of the earth's surface, fix almost half of the biosphere's total energy. The photograph on the opposite page, which was made in the Mazumbai forest in Tanzania, illustrates the rich diversity typical of a relatively mature ecosystem, with many species arranged in a structure that apportions the available solar energy as effectively as possible.

STRUCTURE OF FORESTS changes with disturbance according to well-defined patterns. The photographs show the loss of structure in an oak-pine forest at the Brookhaven National Laboratory as a result of continued exposure to gamma radiation. Exposure of the intact forest (*top left*) to radiation first destroys pine trees and then other trees, leaving tree sprouts, shrubs and ground cover (*top right*). Longer exposure kills shrubs (*bottom left*) and finally the sedge, grasses and herbs of the ground cover (*bottom right*).

location, including its input of energy, among an ever increasing number of different kinds of users, which we recognize as plant and animal species.

The arrangement of these species in today's ecosystems is a comparatively recent event, and the ecosystems continue to be developed by migration and continuing evolution. Changes accrue slowly through a conjoint evolution that is not only biological but also chemical and physical. The entire process appears to be open-ended, continuous, self-augmenting and endlessly versatile. It builds on itself, not merely preserving life but increasing the capacity of a site to support life. In so doing it stabilizes the site and the biota. Mineral nutrients are no longer leached rapidly into watercourses; they are conserved and recirculated, offering opportunities for more evolution. Interactions among ecosystems are exploited and stabilized, by living systems adapted to the purpose. The return of the salmon and other fishes from years at sea to the upper reaches of rivers is one example; impoverished upland streams are thus fertilized with nutrients harvested in the ocean, opening further possibilities for life.

The time scale for most of these developments, particularly in the later stages when many of the species have large bodies and long life cycles, is very long. Such systems are for all practical purposes stable. These are the living systems that have shaped the biosphere. They are self-regulating and remarkably resilient. Now human activities have become so pervasive as to affect these systems all over the world. What kinds of change can we expect? The answers depend on an understanding of the patterns of evolution and on a knowledge of the structure and function of ecosystems. And the fixation and flow of energy is at the core.

Much of our current understanding of ecosystems has been based on a paper published in *Ecology* in 1942 by Raymond L. Lindeman, a young colleague of G. Evelyn Hutchinson's at Yale University. (It was Lindeman's sixth and last paper; his death at the age of 26 deprived ecology of one of its most outstanding intellects.) Lindeman drew on work by earlier scholars, particularly Arthur G. Tansley and Charles S. Elton of England and Frederick E. Clements and Victor E. Shelford of the U.S., to examine what he called the "trophic-dynamic aspect" of ecology. He called attention to the fixation of energy by natural ecosystems and to the quantitative relations that must exist in nature be-

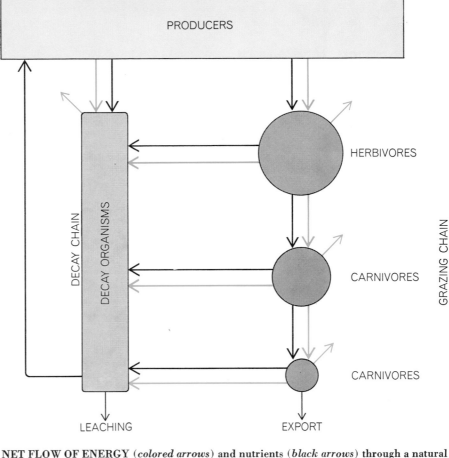

NET FLOW OF ENERGY (*colored arrows*) and nutrients (*black arrows*) through a natural community is diagrammed in simplified form. In a mature community all the energy fixed by the primary producers, the plants, is dissipated as heat in the respiration of the plants, the consumers (herbivores and successive echelons of carnivores) and decay organisms. Almost all nutrients are eventually recycled, however, to renew plant and animal populations.

tween the different users of this energy as it is divided progressively among the various populations of an ecosystem.

Lindeman's suggestions were provocative. They stimulated a series of field and laboratory studies, all of which strengthened his synthesis. One of the most useful generalizations of his approach, sometimes called "the 10 percent law," simply states that in nature some fraction of the energy entering any population is available for transfer to the populations that feed on it without serious disruption of either. The actual amount of energy transferred probably varies widely. It seems fair to assume that in the grazing chain perhaps 10 to 20 percent of the energy fixed by the plant community can be transferred to herbivores, 10 to 20 percent of the energy entering the herbivore community can be transferred to the first level of carnivores and so on. In this way what is called a mature community may support three or four levels of animal popu-

lations, each related to its food supply quantitatively on the basis of energy fixation.

No less important than the grazing food chains are the food chains of decay. On land these chains start with dead organic matter: leaves, bits of bark and branches. In water they originate in the remains of algae, fecal matter and other organic debris. The organic debris may be totally consumed by the bacteria, fungi and small animals of decay, releasing carbon dioxide, water and heat. It may enter far more complex food webs, potentially involving larger animals such as mullet, carp, crabs and ultimately higher carnivores, so that although it is convenient to think of the grazing and decay routes as being distinct, they usually overlap.

The decay food chain does not always function efficiently. Under certain circumstances it exhausts all the available oxygen. Decay is then incomplete; its products include methane, alcohols, amines, hydrogen sulfide and partially decomposed organic matter. Its connections to the grazing food chain are reduced or broken, with profound effects on living systems. Such shifts are occurring more frequently in an increasingly man-dominated world.

How much energy is fixed by the major ecosystems of the biosphere? The question is more demanding than it may appear because measuring energy fixation in such diverse vegetations as forests, fields and the oceans is most difficult. Rates of energy fixation vary from day to day—even from minute to minute—and from place to place. They are affected by many factors, including light and the concentration of carbon dioxide, water and nutrients.

In spite of the difficulties in obtaining unequivocal answers several attempts have been made to appraise the total amounts of energy fixed by the earth's ecosystems. Most recently Robert H.

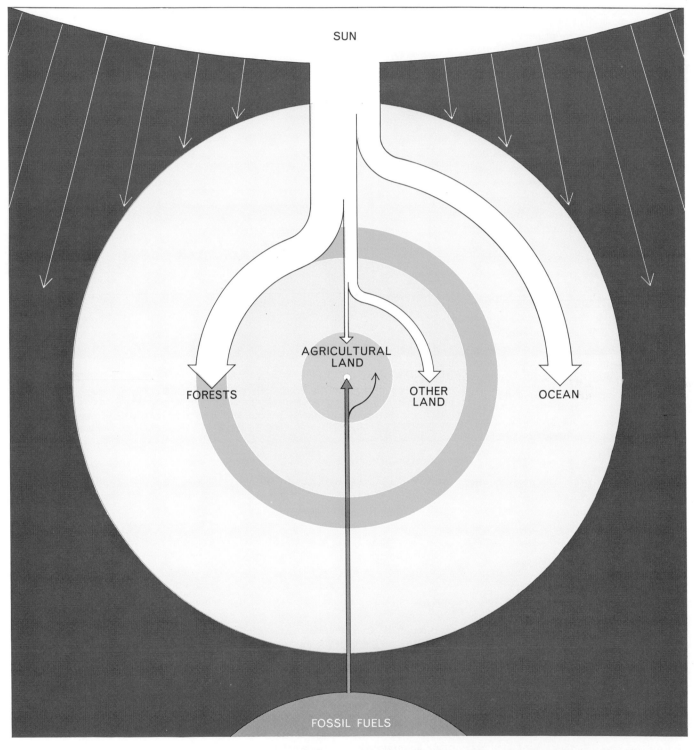

ENERGY FIXED by the earth's primary producers is equivalent to about 164 billion metric tons of dry organic matter a year, according to Robert H. Whittaker and Gene E. Likens of Cornell University. About 5 percent of the energy is fixed by agricultural ecosystems and is utilized directly by man, one species among millions. Man also draws annually on fossil fuel reserves for about the same amount of energy. In this anthropocentric view of the biosphere the area of the concentric rings is proportional to the major ecosystems' share of the surface area of the earth (indicated in millions of square kilometers). The width of the arrows is proportional to the amount of energy fixed in each ecosystem and contributed by fossil fuels (indicated in billions of metric tons of dry matter per year). The intensity of the color in each ring suggests the productivity (production per unit area) of each ecosystem.

Whittaker and Gene E. Likens of Cornell University have estimated that in all the earth's ecosystems, both terrestrial and marine, 164 billion metric tons of dry organic matter is produced annually, about a third of it in the oceans and two-thirds of it on land. This "net production" represents the excess of organic production over what is required to maintain the plants that fixed the energy; it is the energy potentially available for consumers.

Virtually all the net production of the earth is consumed annually in the respiration of organisms other than green plants, releasing carbon dioxide, water and the heat that is reradiated into space. The consumers are animals, including man, and the organisms of decay. The energy that is not consumed is either stored in the tissues of living organisms or in humus and organic sediments.

The relations between the producers and the consumers are clarified by two simple formulas. Consider the growth of a single green plant, an "autotroph" that is capable of fixing its own solar energy. Some of the energy it fixes is stored in organic matter that accumulates as new tissue. The amount of the new tissue, measured as dry weight, is the net production. This does not, however, represent all the energy fixed. Some energy is required just to support the living tissues of the plant. This is energy used in respiration.

The total energy fixed, then, is partitioned immediately within the plant according to the equation $GP - Rs_A = NP$. The total amount of energy fixed is gross production (GP); Rs_A is the energy used in the respiration of the autotrophic plant, and the amount of energy left over is net production (NP). The growth of a plant is measurable as net production, which can be expressed in any of several different ways, including energy stored and dry weight.

The same relations hold for an entire plant community and for the biosphere as a whole. If we consider not only the plants but also the consumers of plants and the entire food web, including the organisms of decay, we must add a new unit of respiration without adding any further producers. That is what happens as an ecosystem matures: consumer populations increase substantially, adding to the respiration of the plants the respiration (Rs_H) of the heterotrophs, the organisms that obtain their energy from the photosynthesizing plants. For an ecosystem (the total biota of any unit of the earth's surface) NEP equals $GP - (Rs_A + Rs_H)$. NEP is the net ecosystem

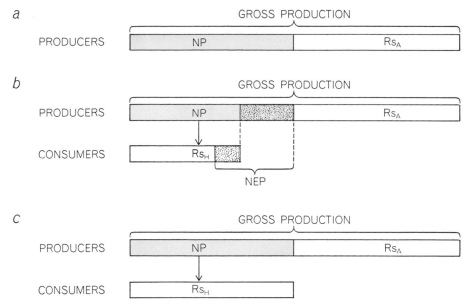

ENERGY IS UTILIZED by producers and consumers as shown here. In the case of a single green plant (*a*) some of the total energy fixed, or gross production, is expended in the plant's own respiration (Rs_A) and the rest goes into net production (NP), or new tissue. In a successional plant-and-animal community (*b*) some of the net production is stored as growth, contributing to net ecosystem production (NEP); the rest is used by consumers, which expend most of it in respiration (Rs_H) and store some as growth, adding to net ecosystem production. In a mature community (*c*) all the energy fixed is used in respiration.

production, the net increase in energy stored within the system. $Rs_A + Rs_H$ is the total respiration of the ecosystem.

This last equation establishes the important distinction between a "successional," or developmental, ecosystem and a "climax," or mature, one. In the successional system the total respiration is less than the gross production, leaving energy (NEP) that is built into structure and adds to the resources of the site. (A forest of large trees obviously has more space in it, more organic matter and probably a wider variety of microhabitats than a forest of small trees.) In a climax system, on the other hand, all the energy fixed is used in the combined respiration of the plants and the heterotrophs. NEP goes to zero: there is no energy left over and no net annual storage. Climax ecosystems probably represent a most efficient way of using the resources of a site to sustain life with minimum impact on other ecosystems. It is of course such ecosystems that have dominated the biosphere throughout recent millenniums.

These general relations are clarified if one asks, with regard to a specific ecosystem, how much energy is fixed and how it is used, and how efficient the ecosystem is in harvesting solar energy and supporting life. The answers are found by solving the simple production equations, but in order to solve them one must measure the metabolism of an en-

tire unit of landscape. Such studies are being attempted in many types of ecosystem under the aegis of the International Biological Program, a major research effort designed to examine the productivity of the biosphere. The example I shall give is drawn from research in an oak-pine forest at the Brookhaven National Laboratory.

The research has spanned most of a decade and has involved many contributors. A most important contribution was made by Whittaker, who collaborated with me in completing a detailed description of the structure of the forest, including the total amount of organic matter, the weight and area of leaves, the weight of roots and the amount of net production. The techniques developed in that work are now being used in many similar studies. Such data are necessary to relate other measurements, including measurements of the gas exchange between leaves and the atmosphere, to the entire forest and so provide an additional measurement of net production and respiration.

A major problem was measuring the forest's total respiration. We used two techniques. First, Winston R. Dykeman and I took advantage of the frequent inversions of temperature that occur in central Long Island and used the rate of accumulation of carbon dioxide during these inversions as a direct measurement of total respiration. The inversions are nocturnal; this eliminates the effect of photosynthesis, which of course proceeds only in daylight.

During an inversion the temperature of the air near the ground is (contrary to the usual daytime situation) lower than that of the air at higher elevations. Since the cooler air is denser, the air column remains vertically stable for as much as several hours; the carbon dioxide released by respiration accumulates, and its buildup at a given height is an index of the rate of respiration at that height. The calculation of the buildup during more than 40 inversions in the course of a year provided one measure of total respiration [*see top illustration on page 34*]. A second measurement came from a detailed study of the rates of respiration of various segments of the forest (including the branches and stems of trees) and the soil.

The estimates available from these studies and others are converging on the following solution of the production equations, all in terms of grams of dry organic matter per square meter per year: The gross production is 2,650 grams; the net production, 1,200 grams; the net ecosystem production, or net storage, 550 grams, and the total respiration, or energy loss, 2,100 grams, of which Rs_A is 1,450 and Rs_H is 650 [*see illustration on these two pages*]. The forest is obviously immature in the sense that it is still storing energy (NEP) in an increased plant population. The ratio of total respiration to gross production (2,100/2,650) suggests that the forest is at about 80 percent of climax and confirms other studies that show that the forest is "late successional."

The net production of the Brookhaven forest of 1,200 grams per square meter per year is in the low middle range for forests and is typical of the productivity of small-statured forests. The efficiency of this forest in using the annual input of solar energy effective in photosynthesis is about .9 percent. Large-statured forests (moist forests of the Temperate Zone, where nutrients are abundant, and certain tropical rain forests) have a net productivity ranging up to several thousand grams per square meter per year. They may have an efficiency approaching 3 percent of the usable energy available throughout the year at the surface of the ground, but usually not much more.

Sugarcane productivity in the Tropics has been reported as exceeding 9,000 grams per square meter per year. The new strains of rice that are contributing to the "green revolution" have a maximum yield under intensive triple-cropping regimes that may approach 2,000 grams of rice per square meter per year. Over large areas the yield is much lower, seldom exceeding 350 to 400 grams of milled rice per square meter per year. These yields are to be compared with corn yields in the U.S., which approach 500 grams. (The rice and corn yields are expressed as grain, not as total net production as we have been discussing it. Net production including the chaff, stems, leaves and roots is between three and five times the harvest of grain. Thus the net production of the most productive agriculture is 6,000 to 10,000 grams, probably the highest net production in the world. Most agriculture, however, has net production of 1,000 to 3,000 grams, the same range as most forests.)

The high productivities of agriculture are somewhat misleading in that they are bought with a contribution of energy from fossil fuels: energy that is applied to cultivate and harvest the crop, to manufacture and transport pesticides and fertilizers and to provide and control irrigation. The cost accounting is incomplete; these systems "leak" pesticides, fertilizers and often soil itself, injuring other ecosystems. It is clear, however, that the high yields of agriculture are dependent on a subsidy of energy that was fixed as fossil fuels in previous ages and is available now (and for some decades to come) to support large human populations. Without this subsidy or some other source of power, yields would drop. They may suffer in any case as it becomes increasingly necessary to reduce the interactions between agriculture and other ecosystems. One sign is the progressive restriction in the use of insecticides because of hazards far from where they are applied. Similar restraint may soon be necessary in the use of herbicides and fertilizers.

The oceans appear unproductive compared with terrestrial ecosystems. In separate detailed analyses of the fish production of the world's oceans William E. Ricker of the Fisheries Research Board of Canada and John H. Ryther of the Woods Hole Oceanographic Institution recently emphasized that the oceans are far from an unlimited resource. The net production of the open ocean is about

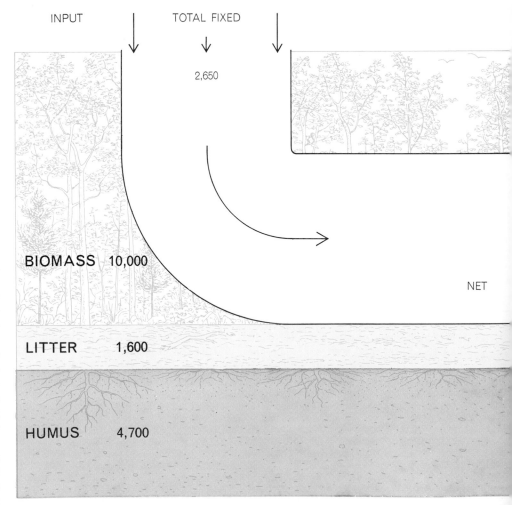

INPUT   TOTAL FIXED

2,650

BIOMASS   10,000

NET

LITTER   1,600

HUMUS   4,700

ENERGY RELATIONSHIPS were worked out for an oak-pine forest at the Brookhaven National Laboratory. Of the annual gross production of 2,650 grams of dry matter per

50 grams of fixed carbon per square meter per year. Areas of very high productivity, including coastal areas and areas of upwelling where nutrients are abundant, do not average more than 300 grams of carbon. The mean productivity of the oceans, according to this analysis, would be about 55 grams of carbon, equivalent to between 120 and 150 grams of dry organic matter.

Inasmuch as the highest productivity of enriched areas of the ocean barely approaches that of diminutive forests such as Brookhaven's, the oceans do not appear to represent a vast potential resource. On the contrary, Ryther suggests on the basis of an elaborate analysis of the complex trophic relations of the oceans that "it seems unlikely that the potential sustained yield of fish to man is appreciably greater than 100 million [metric] tons [wet weight]. The total world fish landings for 1967 were just over 60 million tons, and this figure has been increasing at an average rate of about 8 percent per year for the past 25 years.... At the present rate, the in-

dustry can expand for no more than a decade." Ricker comes to a similar conclusion. Neither he nor Ryther appraised the effects on the productivity of the oceans of the accumulation of toxic substances such as pesticides, of industrial and municipal wastes, of oil production on the continental shelves, of the current attempts at mining the sea bottom and of other exploitation of the seas that is inconsistent with continued harvesting of fish.

The available evidence suggests that, in spite of the much larger area of the oceans, by far the greater amount of energy is fixed on land. The oceans, even if their productivity can be preserved, do not represent a vast unexploited source of energy for support of larger human populations. They are currently being exploited at close to the maximum sustainable rate, and their continued use as a dump for wastes of all kinds makes it questionable whether that rate will be sustained.

A brief consideration of the utilization of the energy fixed in the Brookhaven forest will help to clarify this

point. The energy fixed by this late-successional forest is first divided between net production and immediate use in plant respiration, with about 55 percent being used immediately. (The ratio of 55 percent going directly into respiration appears consistent for the Temperate Zone forests examined so far; the ratio appears to rise in the Tropics and to decline in higher latitudes.) The net production is divided among herbivores, decay and storage. In the Brookhaven forest herbivore populations have been reduced by the exclusion of deer, leaving as the principal herbivores insects and limited populations of small mammals.

Our estimates indicate that only a few percent of the net production is consumed directly by herbivores (a low rate in comparison with other ecosystems). Practically all this quantity is consumed immediately in animal respiration, so that the animal population shows virtually no annual increase, or contribution to the net ecosystem production. The principal contribution to the net ecosystem production is the growth of the plant populations, which

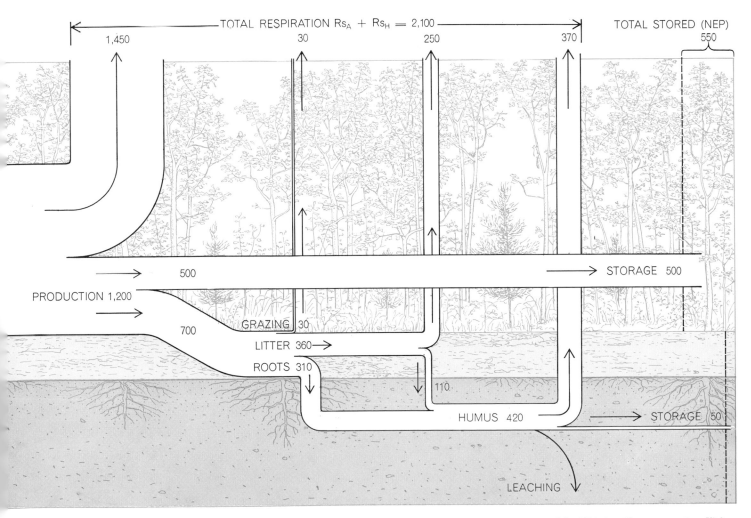

square meter, some 2,100 grams are lost in respiration, leaving 550 stored as new plant growth, litter and humus. The animal population is not increasing appreciably. This is a "late successional" forest in which 80 percent of the production is expended in respiration.

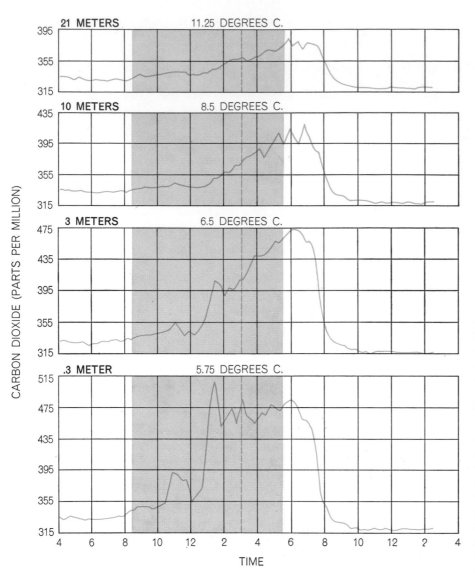

RATE OF RESPIRATION of the forest was determined by measuring the rate at which carbon dioxide, a product of respiration, accumulated during nights when the air was still because of a temperature inversion. The curves give the carbon dioxide concentration at four elevations in the course of one such night. (Note that the temperature, recorded at 3:00 A.M., was lower near the ground than at greater heights.) The hourly increase in carbon dioxide concentration, which was calculated from these curves, yielded rate of respiration.

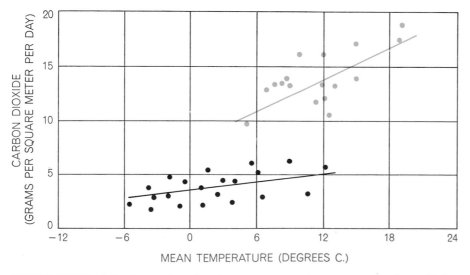

RESPIRATION of the forest, plotted against temperature, is seen to proceed at a higher rate in summer (*colored curve*) than in winter (*black curve*). Annual respiration was calculated in grams of carbon dioxide, then converted to yield the total respiration, 2,100 grams.

accounts for more than 40 percent of the net production. The remainder of the net production enters the food chains of decay, which are obviously well developed. Clearly the elimination of deer, combined with poorly developed herbivore and carnivore populations, has resulted in a diversion of energy from the grazing chain into the food chains of decay.

This is precisely what happens in aquatic systems as they are enriched with nutrients washed from the land; the shift to decay is also caused by the accumulation of any toxic substance, whether it affects plants or animals. Any reduction in populations of grazers shifts the flow of energy toward decay. Any effect on the plants shifts plant populations away from sensitive species toward resistant species that may not be food for the indigenous herbivores, thereby eliminating the normal food chains and also shifting the flow of energy into decay.

These observations simply show that the structure and function of major ecosystems are sensitive to many influences. Clearly the amount of living tissue that can be supported in any ecosystem depends on the amount of net production. Net production, however, is coupled to both photosynthesis and respiration, both of which can be affected by many factors. Photosynthesis is sensitive to light intensity and duration, to the availability of water and mineral nutrients and to temperature. It is also sensitive to the concentration of carbon dioxide; on a worldwide basis the amount of carbon dioxide in the atmosphere may exert a major control over rates of net production. Greenhouse men have recognized the sensitivity of photosynthesis to carbon dioxide concentration for many years and sometimes increase the concentration artificially to stimulate plant growth. Has the emission of carbon dioxide from the combustion of fossil fuels in the past 150 years caused a worldwide increase in net production, and if so, how much of an increase?

With equipment specially designed at Brookhaven, Robert Wright and I supplied air with enhanced levels of carbon dioxide to trees and determined the effect on net photosynthesis by measuring the uptake of the gas by leaves. The net amount of carbon dioxide that was fixed increased linearly with the increase in the carbon dioxide concentration in the air. Such small increases in carbon dioxide concentration have virtually no effect on rates of respiration. The data suggest that the increase of about 10 percent (30 parts per million) in the carbon dioxide concentration of the atmosphere since the middle of the 19th century caused by the industrial revolution may have increased net production by as much as 5 to 10 percent. This increase, if applicable worldwide and considered alone, would increase the total energy (and carbon) stored in natural ecosystems by an equivalent amount, and would result in an equivalent improvement in the yields of agriculture. The increase in net production also tends to stabilize the carbon dioxide content of the atmosphere by storing more carbon in living organic matter, particularly in forests, and in the nonliving organic matter of sediments and humus. Such changes have almost certainly occurred on a worldwide basis as an inadvertent result of human activities in the past 100 years or so.

Such simple single-factor analyses of environmental problems, however, are almost always misleading. As the carbon dioxide concentration in the atmosphere has been increasing, many other factors have changed. There was a period of rising temperature, possibly due to the increased carbon dioxide concentration. More recently, however, there has been a decline in world temperatures that continues. This can be expected to reduce net production worldwide by reducing the periods favorable for plant growth. Added to the effects of changing temperature—and indeed overriding it—is the accumulation of toxic wastes from human activities. The overall effect is to reduce the structure of ecosystems. This in turn shortens food chains and favors (1) populations of small hardy plants, (2) small-bodied herbivores that reproduce rapidly and (3) the food chains of decay. The loss of structure also implies a loss of "regulation"; the simplified communities are subject to rapid changes in the density of these smaller, more rapidly reproducing organisms that have been released from their normal controls.

Local increases in water temperature also give rise to predictable effects. There is talk, for example, of warming the waters of the New York region with waste heat from reactors to produce a rich "tropical" biota, but such manipulation would produce a degraded local biota supplemented by a few hardy species of more southerly ecosystems. Such circumstances again favor productivity not by complex, highly integrated arrays of specialized organisms but by simple arrays of generalized ones. Energy then is funneled not into intricate food webs capped by tuna, mackerel, petrels, dolphins and other highly specialized carni-

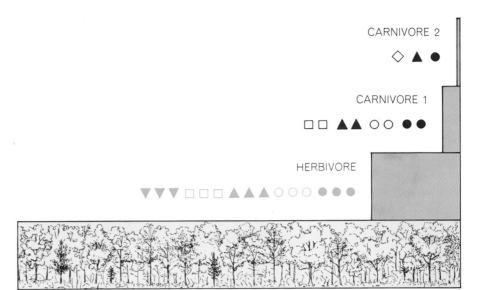

INTACT NATURAL ECOSYSTEM is exemplified by a mature oak-hickory forest that supports several stages of consumers in the grazing food chain, with from 10 to 20 percent of the energy in each trophic level being passed along to the next level. The symbols represent different herbivore and carnivore species. Complexity of structure regulates population sizes, maintaining the same pattern of energy distribution in the system from year to year.

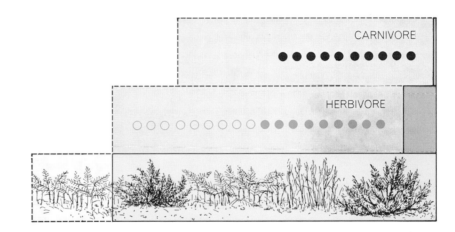

DEGRADED ECOSYSTEM has a truncated grazing chain. The annual production of the sparse grasses, herbs and shrubs fluctuates (*shaded area*). So do populations of herbivores and carnivores, which are characterized by large numbers of individuals but few different species. Under extreme conditions most of the net production may be consumed, leading to the starvation of herbivores and accentuating the characteristic fluctuation in populations.

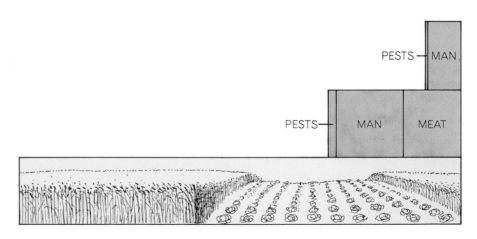

AGRICULTURAL ECOSYSTEM is a special case, yielding a larger than normal harvest of net production for herbivores, including man and animals that provide meat for man. Stability is maintained through inputs of energy in cultivation, pesticides and fertilizer.

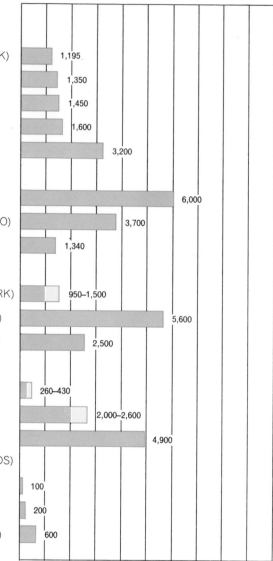

NATURAL ECOSYSTEMS

TEMPERATE TERRESTRIAL ZONE

OAK-PINE FOREST (NEW YORK) — 1,195

BEECH FOREST (DENMARK) — 1,350

SPRUCE FOREST (GERMANY) — 1,450

SCOTCH PINE (ENGLAND) — 1,600

GRASSLAND (NEW ZEALAND) — 3,200

TROPICAL TERRESTRIAL ZONE

FOREST (WEST INDIES) — 6,000

OIL-PALM PLANTATION (CONGO) — 3,700

FOREST (IVORY COAST) — 1,340

FRESHWATER

FRESHWATER POND (DENMARK) — 950–1,500

SEWAGE PONDS (CALIFORNIA) — 5,600

CATTAIL SWAMP (MINNESOTA) — 2,500

MARINE

ALGAE (DENMARK) — 260–430

SEAWEED (NOVA SCOTIA) — 2,000–2,600

ALGAE ON CORAL REEF (MARSHALL ISLANDS) — 4,900

OPEN OCEAN (AVERAGE) — 100

COASTAL ZONE (AVERAGE) — 200

UPWELLING AREAS (AVERAGE) — 600

AGRICULTURAL ECOSYSTEMS

TEMPERATE ZONE

CORN (MINNESOTA) — 1,390

CORN (ISRAEL) — 3,600

CORN (U.S. AVERAGE) — 2,500–4,000

RICE (JAPAN AVERAGE) — 1,000–1,200

TROPICAL ZONE

SUGARCANE (HAWAII) — 7,200–7,800

SUGARCANE (JAVA) — 9,400

RICE (CEYLON AVERAGE) — 340–550

RICE (WEST PAKISTAN AVERAGE) — 560–700

0   2,000   4,000   6,000   8,000   10,000

NET PRODUCTION
(GRAMS PER SQUARE METER PER YEAR)

NET PRODUCTION LEVELS of a number of natural and agricultural ecosystems are compared. (The total net production of U.S. corn and of rice is calculated from grain yields.)

vores but into simple food webs dominated by hardy scavengers such as gulls and crabs and into the food webs of decay. As the annual contribution to decay increases, these webs in water become overloaded; the oxygen dissolved in the water is used up and metabolism shifts from the aerobic form where oxygen is freely available to the much less efficient anaerobic respiration; organic matter accumulates, releasing methane, hydrogen sulfide and other noxious gases that only reinforce the tendency.

The broad pattern of these changes is clear enough. On the one hand, an increasing fraction of the total energy fixed is being diverted to the direct support of man, replacing the earth's major ecosystems with cities and land devoted to agriculture—the simplified ecosystems of civilization that require continuing contributions of energy under human control for their regulation. On the other hand, the leakage of toxic substances from the man-dominated provinces of the earth is reducing the structure and self-regulation of the remaining natural ecosystems. The trend is progressive. The simplification of the earth's biota is breaking down the insulation of large units of the earth's surface, increasing the interactions between terrestrial and aquatic systems, between upland and lowland, between river and estuary. The long-term trend of evolution toward building complex, integral, stable ecosystems is being reversed. Although the changes are rapid, accelerating and important, they do not mean that the earth will face an oxygen crisis; photosynthesis will continue for a long time yet, perhaps at an accelerated rate in certain places, stimulated by increased carbon dioxide concentrations in air and the availability of nutrients in water. A smaller fraction of the earth's fixed energy is easily available to man, however. The energy flows increasingly through smaller organisms such as the hardy shrubs and herbs of the irradiated forest at Brookhaven, the scrub oaks that are replacing the smog-killed pines of the Los Angeles basin, the noxious algae of eutrophic lakes and estuaries, into short food chains, humus and anaerobic sediments.

These are major man-caused changes in the biosphere. Many aspects of them are irreversible; their implications are poorly known. Together they constitute a major series of interlocking objectives for science and society in the next decade focused on the question: "How much of the energy that runs the biosphere can be diverted to the support of a single species: man?"

IV

The Water Cycle

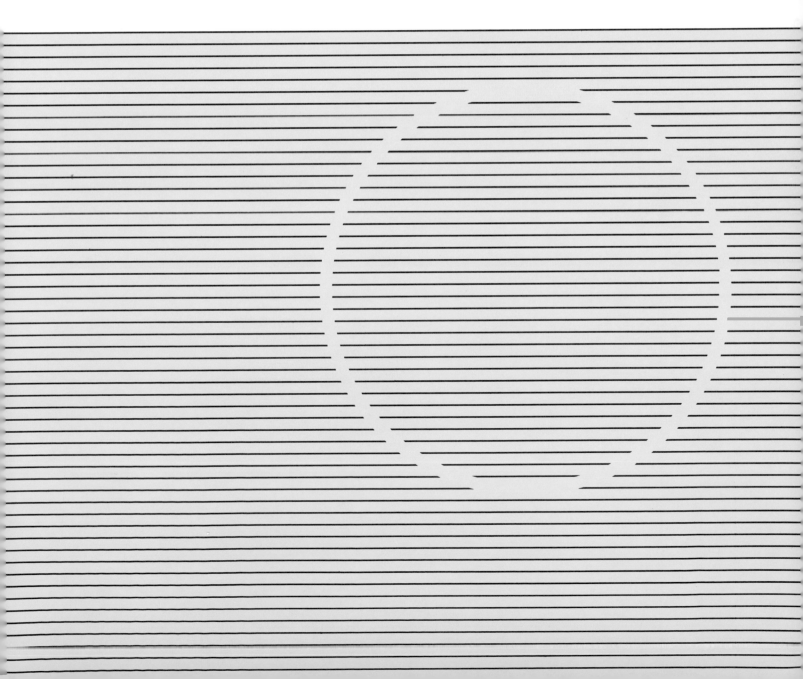

The Water Cycle

by H. L. PENMAN

Water is the medium of life processes and the source of their hydrogen. It flows through living matter mainly in the stream of transpiration: from the roots of a plant through its leaves

By far the most abundant single substance in the biosphere is the familiar but unusual inorganic compound called water. The earth's oceans, ice caps, glaciers, lakes, rivers, soils and atmosphere contain 1.5 billion cubic kilometers of water in one form or another. In nearly all its physical properties water is either unique or at the extreme end of the range of a property. Its extraordinary physical properties, in turn, endow it with a unique chemistry. From these physical and chemical characteristics flows the biological importance of water. It is the purpose of this chapter to describe some of water's principal qualities and their significance in the biosphere.

Water remains a liquid within the temperature range most suited to life processes, yet in due season there are occasions when liquid water exists in equilibrium with its solid and gaseous form, for example as ice on the top of a lake with water vapor in the air above it. Freezing starts at the surface of the water and proceeds downward; this follows from one of water's many peculiar attributes. Like everything else, ice included, liquid water contracts when it is cooled, but the shrinkage ceases before solidification, at about four degrees Celsius. From that temperature down to the freezing point the water expands, and because of its decreased density the cooler water floats on top of the warmer. Ice has a density of .92 with respect to the maximum density of water and hence an unconstrained block of ice will float in water with about an eleventh of its volume projecting above the surface. The biological significance of freezing from the surface downward, rather than from the bottom upward, is too well known to need repetition here.

Among its other thermal properties water has the greatest specific heat known among liquids (the ability to store heat energy for a given increase in temperature). The same is true of water's latent heat of vaporization: at 20 degrees C. (68 degrees Fahrenheit), 585 calories are required to evaporate one gram of water. Finally, with the exception of mercury, water has the greatest thermal conductivity of all liquids. Some consequences of water's large latent heat of evaporation, which is a major energizer of the atmosphere, will be considered below. Its great specific heat means that, for a given rate of energy input, the temperature of a given mass of water will rise more slowly than the temperature of any other material. Conversely, as energy is released its temperature will drop more slowly. This slow warming and cooling, together with other important factors, affects yearly, daily and even hourly changes in the temperature of oceans and lakes, which are quite different from the corresponding changes in the temperature of land. Among other things, this can lead to differences in the thermal regimes of soils that are of major importance in ecology. The type of soil, interacting with water, determines the earliness or lateness of plant growth at a given site; the interaction may also affect the local risk of frost.

In basic structure the water molecule has a small dipole moment and is feebly ionized. Water will dissolve almost anything to some extent (fortunately the extent is extremely small for many substances). The dissolved material tends to remain in solution because of another of water's exceptional attributes. The values given by the inverse-square law for the force that attracts separated positive and negative ions are determined by multiplying the square of the distance separating the ions by a constant that varies according to the nature of the separating medium. Known as the dielectric constant, this constant is greater for water than for any other substance. To get the same attractive force in water as in air, for example, the water separation has to be cut down to a ninth of the separation in air.

Because of its extreme dielectric constant liquid water in the biosphere is not chemically pure (unlike water vapor, which is always pure, or ice, which can be and often is pure). Instead liquid water is an ionic solution and one that always contains some hydrogen ions because the water itself can supply them. The concentration of hydrogen ions, expressed as a degree of dilution, gives the physical chemist a numerical index that describes the state of various water samples. The number is the logarithm (to the base 10) of the degree of dilution; the chemist labels it pH. For his tests he is armed with a pH meter, calibrated from zero to 14. Fourteen orders of magnitude is an enormous range for any terrestrial

WATER AT WORK for millenniums in the form of rainfall and stream runoff has produced the dissected land surface seen in the side-looking radar image on the opposite page. The annual work of terrain modeling by rainfall and runoff has been estimated to equal the work of one horse-drawn scraper busy day and night on every 10 acres of land surface. This area, in the vicinity of Sandy Hook, Ky., is drained by tributaries of the Ohio River. Each inch equals 2.3 miles on the ground. The radar mosaic, made by the Autometric division of the Raytheon Company, is reproduced by the courtesy of the Army Topographic Command.

property, yet the water content of the soil may give a reading anywhere from pH 3 (very acid) to pH 10 (very alkaline), which is equivalent to a range of from one to 10 million. These are extremes, however, and most terrestrial plant growth—including much of the world's agriculture—proceeds in soil with a water content that ranges only a few units on each side of pH 6. The range for marine organisms is even more restrictive: coastal waters are about pH 9 and the general oceanic average is just over pH 8. Below pH 7.5 many marine animals die; eggs are particularly vulnerable. Below pH 7 the carbonate in seawater would remain in solution, rendering production of any kind of skeleton impossible.

Another method of describing the state of a given water sample is independent of hydrogen-ion content. Material in solution, whether it is ionized or not, disturbs the liquid structure of the water; in thermodynamic terms the presence of solutes decreases the free energy of the water. Many soil and plant workers find it convenient to use the symbol pF for such changes in free energy, with the steps between units also representing one order of magnitude. As with the pH range, the range of pF values is very great.

The quantity being measured in pF units is basically a potential, with the same dimensions as pressure. If all the water problems in soils, plants and animals were problems of solutions, it would be sufficient to describe the consequent variations in free energy as variations in osmotic potential, expressed in any of the conventional units of pressure. The free energy of water, however, can be decreased in other ways, notably in capillary systems. The energy to lift the water into a capillary tube (or in nature into the porous and cellular systems of soils and plants) comes out of the free energy of the water. Today this is known as "matric" potential, a term that has replaced the earlier "capillary" potential. In soils and plants the matric potential may be more than the osmotic potential. A comparison of numbers will give an idea of the pF scale and its ranges. The pressure is expressed as the height in centimeters of an equivalent column of water; thus one bar equals one atmosphere, which equals a 1,000-centimeter water column. This is equivalent to pF 3.

In a waterlogged soil, beginning to drain, the matric potential may be between pF 0 and pF 1; in a fully drained soil the potential may be near pF 1.7. In a soil that is as dry as plant uptake and the transpiration of water from leaves can make it, the matric potential will be about pF 4.2, which is close to 16 atmospheres of suction. The osmotic potential of seawater is near pF 4.5, which makes seawater too "dry" for plant roots; the salt content of plant cells might be anywhere in a range from less than pF 4 up to pF 4.5.

Here once again water is extreme. Associated with the matric potential in a capillary system there is a curved liquid-air interface; the value of the potential is found by doubling the known value of the liquid's surface tension and dividing the product by the radius of curvature. Water has the greatest surface tension of any liquid known, so that at any given matric potential the radius of curvature of a water meniscus will be greater than it could be for another liquid. The greater the radius of curvature, the greater the total water content. In a soil this means that more liquid can be retained as water just because it *is* water. In general, but not always, this is an advantage for plant growth.

The effects of a decrease in the free energy of water contained in porous soils or in the tissues of plants include a lowering of the fluid's freezing point and vapor pressure. If the source of the decrease is a matric potential, there is also negative pressure, or suction, that tends to pull all kinds of retaining walls together. The effect of freezing in soils and rocks is worth a brief aside. As the temperature falls the water in the larger soil pores freezes first and the free-energy gradient is such that water will be withdrawn from the smaller pores. As a result ice lenses form in the coarser pore spaces and the finer pore spaces are exposed to greater shrinkage forces. Because water expands on freezing, the ice lenses have a disruptive effect as they make room for themselves. In rock this is the beginning of one method of soil formation. There tends to be a preferred size for the rock fragments produced by ice disruption. This size is near the optimum for transport by wind and is the dominant size in many of the loess soils that have accumulated in areas near glaciers. In soil the ice disruption is the source of "frost tilth," which is sought by farmers when they leave land roughly plowed in the fall and hope for a sufficiently frosty winter.

There are still some uncertainties with respect to the world's water balance, but agreement was reached on probable values or ranges during an international symposium on the subject held in Britain this summer as one of the activities of the International Hydrological Decade. The figures that follow are taken from the proceedings of the symposium.

The world's water exists as liquid (salt and fresh), as solid (fresh) and as vapor (fresh). There is some uncertainty in the value of the total volume, but it is near 1,500 million cubic kilometers (in U.S. usage 1.5 billion). Estimates of the components are most easily expressed as

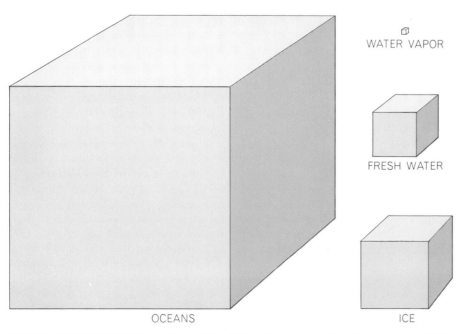

WATER VAPOR

FRESH WATER

OCEANS

ICE

WORLD WATER SUPPLY consists mainly of the salt water contained in the oceans (*left*). The world's fresh water comprises only about 3 percent of the total supply; three-quarters of it is locked up in the world's polar ice caps and glaciers and most of the rest is found as ground water or in lakes. The very small amount of water in the atmosphere at any one time (*top right*) is nonetheless of vital importance as a major energizer of weather systems.

average depths per unit area of the entire surface of the earth, which has a total area of 510 million square kilometers. Oceans and seas—liquid salt water—make up about 97 percent of all water, with an equivalent depth of between 2,700 and 2,800 meters; the greater part is in the Southern Hemisphere. Of the remaining 3 percent, three-quarters is locked up as solid in the polar ice caps and in glaciers. Here measurement is quite difficult, and a spread in estimates is inevitable. The equivalent depth of ice and snow may be near 120 meters, but at the recent symposium a value of 50 meters was not challenged. The other large component of fresh liquid water is subject to similar uncertainty: the estimates for underground water may be near 45 meters, but again a value near 15 meters was not challenged. Estimates for surface water,

mainly in the great lakes of the world, ranged from .4 meter to one meter. There is general agreement on the average water-vapor content of the atmosphere, at an equivalent in liquid of .03 meter. Although this is a very small fraction of the total, size is no measure of importance. Without water in the atmosphere there would be no weather; Leonardo da Vinci's dictum, "Water is the driver of nature," is justified on meteorological grounds alone. A little detail at this point will be helpful as an introduction to another aspect of the world circulation of water.

The amount of water vapor is not the same everywhere, either geographically or seasonally. It is greatest at and near the Equator. If the air there were squeezed dry, it would yield about 44 millimeters of rainfall. In middle lati-

tudes, say from 40 to 50 degrees, the summer yield would be near 20 millimeters and the winter yield near 10 millimeters, with large variations that depend on geography and weather patterns. In the polar regions the yield ranges from two millimeters in winter to as much as eight in summer.

Water vapor enters the atmosphere by evaporation (this term includes transpiration by vegetation), and the main oceanic sources are fairly identifiable. It leaves the atmosphere as rain or snow, and because the precipitation may take place close to the source or thousands of miles away, the residence time may vary from a few hours to a few weeks. A general average is nine or 10 days.

The general balance of evaporation and precipitation needs three sets of figures, one set for the entire earth, one for the oceans and one for the land surface.

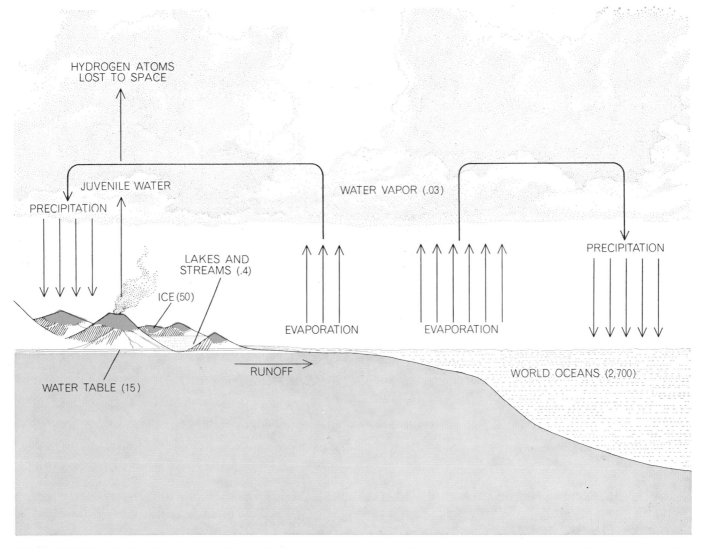

WATER CYCLE in the biosphere requires that worldwide evaporation and precipitation be equal; hydrogen losses to space are presumably replaced by juvenile water. Ocean evaporation, however, is greater than return precipitation; the reverse is true of the land. Excess land precipitation may end up in ice caps and glaciers that contain 75 percent of all fresh water, may replenish supplies taken from the water table by transpiring plants or may enter lakes and rivers, eventually returning to the sea as runoff. Numbers show minimum estimates of the amount of water present in each reserve, expressed as a depth in meters per unit area of the earth's surface.

Here, within a few percent, there is almost complete agreement on values. For the entire earth, average evaporation and precipitation are equal—as they must be—at very nearly 100 centimeters per year. For the oceans, expressed as equivalent depths over the area of the oceans, the average annual precipitation is between 107 and 114 centimeters, the average annual evaporation is between 116 and 124 centimeters and balance is restored by river flow, with an annual value close to 10 centimeters in all estimates. For the land surface the average annual precipitation is near 71 centimeters, the average annual evaporation is near 47 centimeters and the average annual river discharge is near 24 centimeters. (The ocean figure of 10 centimeters corresponds to the 24-centimeter land figure.)

Because half of the land surface—ice caps, deserts, mountains, tundra—contributes little or nothing to evaporation, a better evaporation average would take into consideration only the land compo-

nent of the biosphere where the availability of water is combined with the opportunity for evaporation. Here the average evaporation may total 100 centimeters per year. The evaporation in high latitudes would of course be far less than the evaporation nearer the Equator.

Available measurements support this conclusion. In Finland, at 65 degrees north latitude, the average evaporation is 20 centimeters per year; in southeastern England, at 50 degrees north, it is 50; in North Carolina, at 35 degrees north, it ranges from 80 to 120. On the Equator in the Congo basin the average is 120 centimeters per year; at the same latitude in Kenya it is 150. In the papyrus swamps of the Nile in the southern Sudan, 10 degrees north of the Equator, the average is 240 centimeters per year, but this is a special case. Here the river carries its water into the desert environment of the Sudd; evaporation rates are high not only because of the clear skies and intense sunshine overhead but also because the surrounding desert is a

source of hot dry air that augments evaporation. This kind of advective augmentation operates in many places other than the Sudan, particularly in semiarid regions where irrigation is practiced, and not quite enough is known about it.

Once in the air, water vapor may circulate locally or become part of the general circulation of the atmosphere. The general circulation is one of the three important ways of moving water across the earth. Some indication of the worldwide volumes involved is given by the fact that the total annual precipitation over the U.S. comes to some 6,000 cubic kilometers, whereas the liquid equivalent of the water vapor that passes over the U.S. in a year owing to the general circulation of the atmosphere is 10 times that amount.

Of the two remaining important ways of moving water across the earth, the major ocean currents comprise one and the discharge of rivers comprises the other. Both have substantial effects on

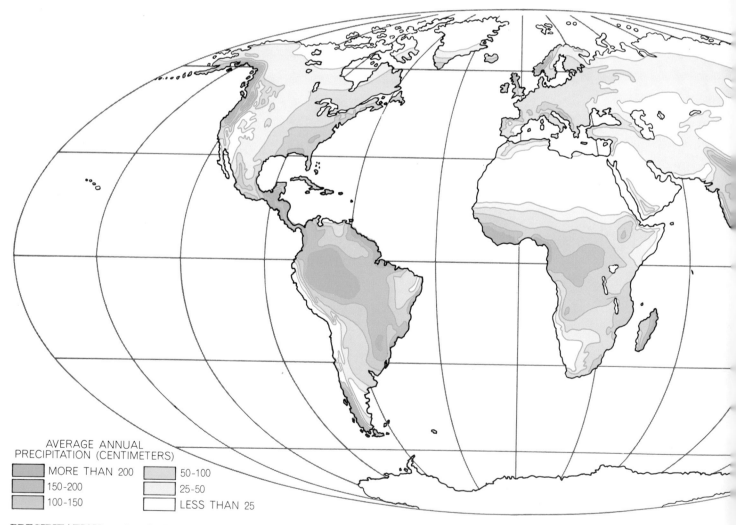

AVERAGE ANNUAL
PRECIPITATION (CENTIMETERS)

MORE THAN 200   50-100
150-200   25-50
100-150   LESS THAN 25

PRECIPITATION reaches the land areas of the world principally in the form of rainfall, which is heaviest at and near the Equator and along some western coasts at higher latitudes (*darker colors*). Variations in precipitation are the result of atmospheric circula-

the biosphere. The ocean currents carry energy surpluses or deficits over great distances; one well-known instance accounts for the extreme contrast between the climates on the west and east sides of the Atlantic in the areas between 50 and 55 degrees north latitude. Without the Gulf Stream northwestern Europe would be a much less pleasant place in which to live and work; indeed, if the cold Labrador Current had replaced the Gulf Stream, the history of civilization would have been very different.

The rivers of the world not only are long-distance movers of water but also serve as conduits for dissolved and suspended material. Because of its chemical and physical properties, water is a very efficient erosive agent; erosion, transport and deposition have to be recognized as geological processes associated with water in the biosphere. They are the processes that have produced lands and soils, now densely populated and intensively cropped, where annual floods and silt deposition are regarded as the mainstay

of life. Elsewhere, notably in the Americas, silt is an embarrassment in the deltas where it settles, and its production is equally unwelcome in river headwaters.

Two further points about river water deserve mention. First, the salt content of river water differs markedly in composition from that of the oceans. This suggests that the oceanic brine is not merely the accumulation of salts from aeons of land-surface leaching. Second, information about river discharge rates is scanty and not always reliable. As an example, it is only recently that a good estimate of the flow of the Amazon has been obtained. It proved to be twice the best previous estimate and indicates that almost a fifth of the world's river discharge comes from this one stream.

It is not possible to do more than guess at the average amount of water the world's plant and animal populations contain. Considered as the equivalent of rainfall, it may amount to about one millimeter over the entire surface of the earth. This is less by one order of mag-

nitude than the amount of water vapor in the atmosphere, and its distribution is even more varied in space and time. For a fully grown good crop of corn in North America or of sugar beet in northwestern Europe the amount might come to the equivalent of five millimeters of rainfall, and its summer residence time would be two to three days. This is a measure of the rate of water supply needed to maintain optimum conditions for growth. Here, at the point of water uptake by the roots of plants, begins the problem with respect to water in the biosphere that makes all other water problems seem trifling.

With unimportant exceptions, the basis of all life on the earth is photosynthesis by green plants, a process that involves physics (in the fixation of solar energy) and chemistry (in the union of carbon dioxide and water to form carbohydrates and more complex biochemical compounds). Water comes into the story in two ways: in transit (as part of the transpiration stream) and in residence (as its hydrogen is chemically bound into the plant structure). The amount that is bound, however, may be less than a fifth of the amount in transit. To give scale to the argument that follows, here are some values based on a real crop in a real climate. In producing 20 fresh-weight tons of crop, 2,000 tons of water will pass into the plants at their roots. At harvest perhaps 15 tons of the water supply will be in transit, leaving the crop with a dry weight of five tons. To produce the five tons of dry matter three tons of water will have been fixed and transformed. The energy fixed in the dry matter will be 1 percent or less of the total solar energy received by the crop; nearly 40 percent of the energy will have been used to evaporate the transpired water. Here is a clear interaction of the kind envisioned in the chapter that introduces this book, in which G. Evelyn Hutchinson describes the biosphere as "a region in which liquid water can exist [and that] receives an ample supply of energy from an external source."

The average value of 40 percent for the net solar radiation income retained by a green crop cover varies, of course, with season and climate. The first loss is to reflectivity: of the solar radiation reaching the crop about 30 percent is reflected. There is also an income of long-wave radiation from the sky, but this is outweighed by the outgo of long-wave radiation from the earth to the atmosphere. When the deficit is met by deducting it from the remaining balance of short-wave solar income, the net re-

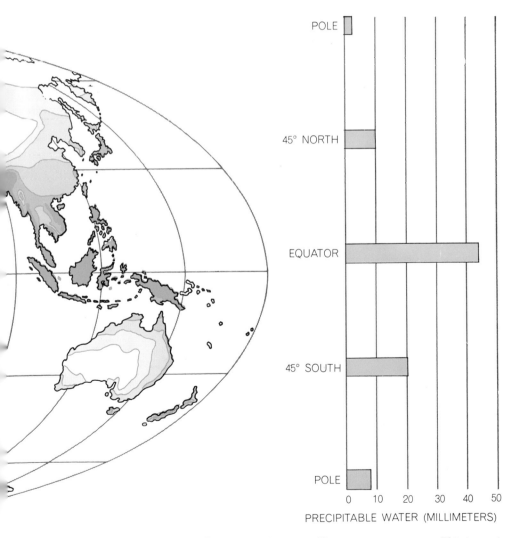

tion patterns and also reflect the amount of precipitable water vapor present. This is greatest at the Equator, least at the poles and more in summer than in winter (*graph at right*).

tained income is decreased to 40 percent of the initial input. As already noted, when the water is available, very nearly all this energy is used in evaporating water.

Here once again water stands at the extreme of a range of physical properties. The volume of water evaporated per unit of energy input is less than it would be for any other liquid. The relevant physical constant, the latent heat of vaporization, is somewhat less than 600 calories per gram at ordinary temperatures, but the rounded figure is adequate for the present purpose. If we let R_I represent the total radiant income in calories per square centimeter over a period of time, then the net radiation is about $.4R_I$ and the evaporation equivalent is near $R_I/$ 1,500 grams per square centimeter (or centimeters of water depth as the equivalent of rainfall). Consider some real midsummer values to show what this means. In a humid temperate climate the value of R_I is close to 450 calories per square centimeter per day. This works out to an evaporation equivalent of three millimeters per day, which is a good estimate for June in southeastern England. For many of the farming areas of the U.S. the R_I value is close to 650 calories per square centimeter, bringing the evaporation rate up to about 4.5 millimeters per day. The maximum rates known, which are found in irrigated areas, range from 4.5 to 7.5 millimeters per day. It is possible that the higher rates are influenced by advection from surrounding nonirrigated areas, as is the case in the papyrus swamps of the Nile.

The most important fact to be considered in connection with this wide range of evaporation rates is that there are only very small variations among the evaporation rates of different kinds of plants. Thus the governing factor in variation is almost exclusively a climatic one. This fact and much other evidence suggest that the supposed water "need" of a crop is dictated not by the plants but by the weather. In this connection the concept of "potential transpiration," which came into use simultaneously and independently in at least two parts of the world, is of great value both in research and in the practical aspects of soil water management. It is worthwhile seeing how potential transpiration is linked with elementary plant physiology and with some of the physics of soil water already considered.

A growing plant takes in water at the roots and, in the absence of immediate replenishment, the process dries the soil so that more and more energy is required for further extraction. The energy requirement is very small, however, compared with the amount of energy needed to evaporate the same quantity of water from the plant's leaves. There can be no serious error in assuming, as Frank J. Veihmeyer of the University of California at Davis does, that all soil water is equally available for transpiration up to the stage marked by the onset of wilting. The purpose of well-managed irrigation, of course, is to make sure that plants never get to the wilting stage. For maximum growth irrigation may have to consist of frequent small applications of water rather than occasional large ones.

Given an adequate supply of water, the chain of consequences is simple. There are maximum values for each of several factors: water content in the plant, hydrostatic pressure in the plant and leaf turgidity. When neither the intensity of the light nor the concentration of carbon dioxide constitutes a limiting factor, maximum leaf turgidity permits maximum opening of the stomatal aperatures in the leaf surface, thus affording the best possible opportunity for movement of carbon dioxide into the leaf. The state of the stomatal opening that allows easy inflow of carbon dioxide, however, also allows equally easy outflow of water vapor. By far the greater part of the water need of plants is actually a "leakage" process that has to be kept going to ensure continued growth. Given a sufficiently wet soil around the plants' roots, the rate of leakage is dictated not by plant physiology but by the physical factors of temperature, humidity and ventilation. The sole constraint is imposed by the law of energy conservation. In its last stages the transpiration stream undergoes a change of state from liquid to vapor, and the rate of change depends on the rate at which energy can reach the system to supply the necessary latent heat of vaporization.

So much for the physics of the process. When the supply of water in the soil approaches exhaustion, plant physiology rather than physics begins to predominate. Plant type, root structure, phase of

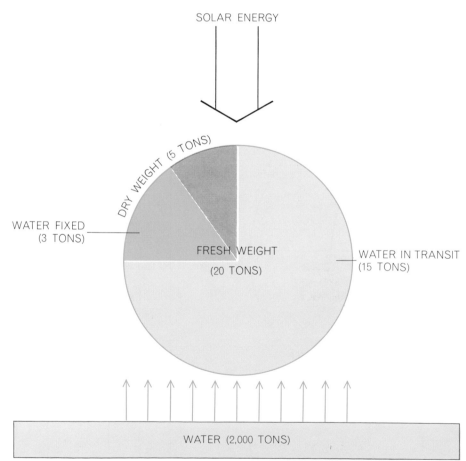

ROLE OF WATER in photosynthesis is quantitatively minor compared with its role in transpiration, as this crop-water graph indicates. To produce 20 fresh-weight tons of crop in a season, some 2,000 tons of water will be drawn from the soil. At the harvest, water in transit will account for some 15 tons of the crop's fresh weight. Drying reduces the crop's weight to five tons. Of these, three tons, or .15 percent of the water used in the season, comprise hydrogen atoms from water molecules, photosynthetically bound to carbon atoms.

plant development, soil type, soil depth—these become the important factors. What is available for utilization has more significance than the weather has, particularly in semiarid zones.

Because agriculture is most active in the more humid zones of the biosphere, it is useful to estimate how much reserve soil water is available on the average in these zones. Factors already described prevent any exact answer to this question. Nonetheless, a cautious estimate, advanced with considerable reservation, would be about 10 centimeters of rainfall equivalent. Three examples will suffice to show the need for caution. There are large agricultural areas of North Carolina and neighboring states where an inert subsoil is covered by no more than 20 centimeters of useful topsoil. Here the entire water reserve available to the agricultural cycle cannot exceed a rainfall equivalent of five centimeters. This is one extreme; the deep volcanic soils of East Africa are at the other. In those soils the roots of many plants go down as much as six meters below the surface. The available water in a profile that deep is equivalent to nearly 50 centimeters of rain, and the plant can extract water throughout a long dry season at something very close to the potential transpiration rate. An example from France falls somewhere in between. There the drying of the soil was observed while a crop of sugar beet transpired at the full potential rate throughout a dry summer. At the driest stage the crop had withdrawn from the soil available water equivalent to 27 centimeters of rainfall.

Soil water and ground water are closely related, but whereas soil water is always biologically important, the importance of ground water may range from being trivial to being all that matters. The soil is a kind of buffer between rainfall and ground water. In general any deficit in soil moisture that has built up in a dry period must be completely restored by rain before there is any water surplus available to move down to ground water. This is an important consideration for the water engineer, who may be drawing a water supply from a stream (permanent streams are sustained by ground water) or may be tapping an aquifer directly by means of a well. In the first instance the engineer will presumably have to work within legal constraints on how much river water he can divert. In the second, if he is to choose a safe aquifer pumping rate, the engineer must (or should!) have some awareness of the current soil-moisture deficit

and of the likely rates of rainfall in the months ahead. The river engineer can use the same information for another purpose: the soil-moisture deficit will enable him to estimate the risk of flooding in the event of a heavy storm.

In some countries the control of ground water is a major outlet for engineering skill, and its exploitation is the basis of farming technique. One need only think on the one hand of the Netherlands and on the other of such semiarid regions as Iran, where deep tunnels tap the buried aquifers and carry ground water to valley bottoms. In many semiarid regions the vegetation along transient streams maintains its luxuriance because the ground-water level there is close to the surface and within reach of plant roots. The plants' effective reach depends both on the soil and on the kind of plant, but in general it is seldom more than a few meters. The movement of any water table deeper than that is unaffected by the plant growth or the evaporation processes taking place above it, and its ground water contributes nothing to the biological activity at the surface.

What has been said about water so far has involved terms that are generally accepted, and the concepts themselves are supported by good reasoning, good evidence or both. The remarks that follow, although also based on reasoning and evidence, are more speculative and personal. If the biosphere is taken to be the place where water and energy interact, can the interaction be expressed quantitatively in terms of biological productivity? The answer has to be no. There are too many variables. All the same, by rearranging some of the water quantities and energy quantities that are known, a suggestive relation can be obtained.

Start with the fact that, for a good crop, 1 percent or less of the incoming solar radiation is fixed as dry matter (here and in what follows the 1 percent refers to the total botanical yield, irrespective of economic value). We shall give this percentage the symbol ε, and express it numerically as 100 per 10,000. This degree of efficiency is achieved only by an experiment station or by an extremely competent commercial farmer. Based on the statistics of world cereal production, including straw as well as grain, the average achievement in highly mechanized industrial farming shows an efficiency of only about 35 per 10,000. This decreases to roughly 17 per 10,000 in North America, and in tropical Africa and Asia subsistence farming rarely shows an efficiency better than 8, even when the pos-

sibility of two crops per year is allowed for. There is obviously room for improvement everywhere and the question in the present context is: Where does water come in, and how?

Some evidence is now being accumulated suggesting that, when there are no limitations on water supply, the total crop growth is proportional to the total of potential transpiration over the period of growth. The factor of proportionality depends on many things: plant variety, management, kinds and quantities of fertilizer, pest and disease controls and the like. Hence the negative answer to the earlier question. Still, something can be done with ratios. There is reason to believe potential transpiration is a fairly constant fraction of the solar radiation income. Combining this fact with the relation between potential transpiration and total crop growth, it is possible to derive a connection between growth rate and utilization of water, assuming that unlimited water is available (by inference, there would be a similar response to timely irrigation). In what may seem too precise a form, the answer is that the increase in yield (t) equals $.39\varepsilon$. Here ε represents efficiency and t can be read, according to preference, as metric tons per hectare per centimeter of water applied or as tons per acre per inch of water. Considering the fivefold (or perhaps tenfold) world variation in efficiency, some uncertainty in the multiplying factor is unimportant; others may prefer, or find, a different value. Taking the illustration already given, suppose the area involved is one acre and the efficiency is exactly or almost 100 per 10,000. The predicted increase in yield in response to water, *applied when it is needed*, is .39 ton of dry matter per acre per inch of water. In terms of fresh weight the gain is about 1.5 tons per acre per inch. This is the kind of response obtained in experiments with irrigated potatoes in Britain.

There are some countries where the value of ε is small because of lack of water, but there are many, including several of the rice-growing nations, where the small value of ε is more truly a measure of the inefficiency of the farming system itself. To get the most out of water, whether it comes from irrigation or from rainfall, the standard of performance elsewhere in the system must be improved: better varieties, better soil management, better crop husbandry, better plant hygiene and better pest control. Then water may be the driver of nature in agriculture as well as in the atmosphere.

V

The Carbon Cycle

The Carbon Cycle

by BERT BOLIN

The main cycle is from carbon dioxide to living matter and back to carbon dioxide. Some of the carbon, however, is removed by a slow epicycle that stores huge inventories in sedimentary rocks

The biosphere contains a complex mixture of carbon compounds in a continuous state of creation, transformation and decomposition. This dynamic state is maintained through the ability of phytoplankton in the sea and plants on land to capture the energy of sunlight and utilize it to transform carbon dioxide (and water) into organic molecules of precise architecture and rich diversity. Chemists and molecular biologists have unraveled many of the intricate processes needed to create the microworld of the living cell. Equally fundamental and no less interesting is the effort to grasp the overall balance and flow of material in the worldwide community of plants and animals that has developed in the few billion years since life began. This is ecology in the broadest sense of the word: the complex interplay between, on the one hand, communities of plants and animals and, on the other, both kinds of community and their nonliving environment.

We now know that the biosphere has not developed in a static inorganic environment. Rather the living world has profoundly altered the primitive lifeless earth, gradually changing the composition of the atmosphere, the sea and the top layers of the solid crust, both on land and under the ocean. Thus a study of the carbon cycle in the biosphere is fundamentally a study of the overall global interactions of living organisms and their physical and chemical environment. To bring order into this world of complex interactions biologists must combine their knowledge with the information available to students of geology, oceanography and meteorology.

The engine for the organic processes that reconstructed the primitive earth is photosynthesis. Regardless of whether it takes place on land or in the sea, it can be summarized by a single reaction: $CO_2 + 2H_2A + light \rightarrow CH_2O + H_2O + 2A + energy$. The formaldehyde molecule CH_2O symbolizes the simplest organic compound; the term "energy" indicates that the reaction stores energy in chemical form. H_2A is commonly water (H_2O), in which case $2A$ symbolizes the release of free oxygen (O_2). There are, however, bacteria that can use compounds in which A stands for sulfur, for some organic radical or for nothing at all.

Organisms that are able to use carbon dioxide as their sole source of carbon are known as autotrophs. Those that use light energy for reducing carbon dioxide are called phototrophic, and those that use the energy stored in inorganic chemical bonds (for example the bonds of nitrates and sulfates) are called chemolithotrophic. Most organisms, however, require preformed organic molecules for growth; hence they are known as heterotrophs. The nonsulfur bacteria are an unusual group that is both photosynthetic and heterotrophic. Chemoheterotrophic organisms, for example animals, obtain their energy from organic compounds without need for light. An organism may be either aerobic or anaerobic regardless of its source of carbon or energy. Thus some anaerobic chemoheterotrophs can survive in the deep ocean and deep lakes in the total absence of light or free oxygen.

There is more to plant life than the creation of organic compounds by photosynthesis. Plant growth involves a series of chemical processes and transformations that require energy. This energy is obtained by reactions that use the oxygen in the surrounding water and air to unlock the energy that has been stored by photosynthesis. The process, which releases carbon dioxide, is termed respiration. It is a continuous process and is therefore dominant at night, when photosynthesis is shut down.

If one measures the carbon dioxide at various levels above the ground in a forest, one can observe pronounced changes in concentration over a 24-hour period [*see top illustration on page 51*]. The average concentration of carbon dioxide in the atmosphere is about 320 parts per million. When the sun rises, photosynthesis begins and leads to a rapid decrease in the carbon dioxide concentration as leaves (and the needles of conifers) convert carbon dioxide into organic compounds. Toward noon, as the temperature increases and the humidity decreases, the rate of respiration rises and the net consumption of carbon dioxide slowly declines. Minimum values of carbon dioxide 10 to 15 parts per million below the daily average are reached around noon at treetop level. At sunset photosynthesis ceases while respiration continues, with the result that the carbon dioxide concentration close to the

CARBON LOCKED IN COAL and oil exceeds by a factor of about 50 the amount of carbon in all living organisms. The estimated world reserves of coal alone are on the order of 7,500 billion tons. The photograph on the opposite page shows a sequence of lignite coal seams being strip-mined in Stanton, N.D., by the Western Division of the Consolidation Coal Company. The seam, about two feet thick, is of low quality and is discarded. The second seam from the top, about three feet thick, is marketable, as is the third seam, 10 feet farther down. This seam is really two seams separated by about 10 inches of gray clay. The upper is some 3½ feet thick; the lower is about two feet thick. Twenty-four feet below the bottom of this seam is still another seam (*not shown*) eight feet thick, which is also mined.

ground may exceed 400 parts per million. This high value reflects partly the release of carbon dioxide from the decomposition of organic matter in the soil and partly the tendency of air to stagnate near the ground at night, when there is no solar heating to produce convection currents.

The net productivity, or net rate of fixation, of carbon dioxide varies greatly from one type of vegetation to another. Rapidly growing tropical rain forests annually fix between one kilogram and two kilograms of carbon (in the form of carbon dioxide) per square meter of land surface, which is roughly equal to the amount of carbon dioxide in a column of air extending from the same area of the earth's surface to the top of the atmosphere. The arctic tundra and the nearly barren regions of the desert may fix as

little as 1 percent of that amount. The forests and cultivated fields of the middle latitudes assimilate between .2 and .4 kilogram per square meter. For the earth as a whole the areas of high productivity are small. A fair estimate is that the land areas of the earth fix into organic compounds 20 to 30 billion net metric tons of carbon per year. There is considerable uncertainty in this figure; published estimates range from 10 to 100 billion tons.

The amount of carbon in the form of carbon dioxide consumed annually by phytoplankton in the oceans is perhaps 40 billion tons, or roughly the same as the gross assimilation of carbon dioxide by land vegetation. Both the carbon dioxide consumed and the oxygen released are largely in the form of gas dissolved near the ocean surface. Therefore most of the carbon cycle in the sea is self-con-

tained: the released oxygen is consumed by sea animals, and their ultimate decomposition releases carbon dioxide back into solution. As we shall see, however, there is a dynamic exchange of carbon dioxide (and oxygen) between the atmosphere and the sea, brought about by the action of the wind and waves. At any given moment the amount of carbon dioxide dissolved in the surface layers of the sea is in close equilibrium with the concentration of carbon dioxide in the atmosphere as a whole.

The carbon fixed by photosynthesis on land is sooner or later returned to the atmosphere by the decomposition of dead organic matter. Leaves and litter fall to the ground and are oxidized by a series of complicated processes in the soil. We can get an approximate idea of the rate at which organic matter in the soil is

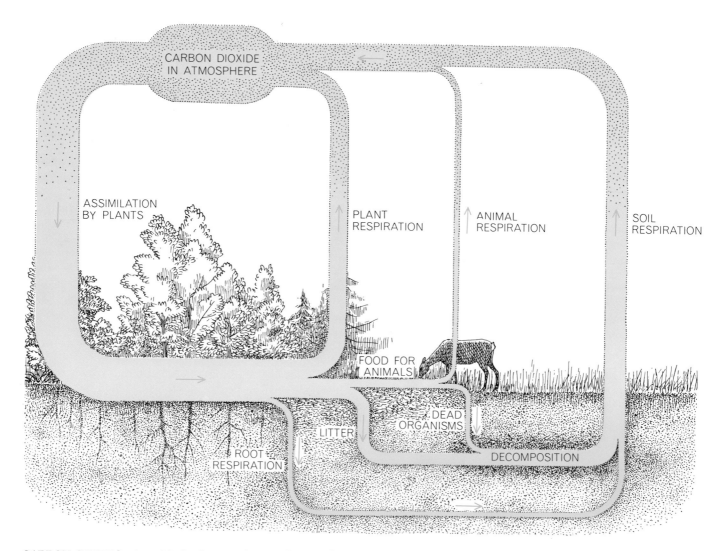

CARBON CYCLE begins with the fixation of atmospheric carbon dioxide by the process of photosynthesis, conducted by plants and certain microorganisms. In this process carbon dioxide and water react to form carbohydrates, with the simultaneous release of free oxygen, which enters the atmosphere. Some of the carbohydrate is directly consumed to supply the plant with energy; the carbon dioxide so generated is released either through the plant's leaves or through its roots. Part of the carbon fixed by plants is consumed by animals, which also respire and release carbon dioxide. Plants and animals die and are ultimately decomposed by microorganisms in the soil; the carbon in their tissues is oxidized to carbon dioxide and returns to the atmosphere. The widths of the pathways are roughly proportional to the quantities involved. A similar carbon cycle takes place within the sea. There is still no general agreement as to which of the two cycles is larger. The author's estimates of the quantities involved appear in the flow chart on page 54.

being transformed by measuring its content of the radioactive isotope carbon 14. At the time carbon is fixed by photosynthesis its ratio of carbon 14 to the nonradioactive isotope carbon 12 is the same as the ratio in the atmosphere (except for a constant fractionation factor), but thereafter the carbon 14 decays and becomes less abundant with respect to the carbon 12. Measurements of this ratio yield rates for the oxidation of organic matter in the soil ranging from decades in tropical soils to several hundred years in boreal forests.

In addition to the daily variations of carbon dioxide in the air there is a marked annual variation, at least in the Northern Hemisphere. As spring comes to northern regions the consumption of carbon dioxide by plants greatly exceeds the return from the soil. The increased withdrawal of carbon dioxide can be measured all the way up to the lower stratosphere. A marked decrease in the atmospheric content of carbon dioxide occurs during the spring. From April to September the atmosphere north of 30 degrees north latitude loses nearly 3 percent of its carbon dioxide content, which is equivalent to about four billion tons of carbon [*see bottom illustration at right*]. Since the decay processes in the soil go on simultaneously, the net withdrawal of four billion tons implies an annual gross fixation of carbon in these latitudes of at least five or six billion tons. This amounts to about a fourth of the annual terrestrial productivity referred to above (20 to 30 billion tons), which was based on a survey of carbon fixation. In this global survey the estimated contribution from the Northern Hemisphere, where plant growth shows a marked seasonal variation, constituted about 25 percent of the total tonnage. Thus two independent estimates of worldwide carbon fixation on land show a quite satisfactory agreement.

The forests of the world not only are the main carbon dioxide consumers on land; they also represent the main reservoir of biologically fixed carbon (except for fossil fuels, which have been largely removed from the carbon cycle save for the amount reintroduced by man's burning of it). The forests contain between 400 and 500 billion tons of carbon, or roughly two-thirds of the amount present as carbon dioxide in the atmosphere (700 billion tons). The figure for forests can be estimated only approximately. The average age of a tree can be assumed to be about 30 years, which implies that about 15 billion tons of carbon

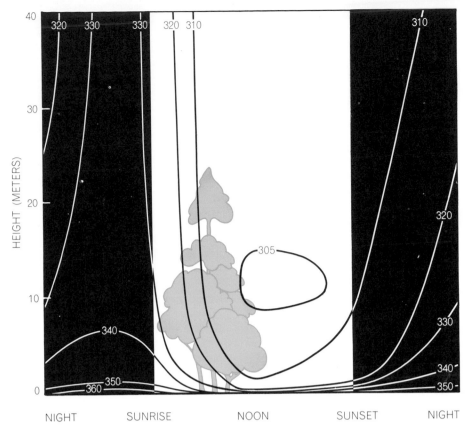

VERTICAL DISTRIBUTION OF CARBON DIOXIDE in the air around a forest varies with time of day. At night, when photosynthesis is shut off, respiration from the soil can raise the carbon dioxide at ground level to as much as 400 parts per million (ppm). By noon, owing to photosynthetic uptake, the concentration at treetop level can drop to 305 ppm.

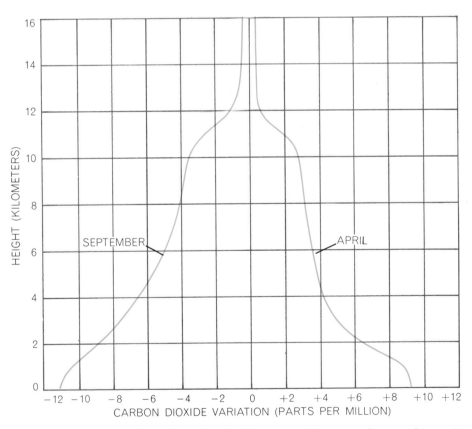

SEASONAL VARIATIONS in the carbon dioxide content of the atmosphere reach a maximum in September and April for the region north of 30 degrees north latitude. The departure from a mean value of about 320 ppm varies with altitude as shown by these two curves.

in the form of carbon dioxide is annually transformed into wood, which seems reasonable in comparison with a total annual assimilation of 20 to 30 billion tons.

The pattern of carbon circulation in the sea is quite different from the pattern on land. The productivity of the soil is mostly limited by the availability of fresh water and phosphorus, and only to a degree by the availability of other nutrients in the soil. In the oceans the overriding limitation is the availability of inorganic substances. The phytoplankton require not only plentiful supplies of phosphorus and nitrogen but also trace amounts of various metals, notably iron.

The competition for food in the sea is so keen that organisms have gradually developed the ability to absorb essential minerals even when these nutrients are available only in very low concentration. As a result high concentrations of nutrients are rarely found in surface waters, where solar radiation makes it possible for photosynthetic organisms to exist. If an ocean area is uncommonly productive, one can be sure that nutrients are supplied from deeper layers. (In limited areas they are supplied by the wastes of human activities.) The most productive waters in the world are therefore near the Antarctic continent, where the deep waters of the surrounding oceans well up and mix with the surface layers. There are similar upwellings along the coast of Chile, in the vicinity of Japan and in the Gulf Stream. In such regions fish are abundant and the maximum annual fixation of carbon approaches .3 kilogram per square meter. In the "desert" areas of the oceans, such

as the open seas of subtropical latitudes, the fixation rate may be less than a tenth of that value. In the Tropics warm surface layers are usually effective in blocking the vertical water exchange needed to carry nutrients up from below.

Phytoplankton, the primary fixers of carbon dioxide in the sea, are eaten by the zooplankton and other tiny animals. These organisms in turn provide food for the larger animals. The major part of the oceanic biomass, however, consists of microorganisms. Since the lifetime of such organisms is measured in weeks, or at most in months, their total mass can never accumulate appreciably. When microorganisms die, they quickly disintegrate as they sink to deeper layers. Soon most of what was once living tissue has become dissolved organic matter.

A small fraction of the organic particulate matter escapes oxidation and settles into the ocean depths. There it profoundly influences the abundance of chemical substances because (except in special regions) the deep layers exchange water with the surface layers very slowly. The enrichment of the deep layers goes hand in hand with a depletion of oxygen. There also appears to be an increase in carbon dioxide (in the form of carbonate and bicarbonate ions) in the ocean depths. The overall distribution of carbon dioxide, oxygen and various minor constituents in the sea reflects a balance between the marine life and its chemical milieu in the surface layers and the slow transport of substances by the general circulation of the ocean. The net effect is to prevent the ocean from becoming saturated with oxygen and to enrich the deeper strata with carbonate and bicarbonate ions.

The particular state in which we find the oceans today could well be quite different if the mechanisms for the exchange of water between the surface layers and the deep ones were either more intense or less so. The present state is determined primarily by the sinking of cold water in the polar regions, particularly the Antarctic. In these regions the water is also slightly saltier, and therefore still denser, because some of it has been frozen out in floating ice. If the climate of the earth were different, the distribution of carbon dioxide, oxygen and minerals might also be quite different. If the difference were large enough, oxygen might completely vanish from the ocean depths, leaving them to be populated only by chemibarotrophic bacteria. (This is now the case in the depths of the Black Sea.)

The time required to establish a new equilibrium in the ocean is determined by the slowest link in the chain of processes that has been described. This link is the oceanic circulation; it seems to take at least 1,000 years for the water in the deepest basins to be completely replaced. One can imagine other conditions of circulation in which the oceans would interact differently with sediments and rocks, producing a balance of substances that one can only guess at.

So far we have been concerned only with the basic biological and ecological processes that provide the mechanisms for circulating carbon through living organisms. Plants on land, with lifetimes measured in years, and phytoplankton in the sea, with lifetimes measured in weeks, are merely the innermost wheels in a biogeochemical machine that embraces the entire earth and that retains important characteristics over much longer time periods. In order to understand such interactions we shall need some rough estimates of the size of the various carbon reservoirs involved and the nature of their contents [see illustration on page 54]. In the context of the present argument the large uncertainties in such estimates are of little significance.

Only a few tenths of a percent of the immense mass of carbon at or near the surface of the earth (on the order of 20×10^{15} tons) is in rapid circulation in the biosphere, which includes the atmosphere, the hydrosphere, the upper portions of the earth's crust and the biomass itself. The overwhelming bulk of near-surface carbon consists of inorganic deposits (chiefly carbonates) and organic fossil deposits (chiefly oil shale, coal and petroleum) that required hundreds of

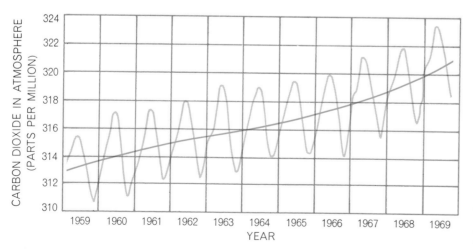

LONG-TERM VARIATIONS in the carbon dioxide content of the atmosphere have been followed at the Mauna Loa Observatory in Hawaii by the Scripps Institution of Oceanography. The sawtooth curve indicates the month-to-month change in concentration since January, 1959. The oscillations reflect seasonal variations in the rate of photosynthesis, as depicted in the bottom illustration on the preceding page. The smooth curve shows the trend.

OIL SHALE is one of the principal sedimentary forms in which carbon has been deposited over geologic time. This photograph, taken at Anvil Points, Colo., shows a section of the Green River Formation, which extends through Colorado, Utah and Wyoming. The formation is estimated to contain the equivalent of more than a trillion barrels of oil in seams containing more than 10 barrels of oil per ton of rock. Of this some 80 billion barrels is considered recoverable. The shale seams are up to 130 feet thick.

WHITE CLIFFS OF DOVER consist of almost pure calcium carbonate, representing the skeletons of phytoplankton that settled to the bottom of the sea over a period of millions of years more than 70 million years ago. The worldwide deposits of limestone, oil shale and other carbon-containing sediments are by far the largest repository of carbon: an estimated 20 quadrillion (10^{15}) tons.

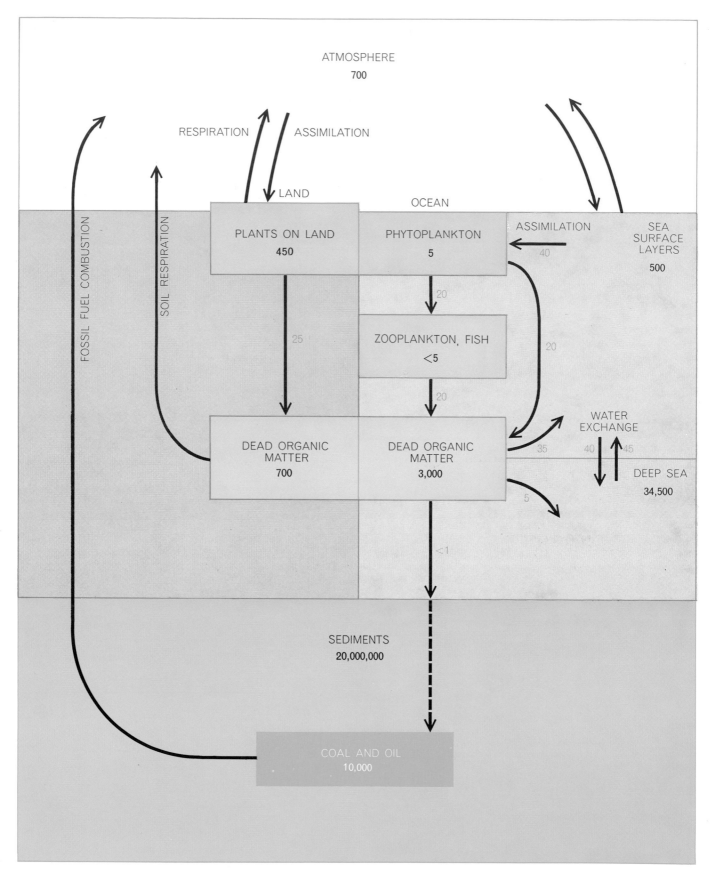

CARBON CIRCULATION IN BIOSPHERE involves two quite distinct cycles, one on land and one in the sea, that are dynamically connected at the interface between the ocean and the atmosphere. The carbon cycle in the sea is essentially self-contained in that phytoplankton assimilate the carbon dioxide dissolved in seawater and release oxygen back into solution. Zooplankton and fish consume the carbon fixed by the phytoplankton, using the dissolved oxygen for respiration. Eventually the decomposition of organic matter replaces the carbon dioxide assimilated by the phytoplank- ton. All quantities are in billions of metric tons. It will be seen that the combustion of fossil fuels at the rate of about five billion tons per year is sufficient to increase the carbon dioxide in the atmosphere by about .7 percent, equivalent to adding some two parts per million to the existing 320 ppm. Since the observed annual increase is only about .7 ppm, it appears that two-thirds of the carbon dioxide released from fossil fuels is quickly removed from the atmosphere, going either into the oceans or adding to the total mass of terrestrial plants. The estimated tonnages are the author's.

millions of years to reach their present magnitude. Over time intervals as brief as those of which we have been speaking—up to 1,000 years for the deep-ocean circulation—the accretion of such deposits is negligible. We may therefore consider the life processes on land and in the sea as the inner wheels that spin at comparatively high velocity in the carbon-circulating machine. They are coupled by a very low gear to more majestic processes that account for the overall circulation of carbon in its various geologic and oceanic forms.

We now know that the two great systems, the atmosphere and the ocean, are closely coupled to each other through the transfer of carbon dioxide across the surface of the oceans. The rate of exchange has recently been estimated by measuring the rate at which the radioactive isotope carbon 14 produced by the testing of nuclear weapons has disappeared from the atmosphere. The neutrons released in such tests form carbon 14 by reacting with the nitrogen 14 of the atmosphere. In this reaction a nitrogen atom ($_7N^{14}$) captures a neutron and subsequently releases a proton, yielding $_6C^{14}$. (The subscript before the letter represents the number of protons in the nucleus; the superscript after the letter indicates the sum of protons and neutrons.)

The last major atmospheric tests were conducted in 1963. Sampling at various altitudes and latitudes shows that the constituents of the atmosphere became rather well mixed over a period of a few years. The decline of carbon 14, however, was found to be rapid; it can be explained only by assuming an exchange of atmospheric carbon dioxide, enriched in carbon 14, with the reservoir of much less radioactive carbon dioxide in the sea. The measurements indicate that the characteristic time for the residence of carbon dioxide in the atmosphere before the gas is dissolved in the sea is between five and 10 years. In other words, every year something like 100 billion tons of atmospheric carbon dioxide dissolves in the sea and is replaced by a nearly equivalent amount of oceanic carbon dioxide.

Since around 1850 man has inadvertently been conducting a global geochemical experiment by burning large amounts of fossil fuel and thereby returning to the atmosphere carbon that was fixed by photosynthesis millions of years ago. Currently between five and six billion tons of fossil carbon per year are being released into the atmosphere. This would be enough to increase the amount of carbon dioxide in the air by 2.3 parts per million per year if the carbon dioxide were uniformly distributed and not removed. Within the past century the carbon dioxide content of the atmosphere has risen from some 290 parts per million to 320, with more than a fifth of the rise occurring in just the past decade [*see illustration on page 52*]. The total increase accounts for only slightly more than a third of the carbon dioxide (some 200 billion tons in all) released from fossil fuels. Although most of the remaining two-thirds has presumably gone into the oceans, a significant fraction may well have increased the total amount of vegetation on land. Laboratory studies show that plants grow faster when the surrounding air is enriched in carbon dioxide. Thus it is possible that man is fertilizing fields and forests by burning coal, oil and natural gas. The biomass on land may have increased by as much as 15 billion tons in the past century. There is, however, little concrete evidence for such an increase.

Man has of course been changing his environment in other ways. Over the past century large areas covered with forest have been cleared and turned to agriculture. In such areas the character of soil respiration has undoubtedly changed, producing effects that might have been detectable in the atmospheric content of carbon dioxide if it had not been for the simultaneous increase in the burning of fossil fuels. In any case the dynamic equilibrium among the major carbon dioxide reservoirs in the biomass, the atmosphere, the hydrosphere and the soil has been disturbed, and it can be said that they are in a period of transition. Since even the most rapid processes of adjustment among the reservoirs take decades, new equilibriums are far from being established. Gradually the deep oceans become involved; their turnover time of about 1,000 years and their rate of exchange with bottom sediments control the ultimate partitioning of carbon.

Meanwhile human activities continue to change explosively. The acceleration in the consumption of fossil fuels implies that the amount of carbon dioxide in the atmosphere will keep climbing from its present value of 320 parts per million to between 375 and 400 parts per million by the year 2000, in spite of anticipated large removals of carbon dioxide by land vegetation and the ocean reservoir [*see illustrations on next page*]. A fundamental question is: What will happen over the next 100 or 1,000 years? Clearly the exponential changes cannot continue.

If we extend the time scale with which we are viewing the carbon cycle by several orders of magnitude, to hundreds of thousands or millions of years, we can anticipate large-scale exchanges between organic carbon on land and carbonates of biological origin in the sea. We do know that there have been massive exchanges in the remote past. Any discussion of these past events and their implications for the future, however, must necessarily be qualitative and uncertain.

Although the plants on land have probably played an important role in the deposition of organic compounds in the soil, the oceans have undoubtedly acted as the main regulator. The amount of carbon dioxide in the atmosphere is essentially determined by the partial pressure of carbon dioxide dissolved in the

GIANT FERN of the genus *Pecopteris*, which fixed atmospheric carbon dioxide 300 million years ago, left the imprint of this frond in a thin layer of shale just above a coal seam in Illinois. The specimen is in the collection of the Smithsonian Institution.

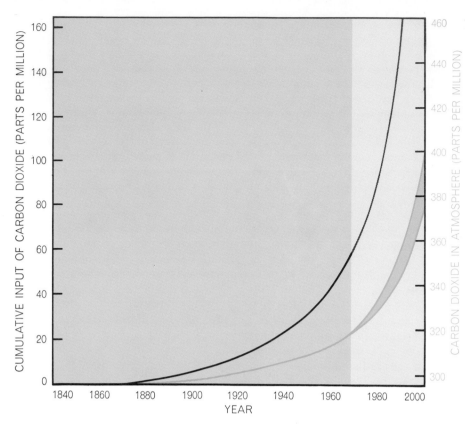

INCREASE IN ATMOSPHERIC CARBON DIOXIDE since 1860 is shown by the lower curve, with a projection to the year 2000. The upper curve shows the cumulative input of carbon dioxide. The difference between the two curves represents the amount of carbon dioxide removed by the ocean or by additions to the total biomass of vegetation on land.

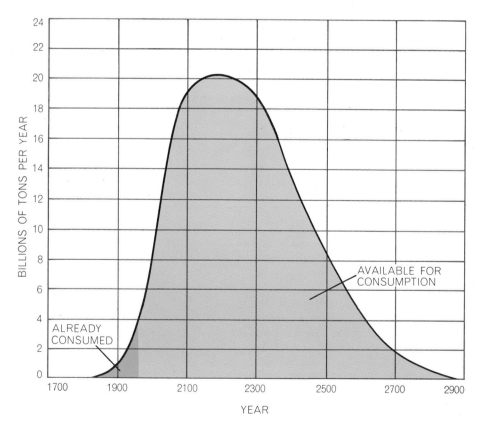

POSSIBLE CONSUMPTION PATTERN OF FOSSIL FUELS was projected by Harrison Brown in the mid-1950's. Here the fuel consumed is updated to 1960. If a third of the carbon dioxide produced by burning it all were to remain in the atmosphere, the carbon dioxide level would rise from 320 ppm today to about 1,500 ppm over the next several centuries.

sea. Over a period of, say, 100,000 years the leaching of calcium carbonates from land areas tends to increase the amount of carbon dioxide in the sea, but at the same time a converse mechanism—the precipitation and deposition of oceanic carbonates—tends to reduce the amount of carbon dioxide in solution. Thus the two mechanisms tend to cancel each other.

Over still longer periods of time—millions or tens of millions of years—the concentrations of carbonate and bicarbonate ions in the sea are probably buffered still further by reactions involving potassium, silicon and aluminum, which are slowly weathered from rocks and carried into the sea. The net effect is to stabilize the carbon dioxide content of the oceans and hence the carbon dioxide content of the atmosphere. Therefore it appears that the carbon dioxide environment, on which the biosphere fundamentally depends, may have been fairly constant right up to the time, barely a moment ago geologically speaking, when man's consumption of fossil fuels began to change the carbon dioxide content of the atmosphere.

The illustration on page 54 represents an attempt to synthesize into a single picture the circulation of carbon in nature, particularly in the biosphere. In addition to the values for inventories and transfers already mentioned, the flow chart contains other quantities for which the evidence is still meager. They have been included not only to balance the books but also to suggest where further investigation might be profitable. This may be the principal value of such an exercise. Such a flow chart also provides a semiquantitative model that enables one to begin to discuss how the global carbon system reacts to disturbances. A good model should of course include inventories and pathways for all the elements that play a significant role in biological processes.

The greatest disturbances of which we are aware are those now being introduced by man himself. Since his tampering with the biological and geochemical balances may ultimately prove injurious —even fatal—to himself, he must understand them much better than he does today. The story of the circulation of carbon in nature teaches us that we cannot control the global balances. Therefore we had better leave them close to the natural state that existed until the beginning of the Industrial Revolution. Out of a simple realization of this necessity may come a new industrial revolution.

VI

The Oxygen Cycle

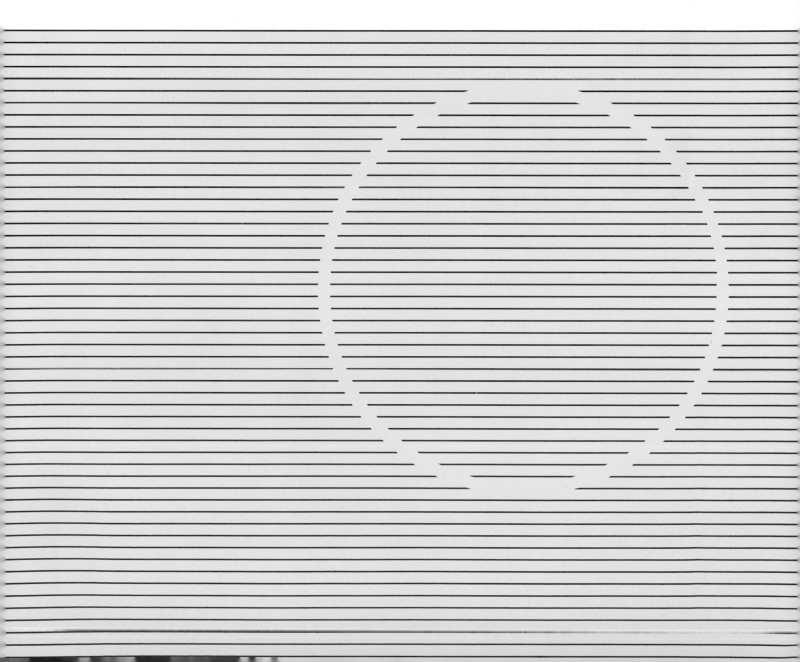

The Oxygen Cycle

by PRESTON CLOUD and AHARON GIBOR

The oxygen in the atmosphere was originally put there by plants. Hence the early plants made possible the evolution of the higher plants and animals that require free oxygen for their metabolism

The history of our planet, as recorded in its rocks and fossils, is reflected in the composition and the biochemical peculiarities of its present biosphere. With a little imagination one can reconstruct from that evidence the appearance and subsequent evolution of gaseous oxygen in the earth's air and water, and the changing pathways of oxygen in the metabolism of living things.

Differentiated multicellular life (consisting of tissues and organs) evolved only after free oxygen appeared in the atmosphere. The cells of animals that are truly multicellular in this sense, the Metazoa, obtain their energy by breaking down fuel (produced originally by photosynthesis) in the presence of oxygen in the process called respiration. The evolution of advanced forms of animal life would probably not have been possible without the high levels of energy release that are characteristic of oxidative metabolism. At the same time free oxygen is potentially destructive to all forms of carbon-based life (and we know no other kind of life). Most organisms have therefore had to "learn" to conduct their oxidations anaerobically, primarily by removing hydrogen from foodstuff rather than by adding oxygen. Indeed, the anaerobic process called fermentation is still the fundamental way of life, underlying other forms of metabolism.

Oxygen in the free state thus plays a role in the evolution and present functioning of the biosphere that is both pervasive and ambivalent. The origin of life

and its subsequent evolution was contingent on the development of systems that shielded it from, or provided chemical defenses against, ordinary molecular oxygen (O_2), ozone (O_3) and atomic oxygen (O). Yet the energy requirements of higher life forms can be met only by oxidative metabolism. The oxidation of the simple sugar glucose, for example, yields 686 kilocalories per mole; the fermentation of glucose yields only 50 kilocalories per mole.

Free oxygen not only supports life; it arises from life. The oxygen now in the atmosphere is probably mainly, if not wholly, of biological origin. Some of it is converted to ozone, causing certain high-energy wavelengths to be filtered out of the radiation that reaches the surface of the earth. Oxygen also combines with a wide range of other elements in the earth's crust. The result of these and other processes is an intimate evolutionary interaction among the biosphere, the atmosphere, the hydrosphere and the lithosphere.

Consider where the oxygen comes from to support the high rates of energy release observed in multicellular organisms and what happens to it and to the carbon dioxide that is respired [*see illustration on page 62*]. The oxygen, of course, comes from the air, of which it constitutes roughly 21 percent. Ultimately, however, it originates with the decomposition of water molecules by light energy in photosynthesis. The 1.5 billion cubic kilometers of water on the earth are split by photosynthesis and reconsti-

tuted by respiration once every two million years or so. Photosynthetically generated oxygen temporarily enters the atmospheric bank, whence it is itself recycled once every 2,000 years or so (at current rates). The carbon dioxide that is respired joins the small amount (.03 percent) already in the atmosphere, which is in balance with the carbon dioxide in the oceans and other parts of the hydrosphere. Through other interactions it may be removed from circulation as a part of the carbonate ion (CO_3^-) in calcium carbonate precipitated from solution. Carbon dioxide thus sequestered may eventually be returned to the atmosphere when limestone, formed by the consolidation of calcium carbonate sediments, emerges from under the sea and is dissolved by some future rainfall.

Thus do sea, air, rock and life interact and exchange components. Before taking up these interactions in somewhat greater detail let us examine the function oxygen serves within individual organisms.

Oxygen plays a fundamental role as a building block of practically all vital molecules, accounting for about a fourth of the atoms in living matter. Practically all organic matter in the present biosphere originates in the process of photosynthesis, whereby plants utilize light energy to react carbon dioxide with water and synthesize organic substances. Since carbohydrates (such as sugar), with the general formula $(CH_2O)_n$, are the common fuels that are stored by plants, the essential reaction of photosynthesis can be written as $CO_2 + H_2O$ + light energy $\rightarrow CH_2O + O_2$. It is not immediately obvious from this formulation which of the reactants serves as the source of oxygen atoms in the carbohydrates and which is the source of free molecular oxygen. In 1941 Samuel Ruben and Mar-

RED BEDS rich in the oxidized (ferric) form of iron mark the advent of oxygen in the atmosphere. The earliest continental red beds are less than two billion years old; the red sandstones and shales of the Nankoweap Formation in the Grand Canyon (*opposite page*) are about 1.3 billion years old. The appearance of oxygen in the atmosphere, the result of photosynthesis, led in time to the evolution of cells that could survive its toxic effects and eventually to cells that could capitalize on the high energy levels of oxidative metabolism.

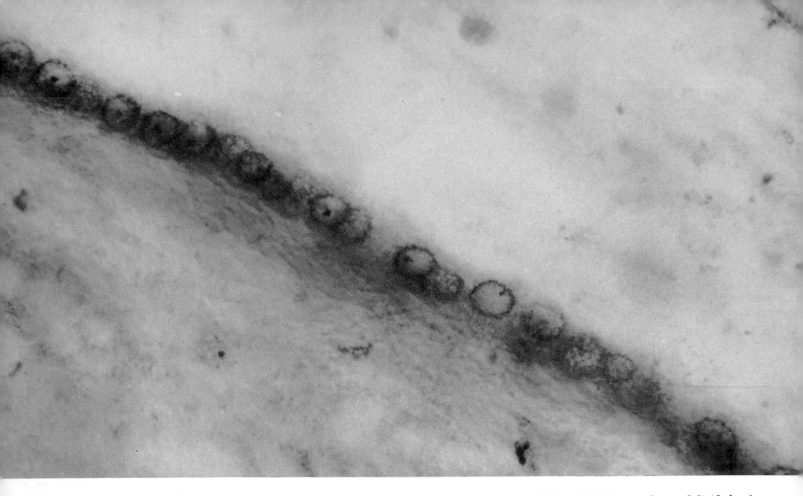

EUCARYOTIC CELLS, which contain a nucleus and divide by mitosis, were, like oxygen, a necessary precondition for the evolution of higher life forms. The oldest eucaryotes known were found in the Beck Spring Dolomite of eastern California by Cloud and his colleagues. The photomicrograph above shows eucaryotic cells with an average diameter of 14 microns, probably green algae. The regular occurrence and position of the dark spots suggest they may be remnants of nuclei or other organelles. Other cell forms, which do not appear in the picture, show branching and large filament diameters that also indicate the eucaryotic level of evolution.

PROCARYOTIC CELLS, which lack a nucleus and divide by simple fission, were a more primitive form of life than the eucaryotes and persist today in the bacteria and blue-green algae. Procaryotes were found in the Beck Spring Dolomite in association with the primitive eucaryotes such as those in the photograph at the top of the page. A mat of threadlike procaryotic blue-green algae, each thread of which is about 3.5 microns in diameter, is seen in the photomicrograph below. It was made, like the one at top of page, by Gerald R. Licari. Cells of this kind, among others, presumably produced photosynthetic oxygen before eucaryotes appeared.

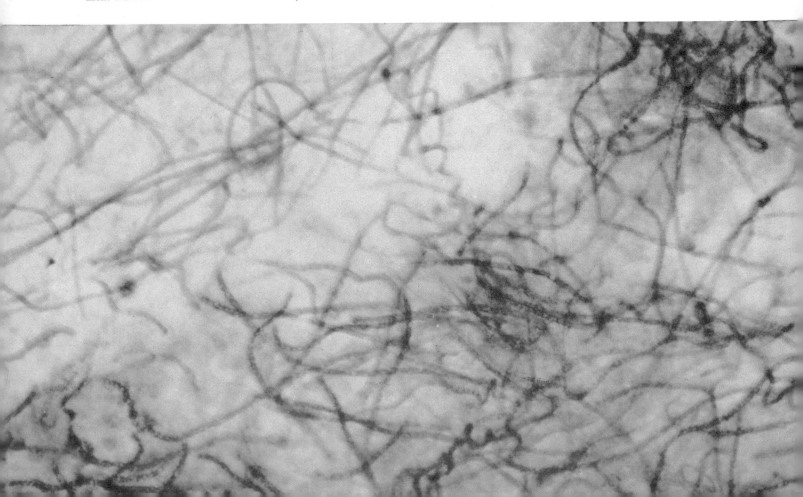

tin D. Kamen of the University of California at Berkeley used the heavy oxygen isotope oxygen 18 as a tracer to demonstrate that the molecular oxygen is derived from the splitting of the water molecule. This observation also suggested that carbon dioxide is the source of the oxygen atoms of the synthesized organic molecules.

The primary products of photosynthesis undergo a vast number of chemical transformations in plant cells and subsequently in the cells of the animals that feed on plants. During these processes changes of course take place in the atomic composition and energy content of the organic molecules. Such transformations can result in carbon compounds that are either more "reduced" or more "oxidized" than carbohydrates. The oxidation-reduction reactions between these compounds are the essence of biological energy supply and demand. A more reduced compound has more hydrogen atoms and fewer oxygen atoms per carbon atom; a more oxidized compound has fewer hydrogen atoms and more oxygen atoms per carbon atom. The combustion of a reduced compound liberates more energy than the combustion of a more oxidized one. An example of a molecule more reduced than a carbohydrate is the familiar alcohol ethanol (C_2H_6O); a more oxidized molecule is pyruvic acid ($C_3H_4O_3$).

Differences in the relative abundance of hydrogen and oxygen atoms in organic molecules result primarily from one of the following reactions: (1) the removal (dehydrogenation) or addition (hydrogenation) of hydrogen atoms, (2) the addition of water (hydration), followed by dehydrogenation; (3) the direct addition of oxygen (oxygenation). The second and third of these processes introduce into organic matter additional oxygen atoms either from water or from molecular oxygen. On decomposition the oxygen atoms of organic molecules are released as carbon dioxide and water. The biological oxidation of molecules such as carbohydrates can be written as the reverse of photosynthesis: $CH_2O + O_2 \rightarrow CO_2 + H_2O +$ energy. The oxygen atom of the organic molecule appears in the carbon dioxide and the molecular oxygen acts as the acceptor for the hydrogen atoms.

The three major nonliving sources of oxygen atoms are therefore carbon dioxide, water and molecular oxygen, and since these molecules exchange oxygen atoms, they can be considered as a common pool. Common mineral oxides such as nitrate ions and sulfate ions are also oxygen sources for living organisms,

which reduce them to ammonia (NH_3) and hydrogen sulfide (H_2S). They are subsequently reoxidized, and so as the oxides circulate through the biosphere their oxygen atoms are exchanged with water.

The dynamic role of molecular oxygen is as an electron sink, or hydrogen acceptor, in biological oxidations. The biological oxidation of organic molecules proceeds primarily by dehydrogenation: enzymes remove hydrogen atoms from the substrate molecule and transfer them to specialized molecules that function as hydrogen carriers [*see top illustration on pages 64 and 65*]. If these carriers become saturated with hydrogen, no further oxidation can take place until some other acceptor becomes available. In the anaerobic process of fermentation organic molecules serve as the hydrogen acceptor. Fermentation therefore results in the oxidation of some organic compounds and the simultaneous reduction of others, as in the fermentation of glucose by yeast: part of the sugar molecule is oxidized to carbon dioxide and other parts are reduced to ethanol.

In aerobic respiration oxygen serves as the hydrogen acceptor and water is produced. The transfer of hydrogen atoms (which is to say of electrons and protons) to oxygen is channeled through an array of catalysts and cofactors. Prominent among the cofactors are the iron-containing pigmented molecules called cytochromes, of which there are several kinds that differ in their affinity for electrons. This affinity is expressed as the oxidation-reduction, or "redox," potential of the molecule; the more positive the potential, the greater the affinity of the oxidized molecule for electrons. For example, the redox potential of cytochrome *b* is .12 volt, the potential of cytochrome *c* is .22 volt and the potential of cytochrome *a* is .29 volt. The redox potential for the reduction of oxygen to water is .8 volt. The passage of electrons from one cytochrome to another down a potential gradient, from cytochrome *b* to cytochrome *c* to the cytochrome *a* complex and on to oxygen, results in the alternate reduction and oxidation of these cofactors. Energy liberated in such oxidation-reduction reactions is coupled to the synthesis of high-energy phosphate compounds such as adenosine triphosphate (ATP). The special copper-containing enzyme cytochrome oxidase mediates the ultimate transfer of electrons from the cytochrome *a* complex to oxygen. This activation and binding of oxygen is seen as the fundamental step, and possibly

the original primitive step, in the evolution of oxidative metabolism.

In cells of higher organisms the oxidative system of enzymes and electron carriers is located in the special organelles called mitochondria. These organelles can be regarded as efficient low-temperature furnaces where organic molecules are burned with oxygen. Most of the released energy is converted into the high-energy bonds of ATP.

Molecular oxygen reacts spontaneously with organic compounds and other reduced substances. This reactivity explains the toxic effects of oxygen above tolerable concentrations. Louis Pasteur discovered that very sensitive organisms such as obligate anaerobes cannot tolerate oxygen concentrations above about 1 percent of the present atmospheric level. Recently the cells of higher organisms have been found to contain organelles called peroxisomes, whose major function is thought to be the protection of cells from oxygen. The peroxisomes contain enzymes that catalyze the direct reduction of oxygen molecules through the oxidation of metabolites such as amino acids and other organic acids. Hydrogen peroxide (H_2O_2) is one of the products of such oxidation. Another of the peroxisome enzymes, catalase, utilizes the hydrogen peroxide as a hydrogen acceptor in the oxidation of substrates such as ethanol or lactic acid. The rate of reduction of oxygen by the peroxisomes increases proportionately with an increase in oxygen concentration, so that an excessive amount of oxygen in the cell increases the rate of its reduction by peroxisomes.

Christian de Duve of Rockefeller University has suggested that the peroxisomes represent a primitive enzyme system that evolved to cope with oxygen when it first appeared in the atmosphere. The peroxisome enzymes enabled the first oxidatively metabolizing cells to use oxygen as a hydrogen acceptor and so reoxidize the reduced products of fermentation. In some respects this process is similar to the oxidative reactions of the mitochondria. Both make further dehydrogenation possible by liberating oxidized hydrogen carriers. The basic difference between the mitochondrial oxidation reactions and those of peroxisomes is that in peroxisomes the steps of oxidation are not coupled to the synthesis of ATP. The energy released in the peroxisomes is thus lost to the cell; the function of the organelle is primarily to protect against the destructive effects of free molecular oxygen.

Oxygen dissolved in water can diffuse

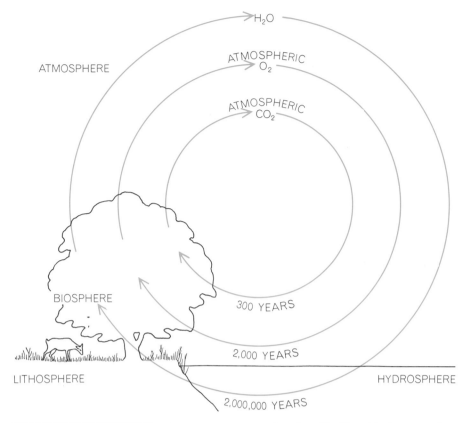

BIOSPHERE EXCHANGES water vapor, oxygen and carbon dioxide with the atmosphere and hydrosphere in a continuing cycle, shown here in simplified form. All the earth's water is split by plant cells and reconstituted by animal and plant cells about every two million years. Oxygen generated in the process enters the atmosphere and is recycled in about 2,000 years. Carbon dioxide respired by animal and plant cells enters the atmosphere and is fixed again by plant cells after an average atmospheric residence time of about 300 years.

across both the inner and the outer membranes of the cell, and the supply of oxygen by diffusion is adequate for single cells and for organisms consisting of small colonies of cells. Differentiated multicellular organisms, however, require more efficient modes of supplying oxygen to tissues and organs. Since all higher organisms depend primarily on mitochondrial aerobic oxidation to generate the energy that maintains their active mode of life, they have evolved elaborate systems to ensure their tissues an adequate supply of oxygen, the gas that once was lethal (and still is, in excess). Two basic devices serve this purpose: special chemical carriers that increase the oxygen capacity of body fluids, and anatomical structures that provide relatively large surfaces for the rapid exchange of gases. The typical properties of an oxygen carrier are exemplified by those of hemoglobin and of myoglobin, or muscle hemoglobin. Hemoglobin in blood readily absorbs oxygen to near-saturation at oxygen pressures such as those found in the lung. When the blood is exposed to lower oxygen pressures as it moves from the lungs to other tissues, the hemoglobin discharges most of its bound oxygen. Myoglobin, which acts as

a reservoir to meet the sharp demand for oxygen in muscle contraction, gives up its oxygen more rapidly. Such reversible bonding of oxygen in response to changes in oxygen pressure is an essential property of biochemical oxygen carriers.

Lungs and gills are examples of anatomical structures in which large wet areas of thin membranous tissue come in contact with oxygen. Body fluids are pumped over one side of these membranes and air, or water containing oxygen, over the other side. This ensures a rapid gas exchange between large volumes of body fluid and the environment.

How did the relations between organisms and gaseous oxygen happen to evolve in such a curiously complicated manner? The atmosphere under which life arose on the earth was almost certainly devoid of free oxygen. The low concentration of noble gases such as neon and krypton in the terrestrial atmosphere compared with their cosmic abundance, together with other geochemical evidence, indicates that the terrestrial atmosphere had a secondary origin in volcanic outgassing from the earth's interior. Oxygen is not known among the gases so released, nor is it

found as inclusions in igneous rocks. The chemistry of rocks older than about two billion years is also inconsistent with the presence of more than trivial quantities of free atmospheric oxygen before that time. Moreover, it would not have been possible for the essential chemical precursors of life—or life itself—to have originated and persisted in the presence of free oxygen before the evolution of suitable oxygen-mediating enzymes.

On such grounds we conclude that the first living organism must have depended on fermentation for its livelihood. Organic substances that originated in non-vital reactions served as substrates for these primordial fermentations. The first organism, therefore, was not only an anaerobe; it was also a heterotroph, dependent on a preexisting organic food supply and incapable of manufacturing its own food by photosynthesis or other autotrophic processes.

The emergence of an autotroph was an essential step in the onward march of biological evolution. This evolutionary step left its mark in the rocks as well as on all living forms. Some fated eobiont, as we may call these early life forms whose properties we can as yet only imagine, evolved and became an autotroph, an organism capable of manufacturing its own food. Biogeological evidence suggests that this critical event may have occurred more than three billion years ago.

If, as seems inescapable, the first autotrophic eobiont was also anaerobic, it would have encountered difficulty when it first learned to split water and release free oxygen. John M. Olson of the Brookhaven National Laboratory recently suggested biochemical arguments to support the idea that primitive photosynthesis may have obtained electrons from substances other than water. He argues that large-scale splitting of water and release of oxygen may have been delayed until the evolution of appropriate enzymes to detoxify this reactive substance.

We nevertheless find a long record of oxidized marine sediments of a peculiar type that precedes the first evidence of atmospheric oxygen in rocks about 1.8 billion years old; we do not find them in significant amounts in more recent strata. These oxidized marine sediments, known as banded iron formations, are alternately iron-rich and iron-poor chemical sediments that were laid down in open bodies of water. Much of the iron in them is ferric (the oxidized form, Fe^{+++}) rather than ferrous (the reduced form, Fe^{++}), implying that there was a source of oxygen in the column of water above them. Considering the

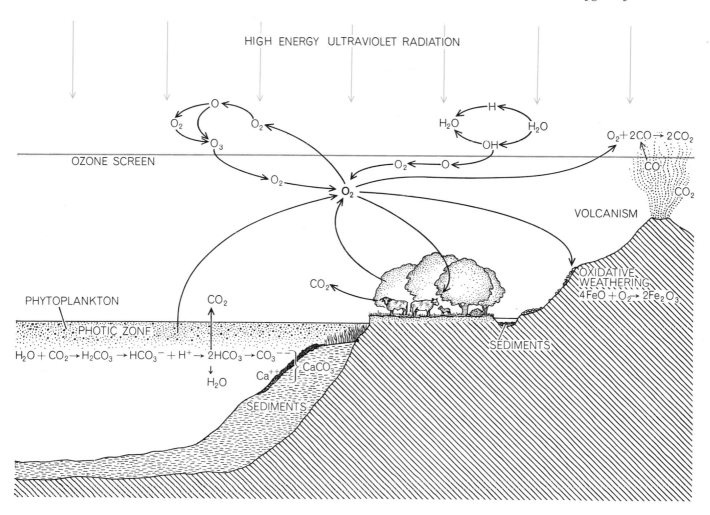

OXYGEN CYCLE is complicated because oxygen appears in so many chemical forms and combinations, primarily as molecular oxygen (O_2), in water and in organic and inorganic compounds. Some global pathways of oxygen are shown here in simplified form.

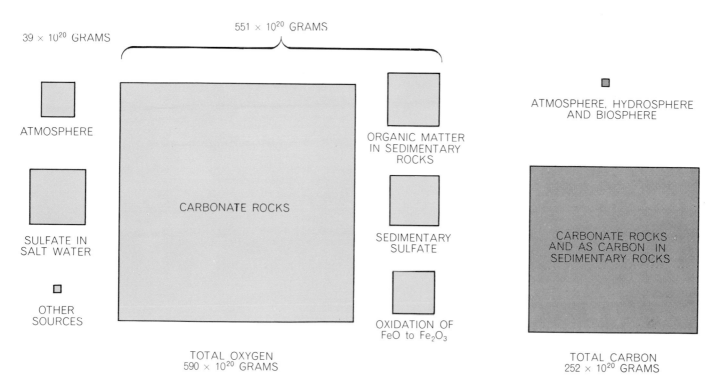

OXYGEN-CARBON BALANCE SHEET suggests that photosynthesis can account not only for all the oxygen in the atmosphere but also for the much larger amount of "fossil" oxygen, mostly in compounds in sediments. The diagram, based on estimates made by William W. Rubey, indicates that the elements are present in about the proportion, 12/32, that would account for their derivation through photosynthesis from carbon dioxide (one atom of carbon, molecular weight 12, to two of oxygen, molecular weight 16).

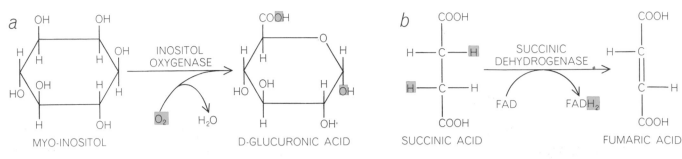

a MYO-INOSITOL → (INOSITOL OXYGENASE, O_2, H_2O) → D-GLUCURONIC ACID

b SUCCINIC ACID → (SUCCINIC DEHYDROGENASE, FAD, $FADH_2$) → FUMARIC ACID

OXIDATION involves a decrease in the number of hydrogen atoms in a molecule or an increase in the number of oxygen atoms. It may be accomplished in several ways. In oxygenation (*a*) oxygen is added directly. In dehydrogenation (*b*) hydrogen is re-

problems that would face a water-splitting photosynthesizer before the evolution of advanced oxygen-mediating enzymes such as oxidases and catalases, one can visualize how the biological oxygen cycle may have interacted with ions in solution in bodies of water during that time. The first oxygen-releasing photoautotrophs may have used ferrous compounds in solution as oxygen acceptors—oxygen for them being merely a toxic waste product. This would have precipitated iron in the ferric form ($4FeO + O_2 \rightarrow 2Fe_2O_3$) or in the ferro-ferric form (Fe_3O_4). A recurrent imbalance of supply and demand might then account for the cyclic nature and differing types of the banded iron formations.

Once advanced oxygen-mediating enzymes arose, oxygen generated by increasing populations of photoautotrophs containing these enzymes would build up in the oceans and begin to escape into the atmosphere. There the ultraviolet component of the sun's radiation would dissociate some of the molecular oxygen into highly reactive atomic oxygen and also give rise to equally reactive ozone. Atmospheric oxygen and its reactive derivatives (even in small quantities) would lead to the oxidation of iron in sediments produced by the weathering of rocks, to the greatly reduced solubility of iron in surface waters (now oxygenated), to the termination of the banded iron formations as an important sedimentary type and to the extensive formation of continental red beds rich in ferric iron [*see illustration on page 58*]. The record of the rocks supports this succession of events: red beds are essentially restricted to rocks younger than about 1.8 billion years, whereas banded iron formation is found only in older rocks.

So far we have assumed that oxygen accumulated in the atmosphere as a consequence of photosynthesis by green plants. How could this happen if the entire process of photosynthesis and respiration is cyclic, representable by the reversible equation $CO_2 + H_2O + energy$

$\rightleftharpoons CH_2O + O_2$? Except to the extent that carbon or its compounds are somehow sequestered, carbohydrates produced by photosynthesis will be reoxidized back to carbon dioxide and water, and no significant quantity of free oxygen will accumulate. The carbon that is sequestered in the earth as graphite in the oldest rocks and as coal, oil, gas and other carbonaceous compounds in the younger ones, and in the living and dead bodies of plants and animals, is the

equivalent of the oxygen in oxidized sediments and in the earth's atmosphere! In attempting to strike a carbon-oxygen balance we must find enough carbon to account not only for the oxygen in the present atmosphere but also for the "fossil" oxygen that went into the conversion of ferrous oxides to ferric oxides, sulfides to sulfates, carbon monoxide to carbon dioxide and so on.

Interestingly, rough estimates made some years ago by William W. Rubey,

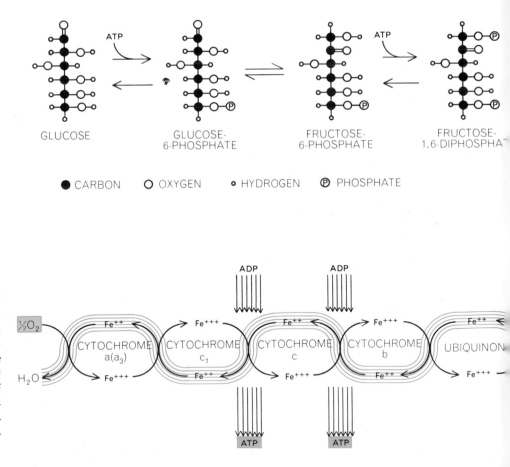

GLUCOSE → (ATP) → GLUCOSE-6-PHOSPHATE → FRUCTOSE-6-PHOSPHATE → (ATP) → FRUCTOSE-1,6-DIPHOSPHATE

● CARBON ○ OXYGEN ∘ HYDROGEN ℗ PHOSPHATE

½O_2 → CYTOCHROME a(a_3) → CYTOCHROME c_1 → CYTOCHROME c → CYTOCHROME b → UBIQUINONE

H_2O

ADP → ATP

Fe^{++} Fe^{+++}

OXIDATIVE METABOLISM provides the energy that powers all higher forms of life. It proceeds in two phases: glycolysis (*top*), an anaerobic phase that does not require oxygen, and aerobic respiration (*bottom*), which requires oxygen. In glycolysis (or fermentation, the anaerobic process by which organisms such as yeast derive their energy) a molecule of the six-carbon sugar glucose is broken down into two molecules of the three-carbon compound pyruvic acid with a net gain of two molecules of adenosine triphosphate, the cellular

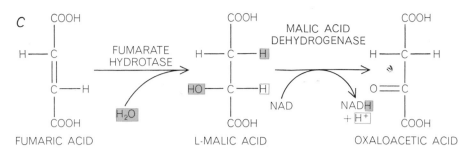

moved. In hydration-dehydrogenation (*c*) water is added and hydrogen is removed. Oxygenation does not occur in respiration, in which oxygen serves only as a hydrogen acceptor.

now of the University of California at Los Angeles, do imply an approximate balance between the chemical combining equivalents of carbon and oxygen in sediments, the atmosphere, the hydrosphere and the biosphere [*see bottom illustration on page 63*]. The relatively small excess of carbon in Rubey's estimates could be accounted for by the oxygen used in converting carbon monoxide to carbon dioxide. Or it might be due to an underestimate of the quantities of sulfate ion or ferric oxide in sediments. (Rubey's estimates could not include large iron formations recently discovered in western Australia and elsewhere.) The carbon dioxide in carbonate rocks does not need to be accounted for, but the oxygen involved in converting it to carbonate ion does. The recycling of sediments through metamorphism, mountain-building and the movement of ocean-floor plates under the continents is a variable of unknown dimensions, but

it probably does not affect the approximate balance observed in view of the fact that the overwhelmingly large pools to be balanced are all in the lithosphere and that carbon and oxygen losses would be roughly equivalent. The small amounts of oxygen dissolved in water are not included in this balance.

Nonetheless, water does enter the picture. Another possible source of oxygen in our atmosphere is photolysis, the ultraviolet dissociation of water vapor in the outer atmosphere followed by the escape of the hydrogen from the earth's gravitational field. This has usually been regarded as a trivial source, however. Although R. T. Brinkmann of the California Institute of Technology has recently argued that nonbiological photolysis may be a major source of atmospheric oxygen, the carbon-oxygen balance sheet does not support that belief, which also runs into other difficulties.

When free oxygen began to accumulate in the atmosphere some 1.8 billion years ago, life was still restricted to sites

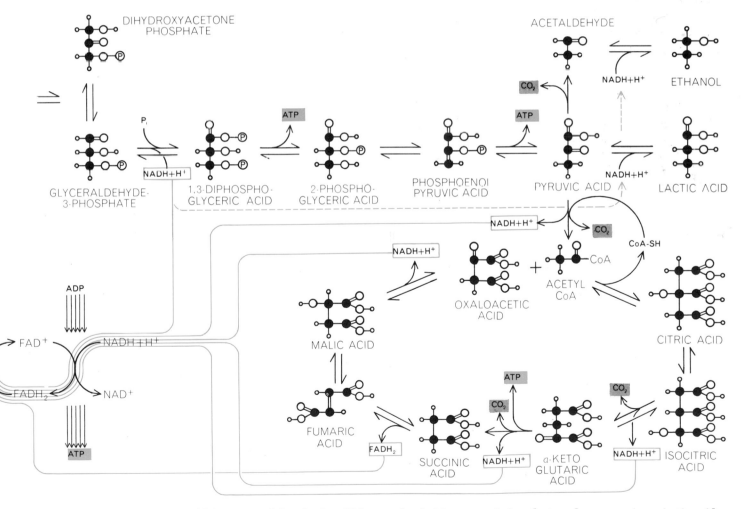

energy carrier. The pyruvic acid is converted into lactic acid in animal cells deprived of oxygen and into some other compound, such as ethanol, in fermentation. In aerobic cells in the presence of oxygen, however, pyruvic acid is completely oxidized to produce carbon dioxide and water. In the process hydrogen ions are removed. The electrons of these hydrogens (and of two removed in glycolysis) are passed along by two electron carriers, nicotinamide adenine dinucleotide (NAD) and flavin adenine dinucleotide (FAD), to a chain of respiratory enzymes, ubiquinone and the cytochromes, which are alternately reduced and oxidized. Energy released in the reactions is coupled to synthesis of ATP, 38 molecules of which are produced for every molecule of glucose consumed.

shielded from destructive ultraviolet radiation by sufficient depths of water or by screens of sediment. In time enough oxygen built up in the atmosphere for ozone, a strong absorber in the ultraviolet, to form a shield against incoming ultraviolet radiation. The late Lloyd V. Berkner and Lauriston C. Marshall of the Graduate Research Center of the Southwest in Dallas calculated that only 1 percent of the present atmospheric level of oxygen would give rise to a sufficient level of ozone to screen out the most deleterious wavelengths of the ultraviolet radiation. This also happens to be the level of oxygen at which Pasteur found that certain microorganisms switch over from a fermentative type of metabolism to an oxidative one. Berkner and Marshall therefore jumped to the conclusion (reasonably enough on the evidence they considered) that this was the stage at which oxidative metabolism arose. They related this stage to the first appearance of metazoan life somewhat more than 600 million years ago.

The geological record has long made it plain, however, that free molecular oxygen existed in the atmosphere well before that relatively late date in geologic time. Moreover, recent evidence is consistent with the origin of oxidative metabolism at least twice as long ago. Eucaryotic cells—cells with organized nuclei and other organelles—have been identified in rocks in eastern California that are believed to be about 1.3 billion years old [see top illustration on page 60]. Since all living eucaryotes depend on oxidative metabolism, it seems likely that these ancestral forms did too. The oxygen level may nonetheless have still been quite low at this stage. Simple diffusion would suffice to move enough oxygen across cell boundaries and within the cell, even at very low concentrations, to supply the early oxidative metabolizers. A higher order of organization and of atmospheric oxygen was required, however, for advanced oxidative metabolism. Perhaps that is why, although the eucaryotic cell existed at least 1.2 billion years ago, we have no unequivocal fossils of metazoan organisms from rocks older than perhaps 640 million years.

In other words, perhaps Berkner and Marshall were mistaken only in trying to make the appearance of the Metazoa coincide with the onset of oxidative metabolism. Once the level of atmospheric oxygen was high enough to generate an effective ozone screen, photosynthetic organisms would have been able to spread throughout the surface waters of the sea, greatly accelerating the rate of oxygen production. The plausible episodes in geological history to correlate with this development are the secondary oxidation of the banded iron formations and the appearance of sedimentary calcium sulfate (gypsum and anhydrite) on a large scale. These events occurred just as or just before the Metazoa first appeared in early Paleozoic time. The attainment of a suitable level of atmospheric oxygen may thus be correlated with the emergence of metazoan root stocks from premetazoan ancestors beginning about 640 million years ago. The fact that oxygen could accumulate no faster than carbon (or hydrogen) was removed argues against the likelihood of a rapid early buildup of oxygen.

That subsequent biospheric and atmospheric evolution were closely interlinked can now be taken for granted. What is not known are the details. Did oxygen levels in the atmosphere increase steadily throughout geologic time, marking regular stages of biological evolution such as the emergence of land plants, of

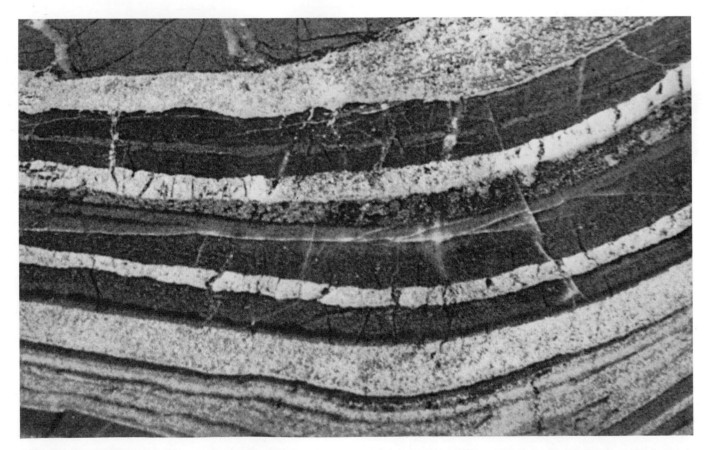

BANDED IRON FORMATION provides the first geological evidence of free oxygen in the hydrosphere. The layers in this polished cross section result from an alternation of iron-rich and iron-poor depositions. This sample from the Soudan Iron Formation in Minnesota is more than 2.7 billion years old. The layers, originally horizontal, were deformed while soft and later metamorphosed.

insects, of the various vertebrate groups and of flowering plants, as Berkner and Marshall suggested? Or were there wide swings in the oxygen level? Did oxygen decrease during great volcanic episodes, as a result of the oxidation of newly emitted carbon monoxide to carbon dioxide, or during times of sedimentary sulfate precipitation? Did oxygen increase when carbon was being sequestered during times of coal and petroleum formation? May there have been fluctuations in both directions as a result of plant and animal evolution, of phytoplankton eruptions and extinctions and of the extent and type of terrestrial plant cover? Such processes and events are now being seriously studied, but the answers are as yet far from clear.

What one can say with confidence is that success in understanding the oxy-

YEARS BEFORE PRESENT	LITHOSPHERE	BIOSPHERE	HYDROSPHERE	ATMOSPHERE
20 MILLION	GLACIATION	MAMMALS DIVERSIFY GRASSES APPEAR		OXYGEN APPROACHES PRESENT LEVEL
50 MILLION	COAL FORMATION VOLCANISM			
100 MILLION		SOCIAL INSECTS, FLOWERING PLANTS MAMMALS		ATMOSPHERIC OXYGEN INCREASES AT FLUCTUATING RATE
200 MILLION	GREAT VOLCANISM COAL FORMATION	INSECTS APPEAR LAND PLANTS APPEAR	OCEANS CONTINUE TO INCREASE IN VOLUME	
500 MILLION	GLACIATION SEDIMENTARY CALCIUM SULFATE	METAZOA APPEAR RAPID INCREASE IN PHYTOPLANKTON	SURFACE WATERS OPENED TO PHYTOPLANKTON	OXYGEN AT 3-10 PERCENT OF PRESENT ATMOSPHERIC LEVEL
1 BILLION	VOLCANISM	EUCARYOTES		OXYGEN AT 1 PERCENT OF PRESENT ATMOSPHERIC LEVEL, OZONE SCREEN EFFECTIVE OXYGEN INCREASING, CARBON DIOXIDE DECREASING
2 BILLION	RED BEDS	ADVANCED OXYGEN-MEDIATING ENZYMES	OXYGEN DIFFUSES INTO ATMOSPHERE	OXYGEN IN ATMOSPHERE
	GLACIATION BANDED IRON FORMATIONS OLDEST SEDIMENTS OLDEST EARTH ROCKS	FIRST OXYGEN-GENERATING PHOTOSYNTHETIC CELLS PROCARYOTES ABIOGENIC EVOLUTION	START OF OXYGEN GENERATION WITH FERROUS IRON AS OXYGEN SINK	NO FREE OXYGEN
5 BILLION	(ORIGIN OF SOLAR SYSTEM)			

CHRONOLOGY that interrelates the evolutions of atmosphere and biosphere is gradually being established from evidence in the geological record and in fossils. According to calculations by Lloyd V. Berkner and Lauriston C. Marshall, when oxygen in the atmosphere reached 1 percent of the present atmospheric level, it provided enough ozone to filter out the most damaging high-energy ultraviolet radiation so that phytoplankton could survive everywhere in the upper, sunlit layers of the seas. The result may have been a geometric increase in the amount of photosynthesis in the oceans that, if accompanied by equivalent sequestration of carbon, might have resulted in a rapid buildup of atmospheric oxygen, leading in time to the evolution of differentiated multicelled animals.

gen cycle of the biosphere in truly broad terms will depend on how good we are at weaving together the related strands of biospheric, atmospheric, hydrospheric and lithospheric evolution throughout geologic time. Whatever we may conjecture about any one of these processes must be consistent with what is known about the others. Whereas any one line of evidence may be weak in itself, a number of lines of evidence, taken together and found to be consistent, reinforce one another exponentially. This synergistic effect enhances our confidence in the proposed time scale linking the evolution of oxygen in the atmosphere and the management of the gaseous oxygen budget within the biosphere [see illustration on page 67].

The most recent factor affecting the oxygen cycle of the biosphere and the oxygen budget of the earth is man himself. In addition to inhaling oxygen and exhaling carbon dioxide as a well-behaved animal does, man decreases the oxygen level and increases the carbon dioxide level by burning fossil fuels and paving formerly green land. He is also engaged in a vast but unplanned experiment to see what effects oil spills and an array of pesticides will have on the world's phytoplankton. The increase in the albedo, or reflectivity, of the earth as a result of covering its waters with a molecule-thick film of oil could also affect plant growth by lowering the temperature and in other unforeseen ways. Reductions in the length of growing seasons and in green areas would limit terrestrial plant growth in the middle latitudes. (This might normally be counterbalanced by increased rainfall in the lower latitudes, but a film of oil would also reduce evaporation and therefore rainfall.) Counteracting such effects, man moves the earth's fresh water around to increase plant growth and photosynthesis in arid and semiarid regions. Some of this activity, however, involves the mining of ground water, thereby favoring processes that cause water to be returned to the sea at a faster rate than evaporation brings it to the land.

He who is willing to say what the final effects of such processes will be is wiser or braver than we are. Perhaps the effects will be self-limiting and self-correcting, although experience should warn us not to gamble on that. Oxygen in the atmosphere might be reduced several percent below the present level without adverse effects. A modest increase in the carbon dioxide level might enhance plant growth and lead to a corresponding increase in the amount of oxygen. Will a further increase in carbon dioxide also have (or renew) a "greenhouse effect," leading to an increase in temperature (and thus to a rising sea level)? Or will such effects be counterbalanced or swamped by the cooling effects of particulate matter in the air or by increased albedo due to oil films? It is anyone's guess. (Perhaps we should be more alarmed about a possible decrease of atmospheric carbon dioxide, on which all forms of life ultimately depend, but the sea contains such vast amounts that it can presumably keep carbon dioxide in the atmosphere balanced at about the present level for a long time to come.) The net effect of the burning of fossil fuels may in the long run be nothing more than a slight increase (or decrease?) in the amount of limestone deposited. In any event the recoverable fossil fuels whose combustion releases carbon dioxide are headed for depletion in a few more centuries, and then man will have other problems to contend with.

What we want to stress is the indivisibility and complexity of the environment. For example, the earth's atmosphere is so thoroughly mixed and so rapidly recycled through the biosphere that the next breath you inhale will contain atoms exhaled by Jesus at Gethsemane and by Adolf Hitler at Munich. It will also contain atoms of radioactive strontium 90 and iodine 131 from atomic explosions and gases from the chimneys and exhaust pipes of the world. Present environmental problems stand as a grim monument to the cumulatively adverse effects of actions that in themselves were reasonable enough but that were taken without sufficient thought to their consequences. If we want to ensure that the biosphere continues to exist over the long term and to have an oxygen cycle, each new action must be matched with an effort to foresee its consequences throughout the ecosystem and to determine how they can be managed favorably or avoided. Understanding also is needed, and we are woefully short on that commodity. This means that we must continue to probe all aspects of the indivisible global ecosystem and its past, present and potential interactions. That is called basic research, and basic research at this critical point in history is gravely endangered by new crosscurrents of anti-intellectualism.

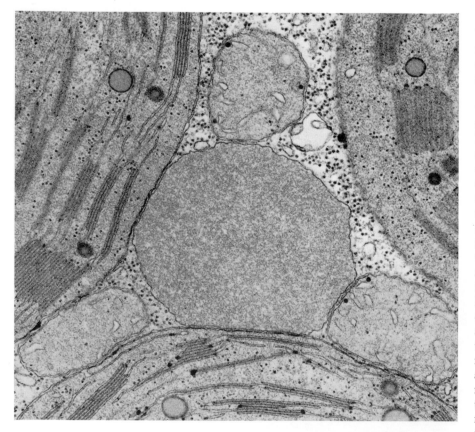

THREE ORGANELLES that are involved in oxygen metabolism in the living cell are enlarged 40,000 diameters in an electron micrograph of a tobacco leaf cell made by Sue Ellen Frederick in the laboratory of Eldon H. Newcomb at the University of Wisconsin. A peroxisome (center) is surrounded by three mitochondria and three chloroplasts. Oxygen is produced in the grana (layered objects) in the chloroplasts and is utilized in aerobic respiration in the mitochondria. Peroxisomes contain enzymes involved in oxygen metabolism.

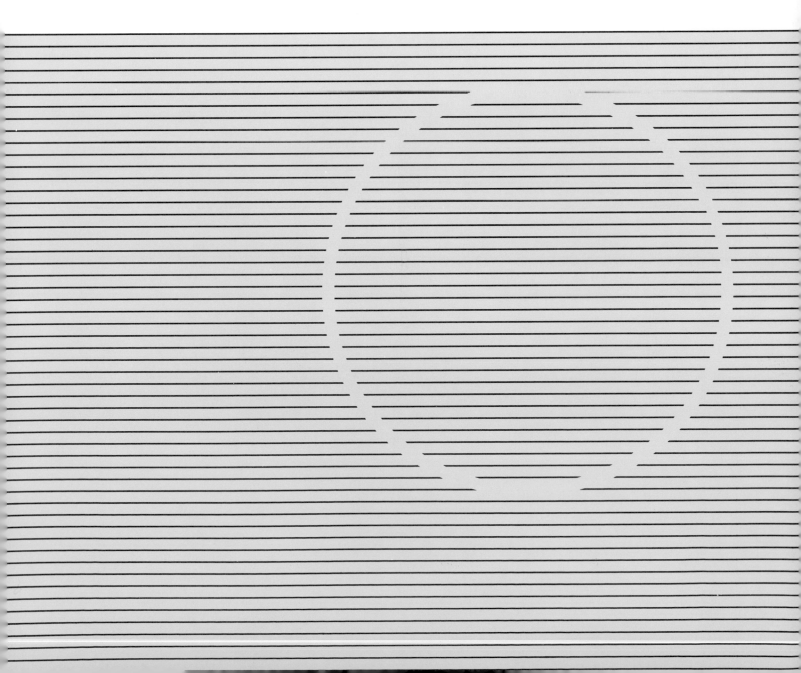

VII

The Nitrogen Cycle

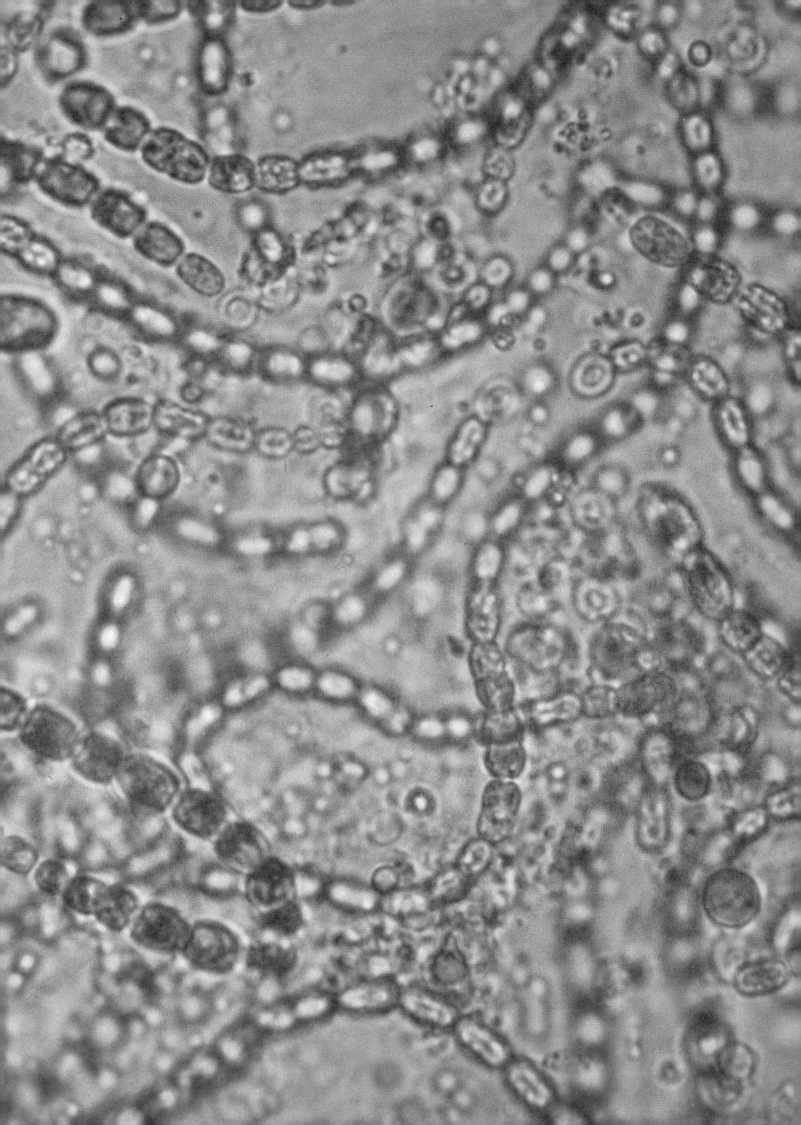

The Nitrogen Cycle

by C. C. DELWICHE

Nitrogen is 79 percent of the atmosphere, but it cannot be used directly by the large majority of living things. It must first be "fixed" by specialized organisms or by industrial processes

Although men and other land animals live in an ocean of air that is 79 percent nitrogen, their supply of food is limited more by the availability of fixed nitrogen than by that of any other plant nutrient. By "fixed" is meant nitrogen incorporated in a chemical compound that can be utilized by plants and animals. As it exists in the atmosphere nitrogen is an inert gas except to the comparatively few organisms that have the ability to convert the element to a combined form. A smaller but still significant amount of atmospheric nitrogen is fixed by ionizing phenomena such as cosmic radiation, meteor trails and lightning, which momentarily provide the high energy needed for nitrogen to react with oxygen or the hydrogen of water. Nitrogen is also fixed by marine organisms, but the largest single natural source of fixed nitrogen is probably terrestrial microorganisms and associations between such microorganisms and plants.

Of all man's recent interventions in the cycles of nature the industrial fixation of nitrogen far exceeds all the others in magnitude. Since 1950 the amount of nitrogen annually fixed for the production of fertilizer has increased approximately fivefold, until it now equals the amount that was fixed by all terrestrial ecosystems before the advent of modern agriculture. In 1968 the world's annual output of industrially fixed nitrogen amounted to about 30 million tons of nitrogen; by the year 2000 the industrial fixation of nitrogen may well exceed 100 million tons.

Before the large-scale manufacture of synthetic fertilizers and the wide cultivation of the nitrogen-fixing legumes one could say with some confidence that the amount of nitrogen removed from the atmosphere by natural fixation processes was closely balanced by the amount returned to the atmosphere by organisms that convert organic nitrates to gaseous nitrogen. Now one cannot be sure that the denitrifying processes are keeping pace with the fixation processes. Nor can one predict all the consequences if nitrogen fixation were to exceed denitrification over an extended period. We do know that excessive runoff of nitrogen compounds in streams and rivers can result in "blooms" of algae and intensified biological activity that deplete the available oxygen and destroy fish and other oxygen-dependent organisms. The rapid eutrophication of Lake Erie is perhaps the most familiar example.

To appreciate the intricate web of nitrogen flow in the biosphere let us trace the course of nitrogen atoms from the atmosphere into the cells of microorganisms, and then into the soil as fixed nitrogen, where it is available to higher plants and ultimately to animals. Plants and animals die and return the fixed nitrogen to the soil, at which point the nitrogen may simply be recycled through a new generation of plants and animals

or it may be broken down into elemental nitrogen and returned to the atmosphere [*see illustration on next two pages*].

Because much of the terminology used to describe steps in the nitrogen cycle evolved in previous centuries it has an archaic quality. Antoine Laurent Lavoisier, who clarified the composition of air, gave nitrogen the name azote, meaning without life. The term is still found in the family name of an important nitrogen-fixing bacterium: the Azotobacteraceae. One might think that fixation would merely be termed nitrification, to indicate the addition of nitrogen to some other substance, but nitrification is reserved for a specialized series of reactions in which a few species of microorganisms oxidize the ammonium ion (NH_4^+) to nitrite (NO_2^-) or nitrite to nitrate (NO_3^-). When nitrites or nitrates are reduced to gaseous compounds such as molecular nitrogen (N_2) or nitrous oxide (N_2O), the process is termed denitrification. "Ammonification" describes the process by which the nitrogen of organic compounds (chiefly amino acids) is converted to ammonium ion. The process operates when microorganisms decompose the remains of dead plants and animals. Finally, a word should be said about the terms oxidation and reduction, which have come to mean more than just the addition of oxygen or its removal. Oxidation is any process that removes electrons from a substance. Reduction is the reverse process: the addition of electrons. Since electrons can neither be created nor destroyed in a chemical reaction, the oxidation of one substance always implies the reduction of another.

One may wonder how it is that some organisms find it profitable to oxidize

BLUE-GREEN ALGAE, magnified 4,200 diameters on the opposite page, are among the few free-living organisms capable of combining nitrogen with hydrogen. Until this primary fixation process is accomplished, the nitrogen in the air (or dissolved in water) cannot be assimilated by the overwhelming majority of plants or by any animal. A few bacteria are also free-living nitrogen fixers. The remaining nitrogen-fixing microorganisms live symbiotically with higher plants. This micrograph, which shows blue-green algae of the genus *Nostoc*, was made by Herman S. Forest of the State University of New York at Geneseo.

71

nitrogen compounds whereas other organisms—even organisms in the same environment—owe their survival to their ability to reduce nitrogen compounds. Apart from photosynthetic organisms, which obtain their energy from radiation, all living forms depend for their energy on chemical transformations.

These transformations normally involve the oxidation of one compound and the reduction of another, although in some cases the compound being oxidized and the compound being reduced are different molecules of the same substance, and in other cases the reactants are fragments of a single molecular species. Ni-

trogen can be cycled because the reduced inorganic compounds of nitrogen can be oxidized by atmospheric oxygen with a yield of useful energy. Under anaerobic conditions the oxidized compounds of nitrogen can act as oxidizing agents for the burning of organic compounds (and a few inorganic com-

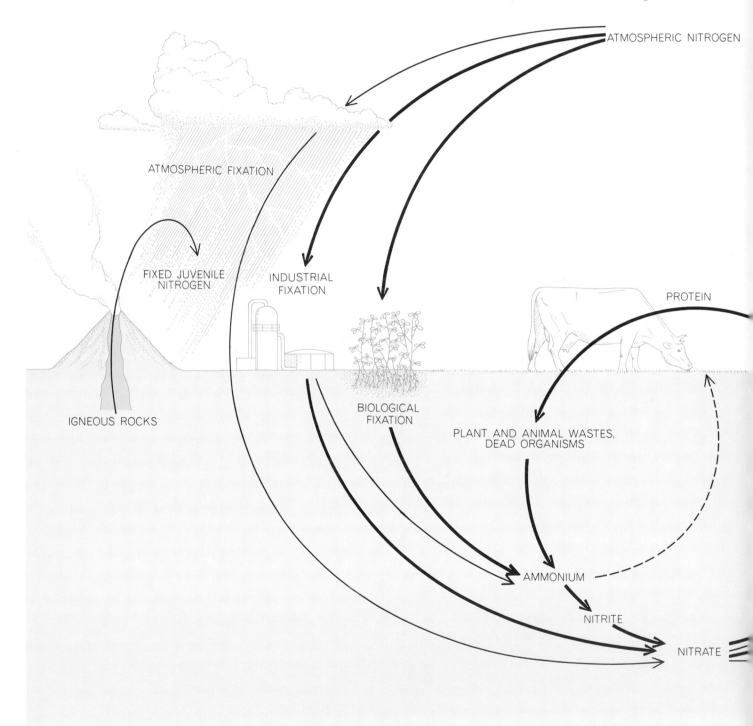

NITROGEN CYCLE, like the water, oxygen and carbon cycles, involves all regions of the biosphere. Although the supply of nitrogen in the atmosphere is virtually inexhaustible, it must be combined with hydrogen or oxygen before it can be assimilated by higher plants, which in turn are consumed by animals. Man has intervened in the historical nitrogen cycle by the large-scale cultivation of nitrogen-fixing legumes and by the industrial fixation of nitrogen. The amount of nitrogen fixed annually by these two expedients now exceeds by perhaps 10 percent the amount of nitrogen fixed by terrestrial ecosystems before the advent of agriculture.

pounds), again with a yield of useful energy.

Nitrogen is able to play its complicated role in life processes because it has an unusual number of oxidation levels, or valences [*see illustration on page 75*]. An oxidation level indicates the number of electrons that an atom in a particular compound has "accepted" or "donated." In plants and animals most nitrogen exists either in the form of the ammonium ion or of amino ($-NH_2$) compounds. In either case it is highly reduced; it has acquired three electrons by its association with three other atoms and thus is said to have a valence of minus 3. At the other extreme, when nitrogen is in the highly oxidized form of the nitrate ion (the principal form it takes in the soil), it shares five of its electrons with oxygen atoms and so has a valence of plus 5. To convert nitrogen as it is found in the ammonium ion or amino acids to nitrogen as it exists in soil nitrates involves a total valence change of eight, or the removal of eight electrons. Conversely, to convert nitrate nitrogen into amino nitrogen requires the addition of eight electrons.

By and large the soil reactions that reduce nitrogen, or add electrons to it, release considerably more energy than the reactions that oxidize nitrogen, or remove electrons from it. The illustration on page 76 lists some of the principal reactions involved in the nitrogen cycle, together with the energy released (or required) by each. As a generalization one can say that for almost every reaction in nature where the conversion of one compound to another yields an energy of at least 15 kilocalories per mole (the equivalent in grams of a compound's molecular weight), some organism or group of organisms has arisen that can exploit this energy to survive.

The fixation of nitrogen requires an investment of energy. Before nitrogen can be fixed it must be "activated," which means that molecular nitrogen must be split into two atoms of free nitrogen. This step requires at least 160 kilocalories for each mole of nitrogen (equivalent to 28 grams). The actual fixation step, in which two atoms of nitrogen combine with three molecules of hydrogen to form two molecules of ammonia (NH_3), releases about 13 kilocalories. Thus the two steps together require a net input of at least 147 kilocalories. Whether nitrogen-fixing organisms actually invest this much energy, however, is not known. Reactions catalyzed by enzymes involve the penetration of activation barriers and not a simple change in energy between a set of initial reactants and their end products.

Once ammonia or the ammonium ion has appeared in the soil, it can be absorbed by the roots of plants and the nitrogen can be incorporated into amino acids and then into proteins. If the plant is subsequently eaten by an animal, the nitrogen may be incorporated into a new protein. In either case the protein ultimately returns to the soil, where it is decomposed (usually with bacterial help) into its component amino acids. Assuming that conditions are aerobic, meaning that an adequate supply of oxygen is present, the soil will contain many microorganisms capable of oxidizing amino acids to carbon dioxide, water and ammonia. If the amino acid happens to be glycine, the reaction will yield 176 kilocalories per mole.

A few microorganisms represented by the genus *Nitrosomonas* employ nitrification of the ammonium ion as their sole source of energy. In the presence of oxygen, ammonia is converted to nitrite ion (NO_2^-) plus water, with an energy yield of about 65 kilocalories per mole, which is quite adequate for a comfortable existence. *Nitrosomonas* belongs to the group of microorganisms termed autotrophs, which get along without an organic source of energy. Photoautotrophs obtain their energy from light; chemoautotrophs (such as *Nitrosomonas*) obtain energy from inorganic compounds.

There is another specialized group of microorganisms, represented by *Nitrobacter,* that are capable of extracting additional energy from the nitrite generated by *Nitrosomonas.* The result is the oxidation of a nitrite ion to a nitrate ion with the release of about 17 kilocalories per mole, which is just enough to support the existence of *Nitrobacter.*

In the soil there are numerous kinds of denitrifying bacteria (for example *Pseudomonas denitrificans*) that, if obliged to exist in the absence of oxygen, are able to use the nitrate or nitrite ion as electron acceptors for the oxidation of organic compounds. In these reactions the energy yield is nearly as large as it would be if pure oxygen were the oxidizing agent. When glucose reacts with oxygen, the energy yield is 686 kilocalories per mole of glucose. In microorganisms living under anaerobic conditions the reaction of glucose with nitrate ion yields about 545 kilocalories per mole of glucose if the nitrogen is reduced to nitrous oxide, and 570 kilocalories if the nitrogen is reduced all the way to its elemental gaseous state.

The comparative value of ammonium and nitrate ions as a source of nitrogen for plants has been the subject of a number of investigations. One might think that the question would be readily resolved in favor of the ammonium ion: its valence is minus 3, the same as the valence of nitrogen in amino acids, whereas the valence of the nitrate ion is plus 5.

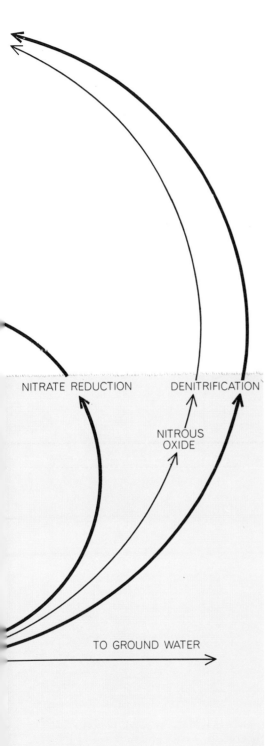

NITRATE REDUCTION   DENITRIFICATION

NITROUS OXIDE

TO GROUND WATER

A cycle similar to the one illustrated also operates in the ocean, but its characteristics and transfer rates are less well understood. A global nitrogen flow chart, using the author's estimates, appears on the next page.

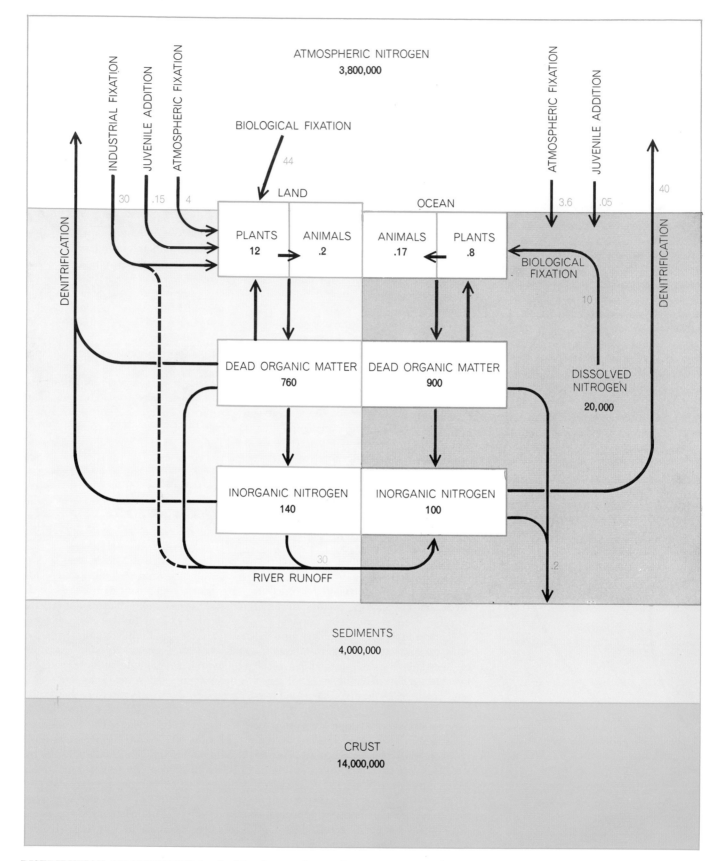

DISTRIBUTION OF NITROGEN in the biosphere and annual transfer rates can be estimated only within broad limits. The two quantities known with high confidence are the amount of nitrogen in the atmosphere and the rate of industrial fixation. The apparent precision in the other figures shown here reflects chiefly an effort to preserve indicated or probable ratios among different inventories. Thus the figures for atmospheric fixation and biological fixation in the oceans could well be off by a factor of 10. The figures for inventories are given in billions of metric tons; the figures for transfer rates (*color*) are given in millions of metric tons. Because of the extensive use of industrially fixed nitrogen the amount of nitrogen available to land plants may significantly exceed the nitrogen returned to the atmosphere by denitrifying bacteria in the soil. A portion of this excess fixed nitrogen is ultimately washed into the sea but it is not included in the figure shown for river runoff. Similarly, the value for oceanic denitrification is no more than a rough estimate that is based on the assumption that the nitrogen cycle was in overall balance before man's intervention.

On this basis plants must expend energy to reduce nitrogen from a valence of plus 5 to one of minus 3. The fact is, however, that there are complicating factors; the preferred form of nitrogen depends on other variables. Because the ammonium ion has a positive charge it tends to be trapped on clay particles near the point where it is formed (or where it is introduced artificially) until it has been oxidized. The nitrate ion, being negatively charged, moves freely through the soil and thus is more readily carried downward into the root zone. Although the demand for fertilizer in solid form (such as ammonium nitrate and urea) remains high, anhydrous ammonia and liquid ammoniacal fertilizers are now widely applied. The quantity of nitrogen per unit weight of ammonia is much greater than it is per unit of nitrate; moreover, liquids are easier to handle than solids.

Until the end of the 19th century little was known about the soil organisms that fix nitrogen. In fact, at that time there was some concern among scientists that the denitrifying bacteria, which had just been discovered, would eventually deplete the reserve of fixed nitrogen in the soil and cripple farm productivity. In an address before the Royal Society of London, Sir William Crookes painted a bleak picture for world food production unless artificial means of fixing nitrogen were soon developed. This was a period when Chilean nitrate reserves were the main source of fixed nitrogen for both fertilizer and explosives. As it turned out, the demand for explosives provided the chief incentive for the invention of the catalytic fixation process by Fritz Haber and Karl Bosch of Germany in 1914. In this process atmospheric nitrogen and hydrogen are passed over a catalyst (usually nickel) at a temperature of about 500 degrees Celsius and a pressure of several hundred atmospheres. In a French version of the process, developed by Georges Claude, nitrogen was obtained by the fractional liquefaction of air. In current versions of the Haber process the source of hydrogen is often the methane in natural gas [see illustration on page 77].

As the biological fixation of nitrogen and the entire nitrogen cycle became better understood, the role of the denitrifying bacteria fell into place. Without such bacteria to return nitrogen to the atmosphere most of the atmospheric nitrogen would now be in the oceans or locked up in sediments. Actually, of course, there is not enough oxygen in the

VALENCE	COMPOUND	FORMULA	VALENCE ELECTRONS
+ 5	NITRATE ION	NO_3^-	
+ 3	NITRITE ION	NO_2^-	
+ 1	NITROXYL	[HNO]	
0	NITROGEN GAS	N_2	
− 1	HYDROXYLAMINE	$HONH_2$	
− 3	AMMONIA	NH_3	

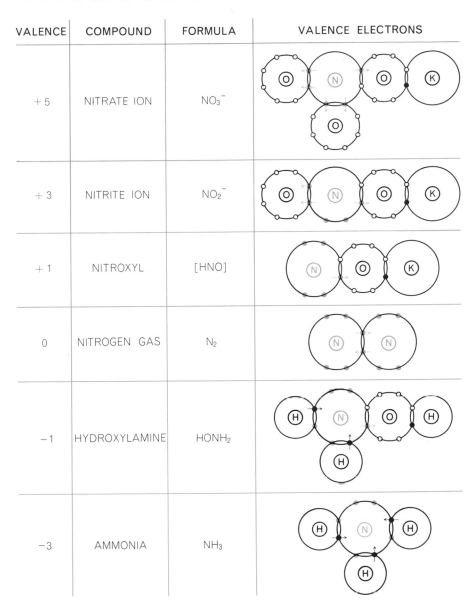

NITROGEN'S VARIETY OF OXIDATION LEVELS, or valence states, explains its ability to combine with hydrogen, oxygen and other atoms to form a great variety of biological compounds. Six of its valence states are listed with schematic diagrams (*right*) showing the disposition of electrons in the atom's outer (valence) shell. The ions are shown combined with potassium (K). In the oxidized (+) states nitrogen's outer electrons complete the outer shells of other atoms. In the reduced (−) states the two electrons needed to complete the outer shell of nitrogen are supplied by other atoms. Actually the outer electrons of two bound atoms spend some time in the shells of both atoms, contributing to the electrostatic attraction between them. Electrons of nitrogen (N) are in color; those of other atoms are black dots or open circles. The nitroxyl radical, HNO, is placed in brackets because it is not stable. It can exist in its dimeric form, hyponitrous acid (HONNOH).

atmosphere today to convert all the free nitrogen into nitrates. One can imagine, however, that if a one-way process were to develop in the absence of denitrifying bacteria, the addition of nitrates to the ocean would make seawater slightly more acidic and start the release of carbon dioxide from carbonate rocks. Eventually the carbon dioxide would be taken up by plants, and if the carbon were then deposited as coal or other hydrocarbons, the remaining oxygen would be available in the atmosphere to be com-

bined with nitrogen. Because of the large number of variables involved it is difficult to predict how the world would look without the denitrification reaction, but it would certainly not be the world we know.

The full story of the biological fixation of nitrogen has not yet been written. One would like to know how the activating enzyme (nitrogenase) used by nitrogen-fixing bacteria can accomplish at ordinary temperatures and pressures what takes hundreds of degrees and thousands of pounds of pressure in a synthetic-ammonia reactor. The total amount of nitrogenase in the world is probably no more than a few kilograms.

The nitrogen-fixing microorganisms are divided into two broad classes: those that are "free-living" and those that live in symbiotic association with higher plants. This distinction, however, is not as sharp as it was once thought to be, because the interaction of plants and microorganisms has varying degrees of intimacy. The symbionts depend directly on the plants for their energy supply and probably for special nutrients as well. The free-living nitrogen fixers are indirectly dependent on plants for their energy or, as in the case of the blue-green algae and photosynthetic bacteria, obtain energy directly from sunlight.

Although the nitrogen-fixation reaction is associated with only a few dozen species of higher plants, these species are widely distributed in the plant kingdom. Among the more primitive plants whose symbionts can fix nitrogen are the cycads and the ginkgos, which can be traced back to the Carboniferous period of some 300 million years ago [see bottom illustration on page 79]. It is probable that the primitive atmosphere of the earth contained ammonia, in which case the necessity for nitrogen fixation did not arise for hundreds of millions of years.

Various kinds of bacteria, particularly the Azotobacteraceae, are evidently the chief suppliers of fixed nitrogen in grasslands and other ecosystems where plants with nitrogen-fixing symbionts are absent. Good quantitative information on the rate of nitrogen fixation in such ecosystems is hard to obtain. Most investigations indicate a nitrogen-fixation rate of only two or three kilograms per hectare per year, with a maximum of perhaps five or six kilograms. Blue-green algae seem to be an important source of fixed nitrogen under conditions that favor their development [see illustration on page 70]. They may be a significant source in rice paddies and other environments favoring their growth. In natural ecosystems with mixed vegetation the symbiotic associations involving such plant genera as *Alnus* (the alders) and *Ceanothus* (the buckthorns) are important suppliers of fixed nitrogen.

For the earth as a whole, however, the greatest natural source of fixed nitrogen is probably the legumes. They are certainly the most important from an agronomic standpoint and have therefore been the most closely studied. The input of nitrogen from the microbial symbionts of alfalfa and other leguminous crops can easily amount to 350 kilograms per hectare, or roughly 100 times the annual rate of fixation attainable by nonsymbiotic organisms in a natural ecosystem.

Recommendations for increasing the world's food supply usually emphasize increasing the cultivation of legumes not only to enrich the soil in nitrogen but also because legumes (for example peas and beans) are themselves a food crop containing a good nutritional balance of amino acids. There are, however, several obstacles to carrying out such recommendations. The first is custom and taste. Many societies with no tradition of growing and eating legumes are reluctant to adopt them as a basic food.

For the farmer legumes can create a more immediate problem: the increased yields made possible by the extra nitrogen lead to the increased consumption of other essential elements, notably potassium and phosphorus. As a consequence farmers often say that legumes are "hard on the soil." What this really means is that the large yield of such crops places

REACTION	ENERGY YIELD (KILOCALORIES)
DENITRIFICATION	
1 $C_6H_{12}O_6 + 6KNO_3 \longrightarrow 6CO_2 + 3H_2O + 6KOH + 3N_2O$ GLUCOSE POTASSIUM NITRATE· POTASSIUM HYDROXIDE NITROUS OXIDE	545
2 $5C_6H_{12}O_6 + 24KNO_3 \longrightarrow 30CO_2 + 18H_2O + 24KOH + 12N_2$ NITROGEN	570 (PER MOLE OF GLUCOSE)
3 $5S + 6KNO_3 + 2CaCO_3 \longrightarrow 3K_2SO_4 + 2CaSO_4 + 2CO_2 + 3N_2$ SULFUR POTASSIUM SULFATE CALCIUM SULFATE	132 (PER MOLE OF SULFUR)
RESPIRATION	
4 $C_6H_{12}O_6 + 6O_2 \longrightarrow 6CO_2 + 6H_2O$ CARBON DIOXIDE WATER	686
AMMONIFICATION	
5 $CH_2NH_2COOH + 1\frac{1}{2}O_2 \longrightarrow 2CO_2 + H_2O + NH_3$ GLYCINE OXYGEN AMMONIA	176
NITRIFICATION	
6 $NH_3 + 1\frac{1}{2}O_2 \longrightarrow HNO_2 + H_2O$ NITROUS ACID	66
7 $KNO_2 + \frac{1}{2}O_2 \longrightarrow KNO_3$ POTASSIUM NITRITE	17.5
NITROGEN FIXATION	
8 $N_2 \longrightarrow 2N$ "ACTIVATION" OF NITROGEN	−160
9 $2N + 3H_2 \longrightarrow 2NH_3$	12.8

ENERGY YIELDS OF REACTIONS important in the nitrogen cycle show the various means by which organisms can obtain energy and thereby keep the cycle going. The most profitable are the denitrification reactions, which add electrons to nitrate nitrogen, whose valence is plus 5, and shift it either to plus 1 (as in N_2O) or zero (as in N_2). In the process glucose (or sulfur) is oxidized. Reactions No. 1 and No. 2 release nearly as much energy as conventional respiration (*No. 4*), in which the agent for oxidizing glucose is oxygen itself. The ammonification reaction (*No. 5*) is one of many that release ammonium for nitrification. The least energy of all, but still enough to provide the sole energetic support for certain bacteria, is released by the nitrification reactions (*No. 6 and No. 7*), which oxidize nitrogen. Only nitrogen fixation, which is accomplished in two steps, calls for an input of energy. The true energy cost of nitrogen fixation to an organism is unknown, however.

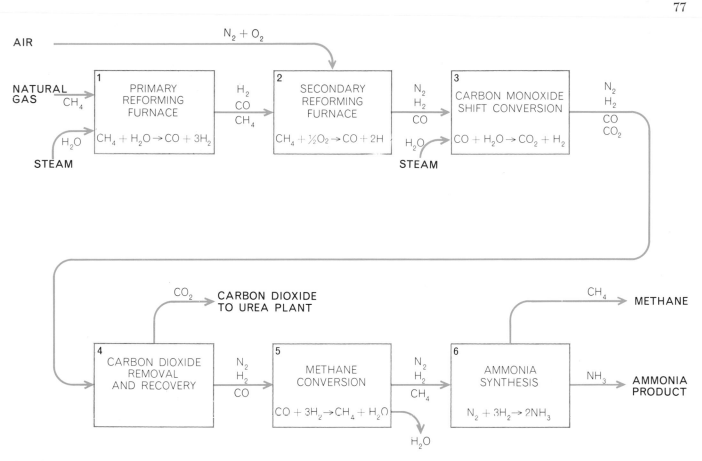

INDUSTRIAL AMMONIA PROCESS is based on the high-pressure catalytic fixation method invented in 1914 by Fritz Haber and Karl Bosch, which supplied Germany with nitrates for explosives in World War I. This flow diagram is based on the process developed by the M. W. Kellogg Company. As in most modern plants, the hydrogen for the basic reaction is obtained from methane, the chief constituent of natural gas, but any hydrocarbon source will do. In Step 1 methane and steam react to produce a gas rich in hydrogen. In Step 2 atmospheric nitrogen is introduced; the oxygen accompanying it is converted to carbon monoxide by partial combustion with methane. The carbon monoxide reacts with steam in Step 3. The carbon dioxide is removed in Step 4 and can be used elsewhere to convert some of the ammonia to urea, which has the formula $CO(NH_2)_2$. The last traces of carbon monoxide are converted to methane in Step 5. In Step 6 nitrogen and hydrogen combine at elevated temperature and pressure, in the presence of a catalyst, to form ammonia. A portion of the ammonia product can readily be converted to nitric acid by reacting it with oxygen. Nitric acid and ammonia can then be combined to produce ammonium nitrate, which, like urea, is another widely used fertilizer.

a high demand on all minerals, and unless the minerals are supplied the full benefit of the crop is not realized.

Symbiotic nitrogen fixers have a greater need for some micronutrients (for example molybdenum) than most plants do. It is now known that molybdenum is directly incorporated in the nitrogen-fixing enzyme nitrogenase. In Australia there were large areas where legumes refused to grow at all until it was discovered that the land could be made fertile by the addition of as little as two ounces of molybdenum per acre. Cobalt turns out to be another essential micronutrient for the fixation of nitrogen. The addition of only 10 parts per trillion of cobalt in a culture solution can make the difference between plants that are stunted and obviously in need of nitrogen and plants that are healthy and growing vigorously.

Although legumes and their symbionts are energetic fixers of nitrogen, there are indications that the yield of a legume crop can be increased still further by direct application of fertilizer instead of depending on the plant to supply all its own needs for fixed nitrogen. Additional experiments are needed to determine just how much the yield can be increased and how this increase compares with the industrial fixation of nitrogen in terms of energy investment. Industrial processes call for some 6,000 kilocalories per kilogram of nitrogen fixed, which is very little more than the theoretical minimum. The few controlled studies with which I am familiar suggest that the increase in crop yield achieved by the addition of a kilogram of nitrogen amounts to about the same number of calories. This comparison suggests that one can exchange the calories put into industrial fixation of nitrogen for the calories contained in food. In actuality this trade-off applies to the entire agricultural enterprise. The energy required for preparing, tilling and harvesting a field and for processing and distributing the product is only slightly less than the energy contained in the harvested crop.

Having examined the principal reactions that propel the nitrogen cycle, we are now in a position to view the process as a whole and to interpret some of its broad implications. As other authors in this discussion of the biosphere have explained, one must be cautious in trying to present a worldwide inventory of a particular element in the biosphere and in indicating annual flows from one part of a cycle to another. The balance sheet for nitrogen [*see top illustration on page 79*] is particularly crude because we do not have enough information to assign accurate estimates to the amounts of nitrogen that are fixed and subsequently returned to the atmosphere by biological processes.

Another source of uncertainty involves the amount of nitrogen fixed by ionizing phenomena in the atmosphere. Although one can measure the amount of fixed nitrogen in rainfall, one is forced to guess

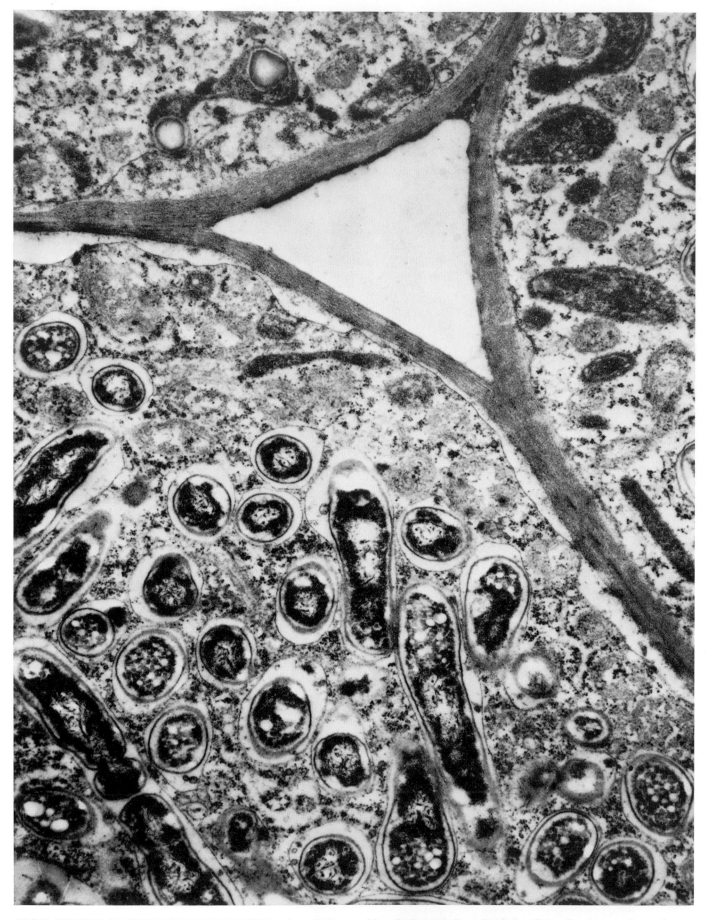

CROSS SECTION OF SOYBEAN ROOT NODULE, enlarged 22,-000 diameters, shows portions of three cells that have been infected by the nitrogen-fixing bacterium *Rhizobium japonicum*. More than two dozen bacteria are visible, each surrounded by a membrane. After the bacteria have divided, within a few days, each membrane will contain four to six "bacteroids." This electron micrograph was made by D. J. Goodchild and F. J. Bergersen of the Commonwealth Scientific and Industrial Research Organization in Australia.

how much is produced by ionization and how much represents nitrogen that has entered the atmosphere from the land or the sea, either as ammonia or as oxides of nitrogen. Because the ocean is slightly alkaline it could release ammonia at a low rate, but that rate is almost impossible to estimate. Land areas are a more likely source of nitrogen oxides, and some reasonable estimates of the rate of loss are possible. One can say that the total amount of fixed nitrogen delivered to the earth by rainfall is of the order of 25 million metric tons per year. My own estimate is that 70 percent of this total is previously fixed nitrogen cycling through the biosphere, and that only 30 percent is freshly fixed by lightning and other atmospheric phenomena.

Another factor that is difficult to estimate is the small but steady loss of nitrogen from the biosphere to sedimentary rocks. Conversely, there is a continuous delivery of new nitrogen to the system by the weathering of igneous rocks in the crust of the earth. The average nitrogen content of igneous rocks, however, is considerably lower than that of sedimentary rocks, and since the quantities of the two kinds of rock are roughly equal, one would expect a net loss of nitrogen from the biosphere through geologic time. Conceivably this loss is just about balanced by the delivery of "juvenile" nitrogen to the atmosphere by volcanic action. The amount of fixed nitrogen reintroduced in this way probably does not exceed two or three million tons per year.

Whereas late-19th-century scientists worried that denitrifying bacteria were exhausting the nitrogen in the soil, we must be concerned today that denitrification may not be keeping pace with nitrogen fixation, considering the large amounts of fixed nitrogen that are being introduced in the biosphere by industrial fixation and the cultivation of legumes. It has become urgent to learn much more about exactly where and under what circumstances denitrification takes place.

We know first of all that denitrification does not normally proceed to any great extent under aerobic conditions. Whenever free oxygen is available, it is energetically advantageous for an organism to use it to oxidize organic compounds rather than to use the oxygen bound in nitrate salts. One can conclude that there must be large areas in the biosphere where conditions are sufficiently anaerobic to strongly favor the denitrification reaction. Such conditions exist wherever the input of organic materials

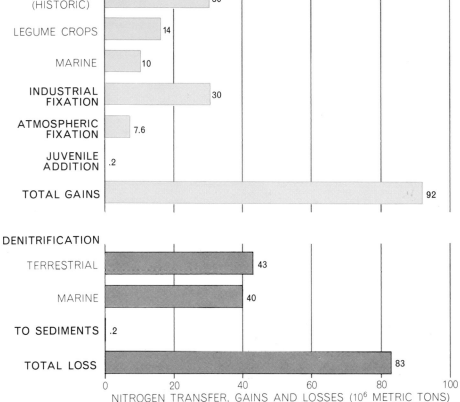

BIOLOGICAL FIXATION

TERRESTRIAL (HISTORIC) — 30
LEGUME CROPS — 14
MARINE — 10
INDUSTRIAL FIXATION — 30
ATMOSPHERIC FIXATION — 7.6
JUVENILE ADDITION — .2
TOTAL GAINS — 92

DENITRIFICATION

TERRESTRIAL — 43
MARINE — 40
TO SEDIMENTS — .2
TOTAL LOSS — 83

NITROGEN TRANSFER, GAINS AND LOSSES (10^6 METRIC TONS)

BALANCE SHEET FOR NITROGEN CYCLE, based on the author's estimates, indicates that nitrogen is now being introduced into the biosphere in fixed form at the rate of some 92 million metric tons per year (*colored bars*), whereas the total amount being denitrified and returned to the atmosphere is only about 83 million tons per year. The difference of some nine million tons may represent the rate at which fixed nitrogen is building up in the biosphere: in the soil, in ground-water reservoirs, in rivers and lakes and in the ocean.

ASSOCIATIONS OF TREES AND BACTERIA are important fixers of nitrogen in natural ecosystems. The ginkgo tree (*left*), a gymnosperm, has shown little outward change in millions of years. The alder (*right*), an angiosperm, is common in many parts of the world.

exceeds the input of oxygen for their degradation. Typical areas where the denitrification process operates close to the surface are the arctic tundra, swamps and similar places where oxygen input is limited. In many other areas where the input of organic material is sizable, however, denitrification is likely to be proceeding at some point below the surface, probably close to the level of the water table.

There are even greater uncertainties regarding the nitrogen cycle in the ocean. It is known that some marine organisms do fix nitrogen, but quantitative information is scanty. A minimum rate of denitrification can be deduced by estimating the amount of nitrate carried into the ocean by rivers. A reasonable estimate is 10 million metric tons per year in the form of nitrates and perhaps twice that amount in the form of organic material, a total of about 30 million tons. Since the transfer of nitrogen into sediments is slight, one can conclude that, at least before man's intervention in the nitrogen cycle, the ocean was probably capable of denitrifying that amount of fixed nitrogen.

The many blanks in our knowledge of the nitrogen cycle are disturbing when one considers that the amount of nitrogen fixed industrially has been doubling about every six years. If we add to this extra nitrogen the amounts fixed by the cultivation of legumes, it already exceeds (by perhaps 10 percent) the amount of nitrogen fixed in nature. Unless fertilizers and nitrogenous wastes are carefully managed, rivers and lakes can become loaded with the nitrogen carried in runoff waters. In such waterways and in neighboring ground-water systems the nitrogen concentration could, and in some cases already does, exceed the levels acceptable for human consumption. Under some circumstances bacterial denitrification can be exploited to control the buildup of fixed nitrogen, but much work has to be done to develop successful management techniques.

The problem of nitrogen disposal is aggravated by the nitrogen contained in the organic wastes of a steadily increasing human and domestic-animal population. Ideally this waste nitrogen should be recycled back to the soil, but efficient and acceptable means for doing so remain to be developed. At present it is economically sounder for the farmer to keep adding industrial fertilizers to his crops. The ingenuity that has been used to feed a growing world population will have to be matched quickly by an effort to keep the nitrogen cycle in reasonable balance.

VIII

Mineral Cycles

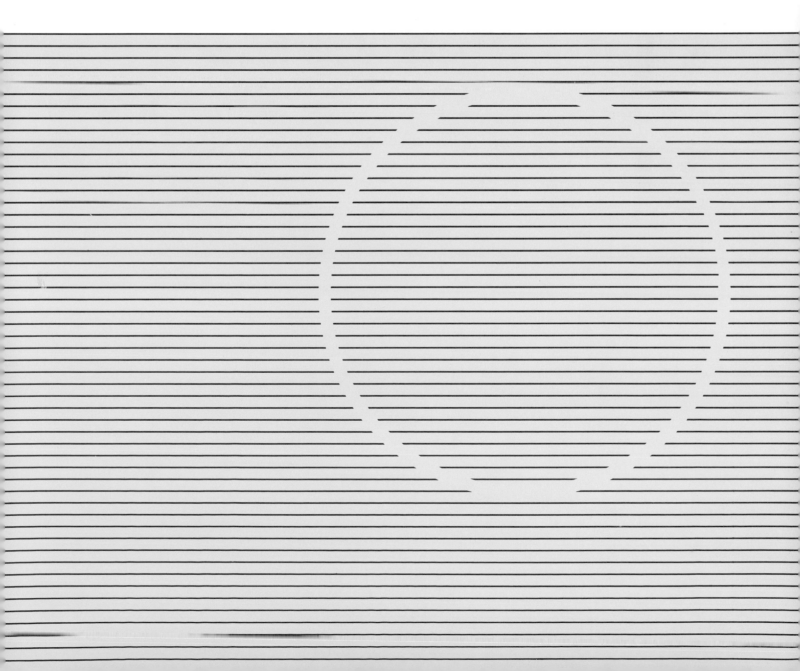

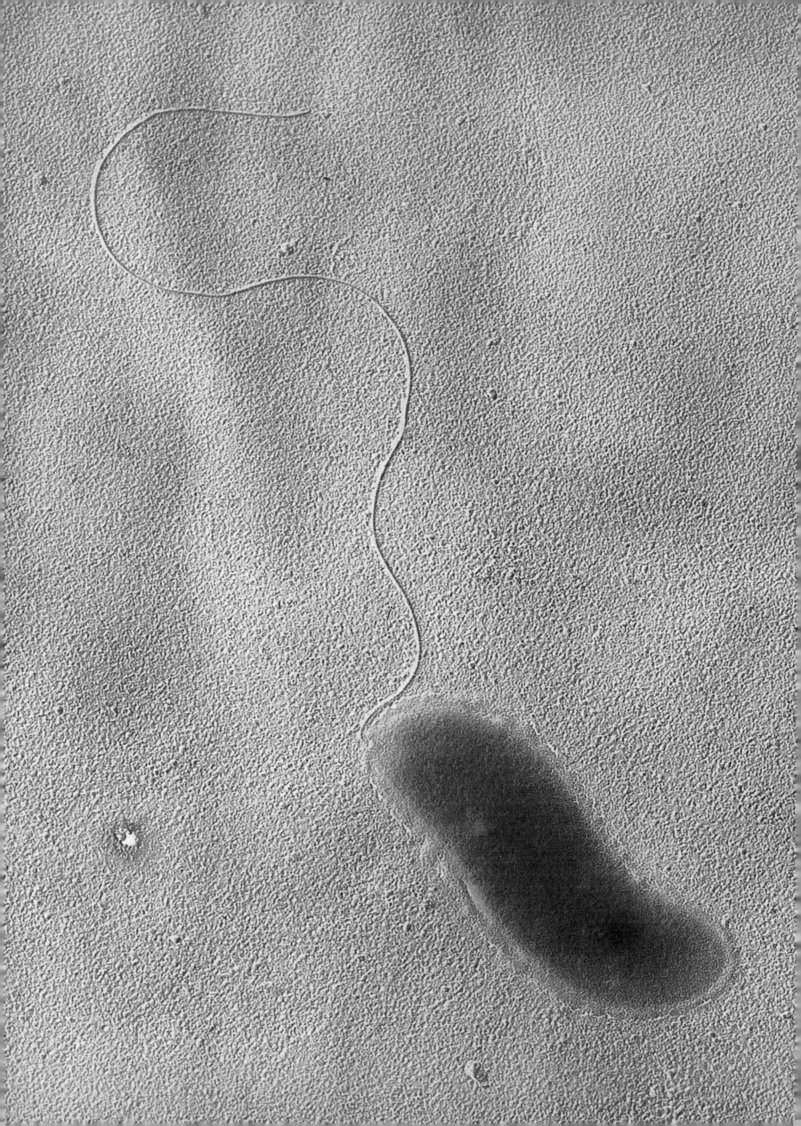

Mineral Cycles

by EDWARD S. DEEVEY, JR.

*Although the biosphere is mainly composed
of hydrogen, carbon, nitrogen and oxygen, other
elements are essential constituents of living matter.
Notable among them are phosphorus and sulfur*

The periodic table lists more than 100 chemical elements. Yet ecologists have defined the biosphere as the locus of interaction of only four of them: hydrogen, carbon, nitrogen and oxygen. In the periodic table these four are numbered 1, 6, 7 and 8. This definition, although it deals handsomely with much of the chemistry of life, turns out to be a little too restrictive. But when we enlarge it to include phosphorus and sulfur, as we do here, we have gone no farther up the table than element No. 16. From this it should be apparent that no element lighter than sulfur can be ignored, either by ecologists or by anyone else. The fact is that most human problems—all environmental ones, anyway—arise from the exceptional reactivity of six of the 16 lightest elements.

Because our definition of the biosphere is based more on reactivity than on atomic number, it is a minimum definition. It is not intended to exclude heavier elements that react with the primary six. As a matter of empirical fact it is known that no element lighter than iron and cobalt, elements No. 26 and No. 27, is unimportant to the biosphere. Beyond copper, No. 29, there are a few conspicuously reactive elements such as the heavy halogens bromine and iodine. Most of the heavies are metals, such as gold, mercury and lead (Nos. 79, 80 and

82), however, and their main effect on the lightweight biosphere is to depress it. Toward the end of the periodic table are some famously overweight metals whose tendency to lighten themselves has disastrous effects on any light substances that get in the way.

In order to understand how it is that many elements interact with the essential six, one must briefly reflect on the biosphere as a whole. Because the biosphere is so reactive, its influence on the hydrosphere, the lithosphere and the atmosphere is inversely proportional to its mass. This mass is very small. An average square centimeter of the earth's surface supports a tiny amount of biosphere: 580 milligrams, less than the weight of two aspirin tablets. A roughly equivalent mass is found in the same area of hydrosphere a single centimeter deep, or in a paper-thin slice of lithosphere. Still, from a worm's-eye view the biosphere has real substance, particularly on land, where it amounts to 200 oven-dry tons on an average hectare.

A glance at a partial list of the elements that compose the biosphere shows why hydrogen, oxygen, carbon and nitrogen dominate conceptions of biosphere chemistry. Together these elements constitute all but a tiny fraction of the average terrestrial vegetation, which in turn constitutes more than 99 percent of the world's standing crop. The quantities are shown in the chart on the next page, based on a splendid compilation by L. E. Rodin and N. I. Basilevich. What I have done is to weight their chemical analyses in proportion to the kinds of land area they represent. The weighting factors, for desert, forest, tundra and so on, are the same ones I used to calculate the earth's production of carbon in an earlier article ["The Human Population," by Edward S. Deevey, Jr.; SCIENTIFIC AMERICAN Offprint 608]. Inciden-

tally, on the basis of this new calculation terrestrial carbon production comes out at 65×10^9 tons of carbon per year, about 15 percent more than the figure I computed before.

What chemical compounds do these elements form? The standard way to determine the chemical composition of an organic substance is to burn it and collect the products. The list of components that results from this destructive procedure expresses some obvious facts, such as the familiar one that the biosphere is mainly carbon dioxide and water. Nitrogen, a major constituent of protein, seems surprisingly scarce (about five parts per 1,000 by weight) until we remember that the biosphere is chiefly wood, that is, not protein but the carbohydrate cellulose.

The destructive procedure would also leave a smudge, about 12 parts per 1,000 of the total, loosely called ash. Its dominant elements calcium, potassium, silicon and magnesium have important biochemical functions. One atom of magnesium, for instance, lies at the center of every molecule of chlorophyll, and silicon, the stuff of sand, is obviously useful for building hard structures. Iron and manganese also play central roles in the biosphere, a fact that could not be guessed from their position in our chart. In biochemistry as in geochemistry the importance of these elements is in governing oxidation-reduction reactions, but the masses involved are small. As for the major cations—ions of such elements as calcium, potassium, magnesium and sodium—new insights have just begun to flood in with their discovery in rainwater.

There are many other metallic elements that appear in trace amounts. Not all of them are listed in the chart because some could be accidental con-

SULFUR-FIXING BACTERIUM shown in the electron micrograph on the opposite page is one of five species that make sulfur available to the biosphere. This bacterium, *Desulfovibrio salexigens*, metabolizes the sulfates in seawater and releases the sulfur as hydrogen sulfide. This sulfur enters the atmosphere and is used by other forms of life. The micrograph enlarges the bacterium 31,000 diameters. It was made by Judith A. Murphy of the University of Illinois.

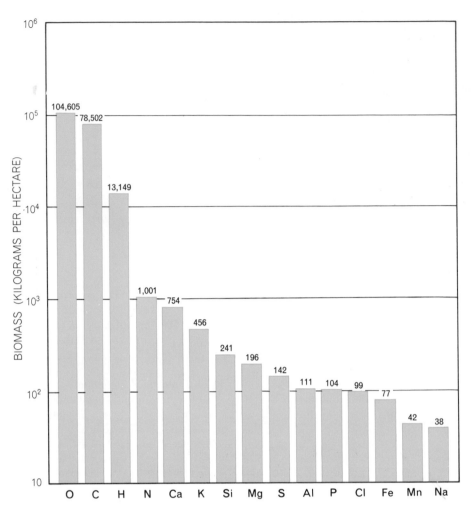

COMPOSITION OF THE BIOSPHERE is dominated by oxygen, carbon and hydrogen, as is indicated by the bars in this logarithmic chart. The units are kilograms per hectare of land surface. Key to the symbols for the chemical elements is at the bottom of the page.

charts on the opposite page can serve as a substitute, we can cast a Holmesian eye over the list. Our thinking will be more productive if we compare the composition of the biosphere with the composition of the lithosphere, the hydrosphere and the atmosphere. For this comparison all four of the "spheres" in the chart are converted from parts by weight to atoms per 100 atoms. (The masses of the four spheres being very different, these percentages will give no idea of the earth's mean or total composition.)

At first glance the four spheres do not seem to belong in the same universe. Not surprisingly, the lithosphere turns out to be a slightly metallic aluminum silicate. ("Here is no water but only rock/Rock and no water and the sandy road," as T. S. Eliot put it in "The Waste Land.") The biosphere, in sharp contrast, is both wet and carbonaceous. A single class of compounds, formaldehyde (CH_2O) and its polymers, including cellulose, could make up more than 98 percent of the total (by weight). Still, even when it is dried in an oven at 110 degrees Celsius, life is mainly hydrogen and oxygen, in close approximation to the proportions known as water. In other words, the biosphere is notably carboxylated: it is both more hydrated and chemically more reduced (hydrogenated) than is the lithosphere from which, in some sense, it came. Among the 10 most abundant elements of the lithosphere there is no obvious source for life's carbon. Hydrogen is also fairly far down the list for rock (and would be farther down if I had not copied some old figures from Frank W. Clarke's *The Data of Geochemistry*, which overweight the acidic rocks of continents).

Even the elementary Dr. Watson might conclude that life's hydrogen comes from some inorganic hydrate—water, for instance—and indeed the hydrosphere provides an ample and ready supply. This will not work for carbon, though, and in trying to account for carboxylation we can make a deduction that is truly elementary in the Holmesian, or nonobvious, sense. We begin

taminants. There remain two, sulfur and phosphorus, each amounting to more than 10 percent of the nitrogen, that do not look like contaminants. To ignore these elements as "traces" or even to think of them as "ash" or "inorganic" elements is to misconstrue the chemical architecture of the biosphere.

A listing of elements and compounds does not reveal that architecture. There is a big difference between a finished house and a pile of building materials. Nevertheless, a list is a useful point of departure. If it is made with care, it can protect ecologists from the kind of mistake that architects sometimes make, such as forgetting the plumbing.

When a list contains as much information as a shopping list—when it shows amounts as well as kinds of materials—some conclusions can be drawn from the relative proportions. (As a former bureaucrat I have learned that a "laundry list" contains even more ambiguous information than a "shopping list"; good bureaucrats keep both.) If a housewife's shopping list showed a pound of coffee, four pork chops and 100 pounds of

sugar, for example, we would know that madame is either hoarding or running a private business. If she also wants a ton of flour, she is evidently baking, not distilling. The inclusion of two dozen light bulbs would suggest that she works mainly at night, but the listing of 10 dozen light bulbs would point to a faulty generator.

As it happens, this kind of semiquantitative ratiocination was applied to ash, and to biogeochemistry, by the master of nonobvious deduction, Sherlock Holmes. Unfortunately no copy of his analytical results (the monograph on cigar ash, cited in Chapter 4 of "A Study in Scarlet") has yet come to light. If the

Al	ALUMINUM	Cl	CHLORINE	Mn	MANGANESE	P	PHOSPHORUS
Ar	ARGON	Fe	IRON	N	NITROGEN	S	SULFUR
B	BORON	H	HYDROGEN	Na	SODIUM	Si	SILICON
C	CARBON	K	POTASSIUM	Ne	NEON	Ti	TITANIUM
Ca	CALCIUM	Mg	MAGNESIUM	O	OXYGEN		

RELATIVE AMOUNTS OF ELEMENTS in the biosphere, the lithosphere, the hydrosphere and the atmosphere are presented in the charts on the opposite page. Here, however, amounts are given not as kilograms per hectare but as atoms per 100 atoms. Here again scale is logarithmic to show less abundant elements, which otherwise could not be compared.

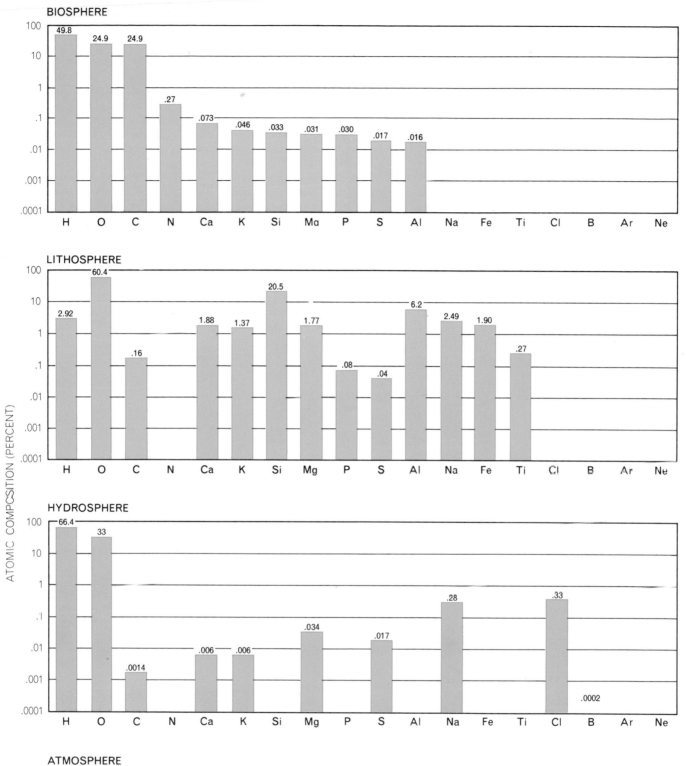

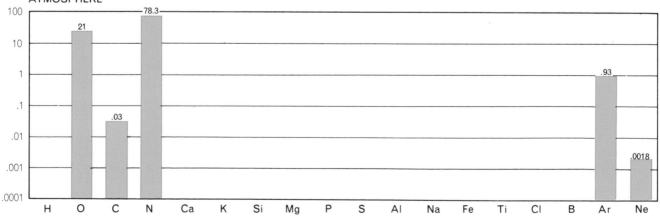

again by noting that life is mainly aqueous, and also that it concentrates carbon in proportions far greater than those in any accessible source. Is it possible that these facts are related? If they are, what do we know about water that throws any light on this relation and on the behavior of carbon? (At this point a lesser detective might reach for the carbonated water and pause for a reply.)

Instead of guessing, Holmes would proceed with his review of the evidence. Water, of course, is continuously recycled near the earth's surface, by runoff, evaporation and condensation. That is, it flows in rivers from the lithosphere to the hydrosphere, and it returns to rewash the land by way of the atmosphere. Any water-soluble elements are certain to track this cycle at least partway, from land to sea, although they may find the sea to be a sink, as boron does. If they

are to get out, they can reach the land as part of an uplifted sea bottom, but that is a chancy mechanism. Recycling is both faster and surer if the element is volatile as well as soluble, so that one of its compounds can move landward through the atmosphere as water does.

In the biosphere there are at least three elements besides those of water—carbon, nitrogen and sulfur—that fall in this doubly mobile class. Among their airborne compounds are carbon dioxide (CO_2), methane (CH_4), free nitrogen (N_2), ammonia (NH_3), hydrogen sulfide (H_2S) and sulfur dioxide (SO_2). It is interesting that when carbon, nitrogen and sulfur are recycled, their valence changes. It may not be an accident that all three are more reduced in the biosphere than they are in the external world. Be that as it may, they all seem

to belong to the biosphere, which is otherwise mainly water. Hence all three must be recycled together, *along with the water* (said Holmes with an air of quiet triumph), if the earth is to sustain its most unusual hydrate. ("And what is that?" I asked. "Why, *carbohydrate*, of course," said Holmes.)

I call this deduction nonobvious, because in an obvious variant it has become so familiar as to inhibit thought. The outlines of the carbon cycle, in organisms at any rate, have been evident since Joseph Priestley's day. The critical step, "obviously," is the photosynthetic reduction of carbon dioxide. That reaction is a hydrogenation, yielding formaldehyde. Its source of hydrogen is the dehydrogenation of water, with the liberation of oxygen. The chemical energy thus captured, by a process unique to green plants, becomes available, inside

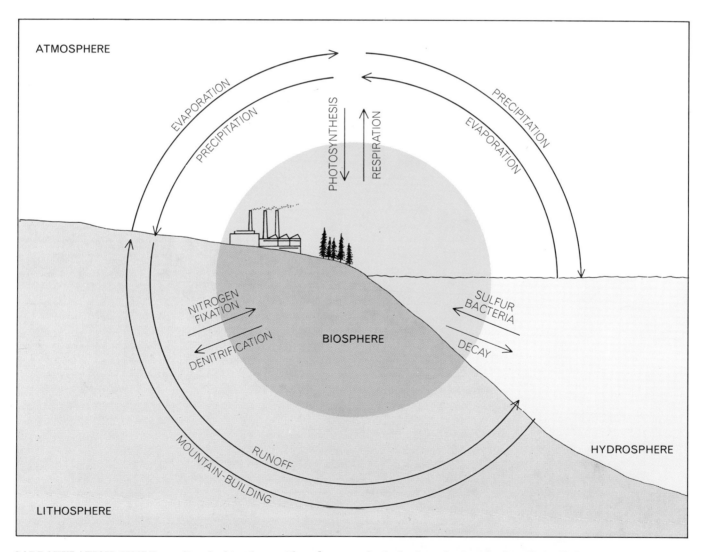

CARBOXYLATION CYCLE supplies the biosphere with carbon, oxygen, hydrogen, nitrogen and sulfur by carrying them from the lithosphere, the hydrosphere and the atmosphere. Curved arrows at upper right and left represent any or all of these five elements that travel from the atmosphere to the lithosphere or to the hydrosphere by precipitation, or back to the atmosphere by evaporation. Curved arrows at bottom indicate direct routes between the lithosphere and the hydrosphere such as runoff, mountain-building and the hydration of minerals. Biosphere (*color*) captures these elements by providing alternative routes. Top pair of straight arrows show exchange between the biosphere and the atmosphere, carbon, for example, being exchanged by photosynthesis and respiration. Pair of straight arrows at right show exchange between the biosphere and the hydrosphere, that of sulfur being mediated by bacteria. Pair of arrows at left indicate soil-biosphere exchanges including nitrogen fixation and denitrification by microorganisms.

the cell, for all other vital reactions (does it not?). After its utilization, which includes consumption by animals, the re-oxidized carbon dioxide can rejoin any geochemical cycles it likes.

All other vital reactions? Well, not quite all. The chemical reduction of nitrogen is one hydrogenation essential to green plants that they cannot perform for themselves. As one result, even elementary textbooks admit, the carbon and nitrogen cycles are necessarily interdependent. Without microorganisms that take nitrogen from the air and hydrogenate it (they can use carbon dioxide as a carbon source), all the nitrogen in the biosphere would soon appear in the atmosphere in stable, oxidized form. (The textbooks concede this point somewhat grudgingly, because much of the biological nitrogen cycle operates below the oxidation state of free nitro-

gen by the reversible reduction of nitrate and nitrite to amino acids and ammonia.)

If, as it turns out, sulfur too is recycled by way of the hydrologic cycle but independently of green plants, it becomes necessary to look beyond carbon and water for the clue to carboxylation. In other words, some biologists are not unlike architects who forget about the plumbing. In their preoccupation with carbon dioxide reduction as the starting point for cell biochemistry they tend to forget two other hydrogenations, those of sulfur and nitrogen, that are just as important.

A check is needed here, to be sure that these two elements are really intrinsic to the biosphere. In the case of sulfur the figures show it to be very scarce, and if it is a contaminant, the whole

argument might be superfluous. Sulfur, however, is no contaminant; no protein can be made without it. In fact, sulfur is the "stiffening" in protein. A protein cannot perform its function unless it is folded and shaped in a particular way. This three-dimensional structure is maintained by bonds between sulfur atoms that link one segment of a protein molecule to another. Without these sulfur bonds a protein would coil randomly, like a carelessly dropped rope.

The reason for the apparent scarcity of sulfur is the low protein content of woody tissue; any animal body contains much more. Cod-meal protein, for example, with 2.26 percent of the sulfurous amino acid methionine, has the empirical formula $H_{555}C_{265}O_{174}N_{83}S$. Although other proteins differ in the proportions, the substance of the biosphere must always contain these five elements.

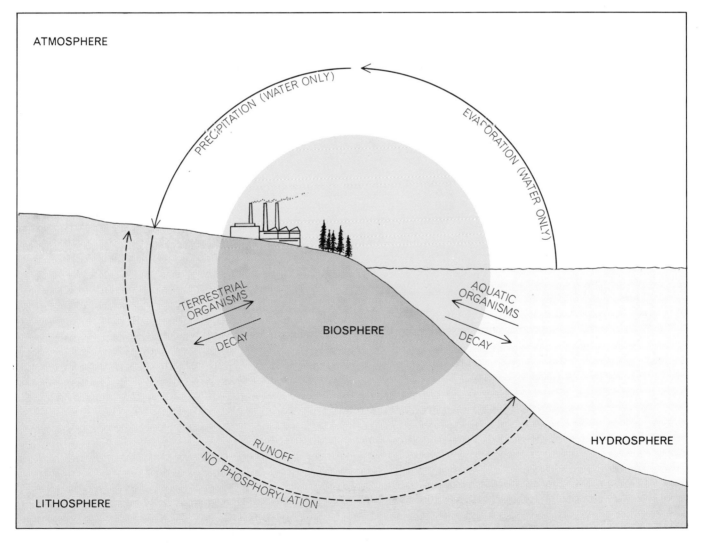

SOLUBLE-ELEMENT CYCLE is followed by minerals such as phosphorus that dissolve in water but are not volatile, that is, they are not carried into the air by evaporation (*curved arrow at right*). The curved arrow at bottom shows that phosphorus is washed from the lithosphere into the hydrosphere by runoff from rainfall (*curved arrow at top left*). The broken curved arrow at bottom indicates that phosphorus in the hydrosphere does not normally return to the lithosphere and that therefore the ocean would be-

come a phosphorus sink. The upper straight arrows at right and left, however, show that the organisms of the biosphere impede this development by absorbing some phosphorus. The straight arrows pointing from the biosphere to the lithosphere and to the hydrosphere indicate the decay of organic matter. On land the soluble-element cycle is continued when decay returns phosphorus to the lithosphere. Without an atmospheric link from ocean to land, however, the cycle is actually a one-way flow with interruptions.

It has been known for many years that sulfur is recycled from the sea back to the land by way of the atmosphere. Calculations confirming this fact by Erik Eriksson of the International Meteorological Institution show that the world's rocks contain too little sulfur, by a factor of about three, to account for the sulfate delivered annually by the world's rivers. About three-quarters of the total budget (in 1940) is therefore inferred to have come from the atmosphere. Of this amount about a third, or a quarter of the total, can have come from industrial sources—better known these days as "sulfur dioxide pollution." The other two-thirds, or half the total budget as of 1940, must take some more natural route from the hydrosphere.

When Eriksson wrote, in 1959, the question was still open, whether the cycled sulfur reaches the land as an aerosol from sea spray or as hydrogen sulfide (H_2S). If the principal volatile compound is a sulfide, it must be made by sulfate-reducing bacteria, because no other "room temperature" source of sulfide is known. M. LeRoy Jensen and Noboyuki Nakai, then working at Yale University, settled this question in favor of the bacteria, by showing that atmospheric sulfur, although it falls in rain as sulfate, contains less of the heavy isotope sulfur 34 than seawater sulfate does. What the natural isotopic label shows is that the sulfate in rain entered the atmosphere not as sea spray but as sulfide, there to be oxidized to sulfur dioxide. After dissolution in rainwater, sulfate (and sulfuric acid) are formed.

The principle of the Jensen-Nakai demonstration is worth noticing, because it applies to the cycling of carbon as well as of sulfur, and barring some technical difficulties it could also apply to nitrogen. The route followed through oxidation-reduction reactions by ordinary sulfur (sulfur 32) is analogous to the route followed by ordinary carbon (carbon 12) in photosynthesis. These lighter, more mobile isotopes appear preferentially in reduced compounds such as hydrogen sulfide, methane and formaldehyde. At equilibrium in a closed system the oxidation products (carbon dioxide or sulfate) have correspondingly more of the heavier isotopes carbon 13 and sulfur 34 without change in the total mass. If, however, a reduced and isotopically light product escapes, as hydrogen sulfide does from the hydrosphere, equilibrium is not attained, and if the gaseous product is trapped and reoxidized in a separate system, the oxide (sulfur dioxide in this case) remains light.

Exactly where within the hydrosphere

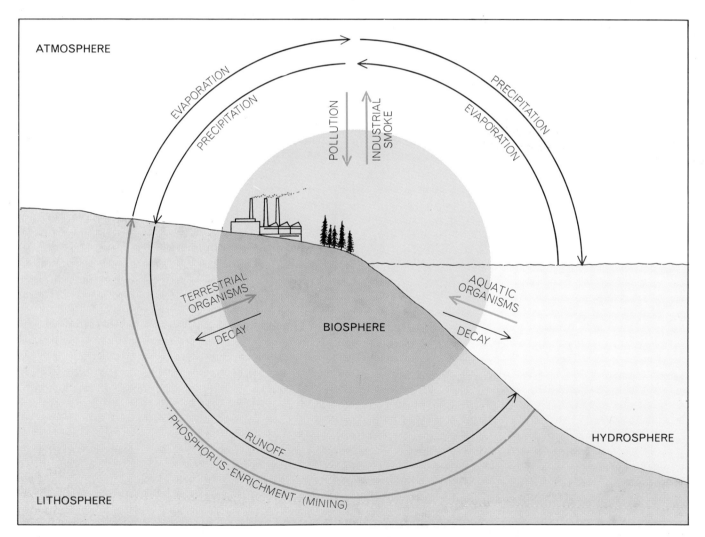

EUTROPHICATION OF THE BIOSPHERE is the intensive cycling of phosphorus, nitrogen and sulfur. Colored curved arrow at bottom represents beginning of the process: the human use of phosphorus as fertilizer, which returns phosphorus to the lithosphere, thereby reversing the phosphorus cycle. Colored straight arrows at left and right indicate that phosphorus added to the lithosphere (and to phosphorus already present) is then taken up by phytoplankton and other organisms as well as by crops. Other straight arrows at right and left show that phosphorus and other elements return to the lithosphere and hydrosphere by decay. Once phosphorus is plentiful, scarcity of nitrogen and sulfur may limit eutrophication. Arrows at top represent carbon dioxide, nitrate and sulfate from industrial activity rising into atmosphere and falling in rain. They may promote eutrophication of dry land since vegetation may reabsorb them from air and soil. Curved arrows indicate routes followed by elements that are both soluble and volatile.

most sulfate-reducers reside is still unclear. The known ones are obligate anaerobes, and their habitat is mud. Swamps, marshes and the floor of eutrophic lakes must all be important, and they may be quantitatively more important than the blue mud of estuaries and continental shelves. The sulfur metabolism of such large systems is not easy to study, even with isotopic tools. Minze Stuiver, now at the University of Washington, injected radioactively labeled sulfate ions into one eutrophic lake, Linsley Pond in Connecticut. Sulfate reduction proved to be intense, as had been expected. This lake, however, has quite a bit of ferrous iron in its deeper waters, and more in the mud itself. In the presence of the ferrous iron all the labeled sulfide was firmly held in the mud as ferrous sulfide, and no hydrogen sulfide escaped. At least for the duration of the radioactive label, with its half-life of 89 days, this mass of mud was not a source of atmospheric sulfur but a sink.

It follows from all of this that the cycling of sulfur in nature is no less relevant to carboxylation than the cycling of carbon and nitrogen. Without downgrading photosynthesis, we can say that carbon fixation is only one of at least three critical steps in the global synthesis of protein. All three are hydrogenations, achieved with the aid of enzymes, which are themselves proteins, and therefore occur only in the biosphere. Of the three reductions, however, only the reduction of carbon calls for green plants and sunlight. The other two, the reduction of nitrogen and of sulfur, are accomplished anaerobically, by microbes. Thus the locus of the nitrogen and sulfur reductions is, broadly speaking, oxygen-deficient soil and mud. Both loci are separated spatially from that airy, sunlit world where green plants (addicted, like human societies, to the external disposal of wastes) are thoughtlessly liberating oxygen.

With three critical steps for five elements, moving through four "spheres" of abstract space, one feels the need for a picture—a "systems model"—just to keep track of the relations. The two-dimensional analogue on page 86 is simple but adequate. Although it fails to specify fluxes, or any chemical quantities, it provides a mental framework for the movement of five elements: hydrogen, oxygen, carbon, nitrogen and sulfur, either alone or in combinations such as water, nitrate, the dioxides of carbon and sulfur, and carbohydrate. The synthetic output is the biosphere, with the

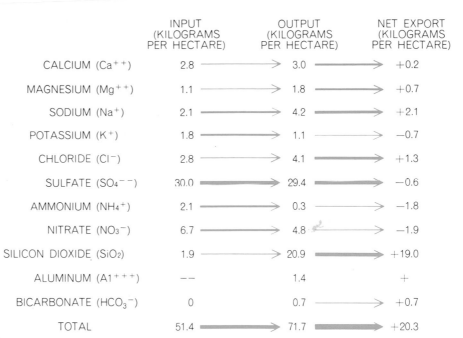

	INPUT (KILOGRAMS PER HECTARE)	OUTPUT (KILOGRAMS PER HECTARE)	NET EXPORT (KILOGRAMS PER HECTARE)
CALCIUM (Ca^{++})	2.8	3.0	+0.2
MAGNESIUM (Mg^{++})	1.1	1.8	+0.7
SODIUM (Na^+)	2.1	4.2	+2.1
POTASSIUM (K^+)	1.8	1.1	−0.7
CHLORIDE (Cl^-)	2.8	4.1	+1.3
SULFATE (SO_4^{--})	30.0	29.4	−0.6
AMMONIUM (NH_4^+)	2.1	0.3	−1.8
NITRATE (NO_3^-)	6.7	4.8	−1.9
SILICON DIOXIDE (SiO_2)	1.9	20.9	+19.0
ALUMINUM (Al^{+++})	— —	1.4	+
BICARBONATE (HCO_3^-)	0	0.7	+0.7
TOTAL	51.4	71.7	+20.3

EUTROPHICATION OF DRY LAND is indicated by the imbalance between the quantity of certain ions falling from the atmosphere on the forest at Watershed No. 6 at Hubbard Brook in New Hampshire and the output of these ions in the brook itself. Input (*smaller arrows at left*) of some elements such as calcium, magnesium and sodium is smaller than the output (*larger arrows at right*). The input of potassium, ammonium, sulfate and nitrate, however, is larger (*larger arrows at left*) than output of these substances (*smaller arrows*). The excess of input indicates that the forest is utilizing these four substances as it grows.

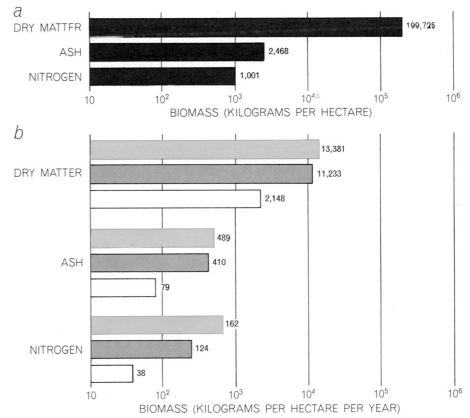

OTHER EVIDENCE FOR EUTROPHICATION is provided by studies of the earth's standing crop on dry land. In *a* biomass, or weighable dry matter that includes ash and nitrogen, totals about 200,000 kilograms per hectare. In *b* the first set of bars shows that the dry matter increases in an average year by 13,381 kilograms per hectare (*color*). About 11,000 kilograms is lost in the form of litter fall (*gray*) such as fallen leaves and branches, giving a "mean increment" of 2,148 kilograms per hectare (*open bar*). The second set of bars shows that ash increases by 489 kilograms per hectare (*color*) but is reduced by litter fall (*gray*) to 79 kilograms (*open bar*). The third set of bars shows that nitrogen increases by 162 kilograms (*color*), a gain that is reduced by litter fall (*gray*) to 38 kilograms per hectare.

empirical composition of protein. The central or regulatory position of the biosphere in this model follows from the fact that for all five elements it is both a source and a temporary sink. For any element that might be tempted to cycle around the edges of the model, the biosphere provides several high-energy alternatives. The most interesting of these are the reductions of carbon, nitrogen and sulfur, each concentrated at a different interface, two being out of immediate contact with air. Water, although it is able in principle to cycle independently, is the source of the hydrogen that energizes the biosphere, and cannot long avoid the biospheric loop as long as the biosphere functions.

It is easy to be bemused by so fascinating a model. Its function, however, is to clarify thought. If further thought disrupts the model, nothing is lost but a few lines on paper. More or less instantly, by reference to the table of biospheric composition, we can see that the model is incomplete. Phosphorus has been left out, along with calcium, potassium, silicon and magnesium, four elements that are commoner in the biosphere than sulfur is. Will any or all of these cycle tamely through the model, or will they disrupt it beyond repair?

For phosphorus, but not yet for the others, the answer is clear: With one significant modification, the model can accommodate phosphorus. First, let us be sure, as we made sure for sulfur, that phosphorus is necessary to the biosphere. It is not a constituent of protein, but no protein can be made without it. The "high-energy phosphate bond," reversibly moving between adenosine diphosphate (ADP) and adenosine triphosphate (ATP), is the universal fuel for all biochemical work within the cell. The photosynthetic fixation of carbon would be a fruitless tour de force if it were not followed by the phosphorylation of the sugar produced. Thus although neither ADP nor ATP contains much phosphorus, one phosphorus atom per molecule of adenosine is absolutely essential. No life (including microbial life) is possible without it.

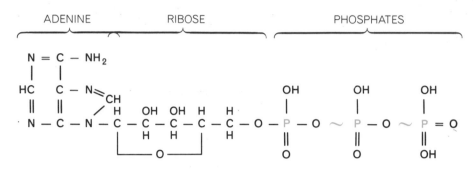

UNIVERSAL FUEL of living matter is adenosine triphosphate (ATP). High-energy phosphate bonds of ATP ($\sim$) each store 12,000 calories and release 7,500 calories when broken.

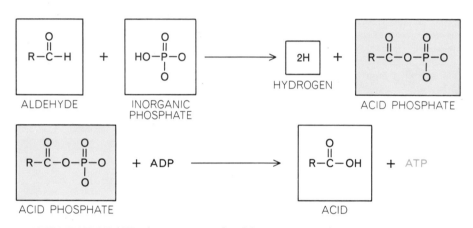

PRODUCTION OF ATP, shown in generalized form, consists of two stages. The first stage begins as aldehyde reacts with an inorganic phosphate to produce hydrogen and acid phosphate. In second stage (*bottom*) acid phosphate (*shading*) reacts with ADP (adenosine diphosphate) to make an organic acid and ATP (*color*). R stands for radicals, or side groups.

Our provisional model of the biosphere has been constructed on two explicit assumptions: (1) the biosphere necessarily contains the five elements of protein and (2) all five are both soluble and volatile. If we now add phosphorus as a sixth necessary element, we can safely assume its solubility in water, and the crucial question concerns its volatility. Except as sea spray in coastal

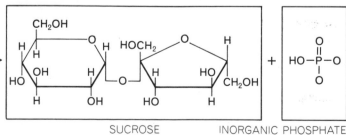

SYNTHESIS OF SUCROSE is an example of a reaction for which ATP (*color*) supplies energy. The reaction begins at upper left as the ATP molecule combines with glucose molecule, releasing 7,500 calories. The reaction produces ADP and glucose-1-phosphate. In a second stage of the reaction (*bottom*) glucose-1-phosphate combines with fructose, yielding sucrose and inorganic phosphate.

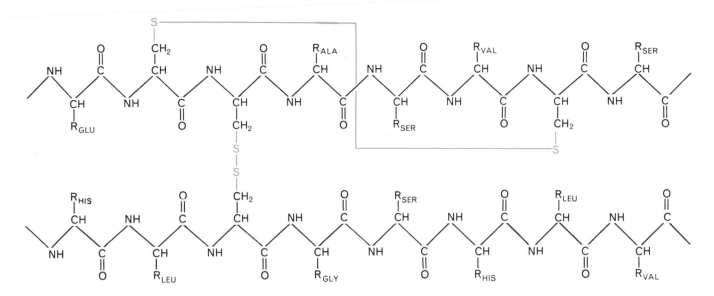

BASIC FUNCTION OF SULFUR in living matter appears to be to provide a linkage between the polypeptide chains in a protein molecule. These linkages help the protein maintain its three-dimensional shape so that it can perform its function. In this segment of a bovine insulin molecule disulfide bonds (*color*) are formed between sulfur atoms, which are present in the amino acid cystine. Cystine is a subunit of both polypeptide chains. Because the molecule is displayed in two dimensions it is flattened. Therefore the bond between the top and bottom cystine groups on the upper chain appears broken. In the normal three-dimensional state, however, this chain is twisted and folded because of the disulfide bond in a way indicated by the colored line that joins the two sulfur atoms. (The other bond is one of two that links the chains.) The shape of the insulin molecule maintained by these bonds enables it to control the metabolism of sugar. The other amino acids in this molecular segment, whose side chains are indicated by the letter *R*, are glutamic acid (GLU), alanine (ALA), serine (SER), valine (VAL), histidine (HIS), leucine (LEU) and glycine (GLY).

zones, or as dust in the vicinity of exposed phosphate rock, phosphorus is unknown in the atmosphere, none of its ordinary compounds has any appreciable vapor pressure. It therefore tracks the hydrologic cycle only partway, from the lithosphere to the hydrosphere, and in a world uncomplicated by a biosphere the ocean would be its only sink. In terms of my model this amounts to uncoupling the atmospheric reservoir (except for water), omitting the half-arrow showing the return of phosphorus from the hydrosphere to the lithosphere and leaving the biosphere's phosphorus as a feedback loop, diverting some of the one-way flow from rock to ocean. Geometrically at least, the model is general enough to accommodate these changes, some version of which will be needed if any permanent sinks are discovered in the system.

For any soluble but nonvolatile element a closed natural cycle is possible only through the biosphere. The model hints at the reason why many elements—vanadium, cobalt, nickel and molybdenum among them—are best known in aquatic organisms and cycle mainly within the hydrosphere. Now, however, the model, nonquantitative though it is, suggests something else. If the biosphere demands such an element as phosphorus (and the cases of iron and manganese should be similar), two alternative inferences are permissible, depending on

the magnitudes of reservoirs and fluxes. If the lithosphere contains an ample supply of phosphorus, or if the flux to the hydrospheric sink is large, the biosphere can take off what it needs and waste the rest. It is commonly believed such elements as sodium and calcium are thus wasted by terrestrial vegetation, although ecologists are beginning to doubt it. On the other hand, if the quantity is scanty or the flux small, the element will be in critically short supply. And if short supply is chronic, the output of the entire system could be expected to be adjusted to the rate of exploitation of one critical element, much as the performance of a bureaucracy is closely geared to the supply of paper clips.

In undisturbed nature the chronic shortage of phosphorus is notorious; that is what most people mean by "soil infertility." In the lithosphere phosphorus is scarcer than carbon, and in the hydrosphere, because phosphorus falls in the parts-per-billion range, it fails to show up at all in the chart of constituents on page 85. Apart from its natural scarcity, phosphorus is freely soluble only in acid solution or under reducing conditions. On the surface of an alkaline and oxidized earth it tends to be immobilized as calcium phosphate or ferric phosphate. In lake waters, where the output of carbohydrate is thriftily attuned to phosphorus concentrations of the order of 50 micro-

grams per liter, doubling the phosphorus input commonly doubles the standing crop of plankton and pondweeds.

Under these conditions the situation in a lake changes drastically. If phosphorus is plentiful, nitrate may become the critically short nutrient for a crop that needs about 15 atoms of nitrogen for one of phosphorus. Blue-green algae may then take over the plankton because by reducing atmospheric nitrogen they escape the dependence that other algae have on nitrate. Meanwhile, judging from much recent experience, the phosphorus input will probably have doubled again—but the subject under discussion is no longer undisturbed nature. What started as "cottage eutrophication," by seepage from a few septic tanks, has been escalated into a noisome mess by "treated" sewage and polyphosphate detergents. To conserve biogeochemical parity the atmosphere has begun to deliver into lakes nitrate and sulfate from the combustion of fossil fuels.

It would be wrong to read too much into a systems model. "Conserving biogeochemical parity" is just a figure of speech, technically hyperbole, and ironical at that. After all, the pollution of the air by nitrate and sulfate is quite independent—technologically, spatially and politically—of the pollution of water by phosphorus. If the accelerated phosphorus cycle in lakes takes advantage of these added inputs, we dare not say that nitrate and sulfate have been drawn into the biosphere from the atmosphere, as U.S. power was drawn to a Canadian circuit breaker in the Northeast blackout of 1965. What the model tells us is that matters can look that way from the standpoint of the biosphere. If the lake segment of the phosphorus cycle is accelerated to the point where nitrogen and sulfur are as critical as phosphorus used to be, and if there is a new source of nitrate and sulfate in the atmosphere, the atmosphere is adequately coupled to all other subsystems to ensure the success of the newly accelerated loop. The loop, known as eutrophication, is thus amplified from a lacustrine nuisance to a systems problem, and around such lakes as Lake Erie it threatens to become a cancer in the global ecosystem.

The trouble started, of course, when the world's one-way phosphorus cycle was first reversed and then accelerated by human activity. Since bird guano was discovered on desert islands, later to be supplemented in fertilizers by phosphate rock, marine phosphate has been restored to the lithosphere in ever increasing amounts. As a device for growing people in ever increasing numbers the practice cannot be faulted, but if people are to continue to flourish in the biosphere, they will have to pay more attention to scarce resources. Phosphorus is much too valuable to be thoughtlessly shared with blue-green algae.

The term eutrophication, which means enrichment, usually inadvertent, is not ordinarily applied to forests and deserts. I dare to extend it to the terrestrial biosphere because two new lines of evidence have suddenly appeared to suggest that the known pollution of air by nitrate and sulfate also encourages the bloom on dry land. The first line of evidence comes from Hubbard Brook, N.H., where F. Herbert Bormann of the Yale School of Forestry and Gene E. Likens of Cornell University have had six forested watersheds under close study since 1963. What interests us here is the difference, per hectare of ecosystem, between the input of ions in rainfall (plus dry fallout, if any) and the output as measured at a dam at the foot of each drainage basin.

Among the common ions entering and leaving Watershed No. 6 at Hubbard Brook, chloride and three positive ions—calcium, magnesium and sodium—show an excess of output over input, pre-sumably derived from the local rocks and soil. These four ions conform, if only barely, to the idea that the biosphere wastes excess salts on their way to the sea. In contrast, potassium and ammonium (NH_4) and the two major negative ions, sulfate and nitrate, are avidly held by this segment of the biosphere, as is indicated by the fact that their input exceeds their output. In the case of potassium all but 700 grams per hectare is captured. Collectively the "nonvolatile" minerals, including silica, that fall from the clear New Hampshire sky amounted to some 13 kilograms per hectare in a typical year. With sulfate, nitrate and ammonium added, the total reached 51.4 kilograms per hectare.

The second line of evidence indicates that the biosphere as a whole is becoming larger. Ecologists expect to find growth in secondary forests, but climax vegetation should be in a steady state, with annual gains balancing losses. According to figures I have recompiled from Rodin and Basilevich, the mean world vegetation is not yet at climax. After the known quantity of dead leaves, branches and other litter is subtracted from the net production of new tissue, the difference is always positive, at an average 2,148 kilograms of new biomass per hectare of land per year. With ash making up 1.2 percent of this biomass, about 26 kilograms of ash is annually withdrawn from an average hectare to sustain the increment of carbohydrate. The input of airborne elements at Hubbard Brook could provide this ash twice over, with no contribution from the local lithosphere.

This comparison is impressionistic, and it may be misleading. Apart from industrial sulfate, which (as sulfuric acid) is perhaps as likely to corrode the biosphere as to nourish it, the world's vegetation may be in no danger of instant eutrophication. (If the biosphere is really becoming larger, the input of industrial carbon dioxide may constitute another major nutrient.) The modes of recycling discovered at Hubbard Brook are nonetheless astonishing. Added to what we know or can safely infer about other volatile elements, such studies underscore the necessity of a global view of biochemistry. What can be said with assurance is that there is a unique and nearly ubiquitous compound, with the empirical formula $H_{2960}O_{1480}C_{1480}N_{16}P_{1.8}S$, called living matter. Its synthesis, on an oxidized and uncarboxylated earth, is the most intricate feat of chemical engineering ever performed—and the most delicate operation that people have ever tampered with.

GUANO-COVERED ISLAND off the coast of Peru is a source of phosphate and nitrate for fertilizer. Guano has been deposited during many millenniums by generations of birds.

IX

Human Food Production as a Process in the Biosphere

Human Food Production as a Process in the Biosphere

by LESTER R. BROWN

Human population growth is mainly the result of increases in food production. This relation raises the question: How many people can the biosphere support without impairment of its overall operation?

Throughout most of man's existence his numbers have been limited by the supply of food. For the first two million years or so he lived as a predator, a herbivore and a scavenger. Under such circumstances the biosphere could not support a human population of more than 10 million, a population smaller than that of London or Afghanistan today. Then, with his domestication of plants and animals some 10,000 years ago, man began to shape the biosphere to his own ends.

As primitive techniques of crop production and animal husbandry became more efficient the earth's food-producing capacity expanded, permitting increases in man's numbers. Population growth in turn exerted pressure on food supply, compelling man to further alter the biosphere in order to meet his food needs. Population growth and advances in food production have thus tended to be mutually reinforcing.

It took two million years for the human population to reach the one-billion mark, but the fourth billion now being added will require only 15 years: from 1960 to 1975. The enormous increase in the demand for food that is generated by this expansion in man's numbers, together with rising incomes, is beginning

to have disturbing consequences. New signs of stress on the biosphere are reported almost daily. The continuing expansion of land under the plow and the evolution of a chemically oriented modern agriculture are producing ominous alterations in the biosphere not just on a local scale but, for the first time in history, on a global scale as well. The natural cycles of energy and the chemical elements are clearly being affected by man's efforts to expand his food supply.

Given the steadily advancing demand for food, further intervention in the biosphere for the expansion of the food supply is inevitable. Such intervention, however, can no longer be undertaken by an individual or a nation without consideration of the impact on the biosphere as a whole. The decision by a government to dam a river, by a farmer to use DDT on his crops or by a married couple to have another child, thereby increasing the demand for food, has repercussions for all mankind.

The revolutionary change in man's role from hunter and gatherer to tiller and herdsman took place in circumstances that are not well known, but some of the earliest evidence of agriculture is found in the hills and grassy plains of the Fer-

tile Crescent in western Asia. The cultivation of food plants and the domestication of animals were aided there by the presence of wild wheat, barley, sheep, goats, pigs, cattle and horses. From the beginnings of agriculture man naturally favored above all other species those plants and animals that had been most useful to him in the wild. As a result of this favoritism he has altered the composition of the earth's plant and animal populations. Today his crops, replacing the original cover of grass or forest, occupy some three billion acres. This amounts to about 10 percent of the earth's total land surface and a considerably larger fraction of the land capable of supporting vegetation, that is, the area excluding deserts, polar regions and higher elevations. Two-thirds of the cultivated cropland is planted to cereals. The area planted to wheat alone is 600 million acres—nearly a million square miles, or an area equivalent to the U.S. east of the Mississippi. As for the influence of animal husbandry on the earth's animal populations, Hereford and Black Angus cattle roam the Great Plains, once the home of an estimated 30 to 40 million buffalo; in Australia the kangaroo has given way to European cattle; in Asia the domesticated water buffalo has multiplied in the major river valleys.

Clearly the food-producing enterprise has altered not only the relative abundance of plant and animal species but also their global distribution. The linkage of the Old and the New World in the 15th century set in motion an exchange of crops among various parts of the world that continues today. This exchange greatly increased the earth's capacity to sustain human populations, partly because some of the crops trans-

EXPERIMENTAL FARM in Brazil, one of thousands around the world where improvements in agricultural technology are pioneered, is seen as an image on an infrared-sensitive film in the aerial photograph on the opposite page. The reflectance of vegetation at near-infrared wavelengths of .7 to .9 micron registers on the film in false shades of red that are proportional to the intensity of the energy. The most reflective, and reddest, areas (*bottom*) are land still uncleared of forest cover. Most of the tilled fields, although irregular in shape, are contour-plowed. Regular patterns (*left and bottom right*) are citrus-orchard rows. The photograph was taken by a National Aeronautics and Space Administration mission in cooperation with the Brazilian government in a joint study of the assessment of agricultural resources by remote sensing. The farm is some 80 miles northwest of São Paulo.

ported elsewhere turned out to be better suited there than to their area of origin. Perhaps the classic example is the introduction of the potato from South America into northern Europe, where it greatly augmented the food supply, permitting marked increases in population. This was most clearly apparent in Ireland, where the population increased rapidly for several decades on the strength of the food supply represented by the potato. Only when the potato-blight organism (*Phytophthora infestans*) devastated the potato crop was population growth checked in Ireland.

The soybean, now the leading source of vegetable oil and principal farm export of the U.S., was introduced from China several decades ago. Grain sorghum, the second-ranking feed grain in the U.S. (after corn), came from Africa as a food store in the early slave ships. In the U.S.S.R. today the principal source of vegetable oil is the sunflower, a plant that originated on the southern Great Plains of the U.S. Corn, unknown in the Old World before Columbus, is now grown on every continent. On the other hand, North America is indebted to the Old World for all its livestock and poultry species with the exception of the turkey.

To man's accomplishments in exploiting the plants and animals that natural evolution has provided, and in improving them through selective breeding over the millenniums, he has added in this century the creation of remarkably productive new breeds, thanks to the discoveries of genetics. Genetics has made possible the development of cereals and other plant species that are more tolerant to cold, more resistant to drought, less susceptible to disease, more responsive to fertilizer, higher in yield and richer in protein. The story of hybrid corn is only one of many spectacular examples. The breeding of short-season corn varieties has extended the northern limit of this crop some 500 miles.

Plant breeders recently achieved a historic breakthrough in the development of new high-yielding varieties of wheat and rice for tropical and subtropical regions. These wheats and rices, bred by Rockefeller Foundation and Ford Foundation scientists in Mexico and the Philippines, are distinguished by several characteristics. Most important, they are short-statured and stiff-strawed, and are highly responsive to chemical fertilizer. They also mature earlier. The first of the high-yielding rices, IR-8, matures in 120

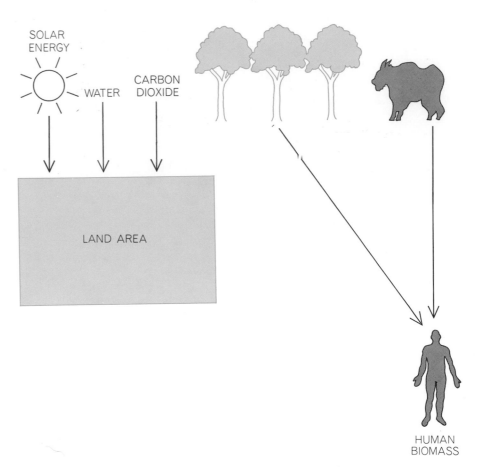

IMPACT OF THE AGRICULTURAL REVOLUTION on the human population is outlined in these two diagrams. The diagram at left shows the state of affairs before the invention of agriculture: the plants and animals supported by photosynthesis on the total land area could support a human population of only about 10 million. The diagram at right shows

days as against 150 to 180 days for other varieties.

Another significant advance incorporated into the new strains is the reduced sensitivity of their seed to photoperiod (length of day). This is partly the result of their cosmopolitan ancestry: they were developed from seed collections all over the world. The biological clocks of traditional varieties of cereals were keyed to specific seasonal cycles, and these cereals could be planted only at a certain time of the year, in the case of rice say at the onset of the monsoon season. The new wheats, which are quite flexible in terms of both seasonal and latitudinal variations in length of day, are now being grown in developing countries as far north as Turkey and as far south as Paraguay.

The combination of earlier maturity and reduced sensitivity to day length creates new opportunities for multiple cropping in tropical and subtropical regions where water supplies are adequate, enabling farmers to harvest two, three and occasionally even four crops per year. Workers at the International Rice Research Institute in the Philippines regularly harvest three crops of rice per

year. Each acre they plant yields six tons annually, roughly three times the average yield of corn, the highest-yielding cereal in the U.S. Thousands of farmers in northern India are now alternating a crop of early-maturing winter wheat with a summer crop of rice, greatly increasing the productivity of their land. These new opportunities for farming land more intensively lessen the pressure for bringing marginal land under cultivation, thus helping to conserve precious topsoil. At the same time they increase the use of agricultural chemicals, creating environmental stresses more akin to those in the advanced countries.

The new dwarf wheats and rices are far more efficient than the traditional varieties in their use of land, water, fertilizer and labor. The new opportunities for multiple cropping permit conversion of far more of the available solar energy into food. The new strains are not the solution to the food problem, but they are removing the threat of massive famine in the short run. They are buying time for the stabilization of population, which is ultimately the only solution to the food crisis. This "green revolution"

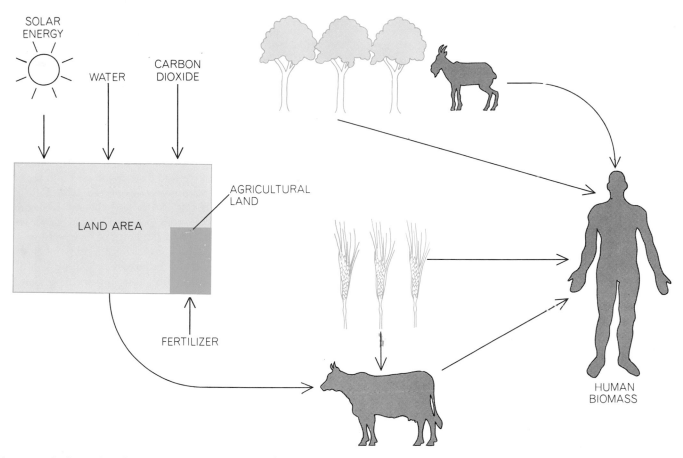

the state of affairs after the invention of agriculture. The 10 percent of the land now under the plow, watered and fertilized by man, is the primary support for a human population of 3.5 billion. Some of the agricultural produce is consumed directly by man; some is consumed indirectly by first being fed to domestic animals. Some of the food for domestic animals, however, comes from land not under the plow (*curved arrow at bottom left*). Man also obtains some food from sources other than agriculture, such as fishing.

may affect the well-being of more people in a shorter period of time than any technological advance in history.

The progress of man's expansion of food production is reflected in the way crop yields have traditionally been calculated. Today the output of cereals is expressed in yield per acre, but in early civilizations it was calculated as a ratio of the grain produced to that required for seed. On this basis the current ratio is perhaps highest in the U.S. corn belt, where farmers realize a four-hundred-fold return on the hybrid corn seed they plant. The ratio for rice is also quite high, but the ratio for wheat, the third of the principal cereals, is much lower, possibly 30 to one on a global basis.

The results of man's efforts to increase the productivity of domestic animals are equally impressive. When the ancestors of our present chickens were domesticated, they laid a clutch of about 15 eggs once a year. Hens in the U.S. today average 220 eggs per year, and the figure is rising steadily as a result of continuing advances in breeding and feeding. When cattle were originally domesticated, they probably did not produce more than 600 pounds of milk per year,

barely enough for a calf. (It is roughly the average amount produced by cows in India today.) The 13 million dairy cows in the U.S. today average 9,000 pounds of milk yearly, outproducing their ancestors 15 to one.

Most such advances in the productivity of plant and animal species are recent. Throughout most of history man's efforts to meet his food needs have been directed primarily toward bringing more land under cultivation, spreading agriculture from valley to valley and continent to continent. He has also, however, invented techniques to raise the productivity of land already under cultivation, particularly in this century, when the decreasing availability of new lands for expansion has compelled him to turn to a more intensive agriculture. These techniques involve altering the biosphere's cycles of energy, water, nitrogen and minerals.

Modern agriculture depends heavily on four technologies: mechanization, irrigation, fertilization and the chemical control of weeds and insects. Each of these technologies has made an important contribution to the earth's in-

creased capacity for sustaining human populations, and each has perturbed the cycles of the biosphere.

At least as early as 3000 B.C. the farmers of the Middle East learned to harness draft animals to help them till the soil. Harnessing animals much stronger than himself enabled man to greatly augment his own limited muscle power. It also enabled him to convert roughage (indigestible by humans) into a usable form of energy and thus to free some of his energy for pursuits other than the quest for food. The invention of the internal-combustion engine and the tractor 5,000 years later provided a much greater breakthrough. It now became possible to substitute petroleum (the product of the photosynthesis of aeons ago) for oats, corn and hay grown as feed for draft animals. The replacement of horses by the tractor not only provided the farmer with several times as much power but also released 70 million acres in the U.S. that had been devoted to raising feed for horses.

In the highly mechanized agriculture of today the expenditure of fossil fuel energy per acre is often substantially greater than the energy yield embodied in the food produced. This deficit in the output is of no immediate consequence, because the system is drawing on energy in the bank. When fossil fuels become scarcer, man will have to turn to some other source of motive energy for agriculture: perhaps nuclear energy or some means, other than photosynthesis, of harnessing solar energy. For the present and for the purposes of agriculture the energy budget of the biosphere is still favorable: the supply of solar energy—both the energy stored in fossil fuels and that taken up daily and converted into food energy by crops—enables an advanced nation to be fed with only 5 percent of the population directly employed in agriculture.

The combination of draft animals and mechanical power has given man an enormous capacity for altering the earth's surface by bringing additional land under the plow (not all of it suited for cultivation). In addition, in the poorer countries his expanding need for fuel has forced him to cut forests far in excess of their ability to renew themselves. The areas largely stripped of forest include mainland China and the subcontinent of India and Pakistan, where much of the population must now use cow dung for fuel. Although statistics are not available, the proportion of mankind using cow dung as fuel to prepare meals may

far exceed the proportion using natural gas. Livestock populations providing draft power, food and fuel tend to increase along with human populations, and in many poor countries the needs of livestock for forage far exceed its self-renewal, gradually denuding the countryside of grass cover.

As population pressure builds, not only is more land brought under the plow but also the land remaining is less suited to cultivation. Once valleys are filled, farmers begin to move up hillsides, creating serious soil-erosion problems. As the natural cover that retards runoff is reduced and soil structure deteriorates, floods and droughts become more severe.

Over most of the earth the thin layer of topsoil producing most of man's food is measured in inches. Denuding the land of its year-round natural cover of grass or forest exposes the thin mantle of life-sustaining soil to rapid erosion by wind and water. Much of the soil ultimately washes into the sea, and some of it is lifted into the atmosphere. Man's actions are causing the topsoil to be removed faster than it is formed. This unstable relationship between man and the land from which he derives his subsistence obviously cannot continue indefinitely.

Robert R. Brooks of Williams College, an economist who spent several years in India, gives a wry description of the process occurring in the state of Rajasthan, where tens of thousands of acres of rural land are being abandoned yearly because of the loss of topsoil: "Overgrazing by goats destroys the desert plants which might otherwise hold the soil in place. Goatherds equipped with sickles attached to 20-foot poles strip the leaves of trees to float downward into the waiting mouths of famished goats and sheep. The trees die and the soil blows away 200 miles to New Delhi, where it comes to rest in the lungs of its inhabitants and on the shiny cars of foreign diplomats."

Soil erosion not only results in a loss of soil but also impairs irrigation systems. This is illustrated in the Mangla irrigation reservoir, recently built in the foothills of the Himalayas in West Pakistan as part of the Indus River irrigation system. On the basis of feasibility studies indicating that the reservoir could be expected to have a lifetime of at least 100 years, $600 million was invested in the construction of the reservoir. Denuding and erosion of the soil in the watershed, however, accompanying a rapid growth of population in the area, has already washed so much soil into the reservoir that it is now expected to be completely filled with silt within 50 years.

A historic example of the effects of man's abuse of the soil is all too plainly visible in North Africa, which once was the fertile granary of the Roman Empire and now is largely a desert or near-desert whose people are fed with the aid of food imports from the U.S. In the U.S. itself the "dust bowl" experience of the 1930's remains a vivid lesson on the folly of overplowing. More recently the U.S.S.R. repeated this error, bringing 100 million acres of virgin soil under the plow only to discover that the region's rainfall was too scanty to sustain continuous cultivation. Once moisture reserves in the soil were depleted the soil began to blow.

Soil erosion is one of the most pressing and most difficult problems threatening the future of the biosphere. Each year it is forcing the abandonment of millions of acres of cropland in Asia, the Middle East, North Africa and Central America. Nature's geological cycle continuously produces topsoil, but its pace is far too slow to be useful to man. Someone once defined soil as rock on its way to the sea. Soil is produced by the weathering of rock and the process takes several centuries to form an inch of topsoil. Man is managing to destroy the topsoil

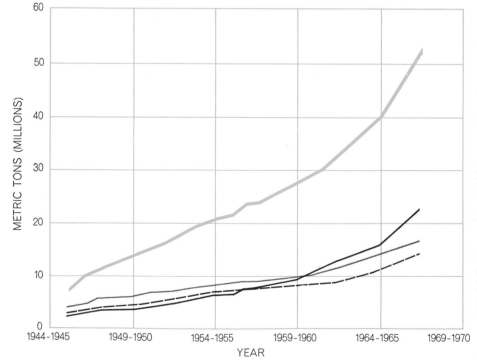

FERTILIZER CONSUMPTION has increased more than fivefold since the end of World War II. The top line in the graph (*color*) shows the tonnage of all kinds of fertilizers combined. The lines below show the tonnages of the three major types: nitrogen (*black*), now the leader, phosphate (*gray*) and potash (*broken line*). Figures, from the most recent report by the UN Food and Agriculture Organization, omit fertilizer consumption in China.

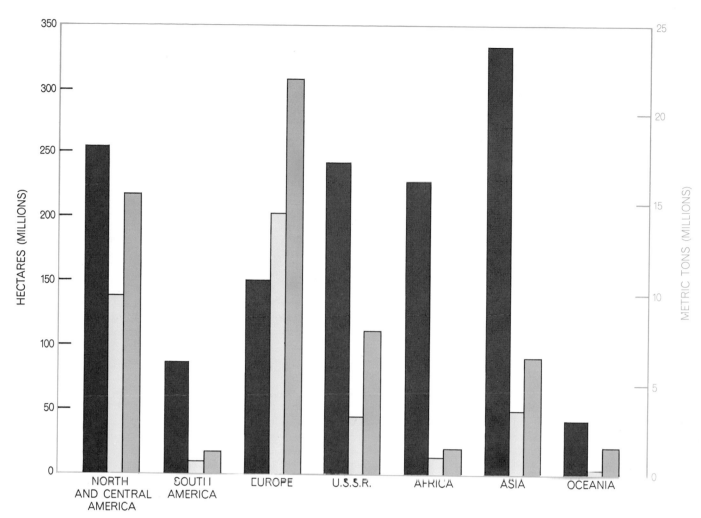

TONS OF FERTILIZER used in seven world areas are compared with the amount of agricultural land in each area. Two tonnages are shown in each instance: the amount used in 1962–1963 (*light color*) and the amount used in 1967–1968 (*solid color*). The great-est use of fertilizer occurs in Europe, the least fertilized area is Africa and the greatest percentage increase in the period was in Australia and New Zealand. Figures, from the Food and Agricul-ture Organization, omit China, North Korea and North Vietnam.

in some areas of the world in a fraction of this time. The only possible remedy is to find ways to conserve the topsoil more effectively.

The dust-bowl era in the U.S. ended with the widespread adoption of con-servation practices by farmers. Twenty million acres were fallowed to accumu-late moisture and thousands of miles of windbreaks were planted across the Great Plains. Fallow land was alternated with strips of wheat ("strip-cropping") to reduce the blowing of soil while the land was idle. The densely populated coun-tries of Asia, however, are in no position to adopt such tactics. Their food needs are so pressing that they cannot afford to take large areas out of cultivation; moreover, they do not yet have the finan-cial resources or the technical skills for the immense projects in reforestation, controlled grazing of cattle, terracing, contour farming and systematic manage-ment of watersheds that would be re-quired to preserve their soil.

The significance of wind erosion goes

far beyond the mere loss of topsoil. As other authors in this issue have observed, a continuing increase in particulate mat-ter in the atmosphere could affect the earth's climate by reducing the amount of incoming solar energy. This particu-late matter comes not only from the technological activities of the richer countries but also from wind erosion in the poorer countries. The poorer coun-tries do not have the resources for un-dertaking the necessary effort to arrest and reverse this trend. Should it be es-tablished that an increasing amount of particulate matter in the atmosphere is changing the climate, the richer coun-tries would have still another reason to provide massive capital and technical as-sistance to the poor countries, joining with them to confront this common threat to mankind.

Irrigation, which agricultural man be-gan to practice at least as early as 6,000 years ago, even earlier than he harnessed animal power, has played its

great role in increasing food production by bringing into profitable cultivation vast areas that would otherwise be un-usable or only marginally productive. Most of the world's irrigated land is in Asia, where it is devoted primarily to the production of rice. In Africa the Volta River of Ghana and the Nile are dammed for irrigation and power pur-poses. The Colorado River system of the U.S. is used extensively for irrigation in the Southwest, as are scores of rivers elsewhere. Still to be exploited for irri-gation are the Mekong of southeastern Asia and the Amazon.

During the past few years there has been an important new irrigation devel-opment in Asia: the widespread installa-tion of small-scale irrigation systems on individual farms. In Pakistan and India, where in many places the water table is close to the surface, hundreds of thou-sands of tube wells with pumps have been installed in recent years. Interest-ingly, this development came about partly as an answer to a problem that had been presented by irrigation itself.

Like many of man's other interventions in the biosphere, his reshaping of the hydrologic cycle has had unwanted side effects. One of them is the raising of the water table by the diversion of river water onto the land. Over a period of time the percolation of irrigation water downward and the accumulation of this water underground may gradually raise the water table until it is within a few feet or even a few inches of the surface. This not only inhibits the growth of plant roots by waterlogging but also results in the surface soil's becoming salty as water evaporates through it, leaving a concentrated deposit of salts in the upper few inches. Such a situation developed in West Pakistan after its fertile plain had been irrigated with water from the Indus for a century. During a visit by President Ayub to Washington in 1961 he appealed to President Kennedy for help: West Pakistan was losing 60,-000 acres of fertile cropland per year because of waterlogging and salinity as its population was expanding 2.5 percent yearly.

This same sequence, the diversion of river water into land for irrigation, followed eventually by waterlogging and salinity and the abandonment of land,

had been repeated many times throughout history. The result was invariably the decline, and sometimes the disappearance, of the civilizations thus intervening in the hydrologic cycle. The remains of civilizations buried in the deserts of the Middle East attest to early experiences similar to those of contemporary Pakistan. These civilizations, however, had no one to turn to for foreign aid. An interdisciplinary U.S. team led by Roger Revelle, then Science Adviser to the Secretary of the Interior, studied the problem and proposed among other things a system of tube wells that would lower the water table by tapping the ground water for intensive irrigation. Discharging this water on the surface, the wells would also wash the soil's salt downward. The stratagem worked, and the salty, waterlogged land of Pakistan is steadily being reclaimed.

Other side effects of river irrigation are not so easily remedied. Such irrigation has brought about a great increase in the incidence of schistosomiasis, a disease that is particularly prevalent in the river valleys of Africa and Asia. The disease is produced by the parasitic larva of a blood fluke, which is harbored by aquatic snails and burrows into the flesh

of people standing in water or in water-soaked fields. The Chinese call schistosomiasis "snail fever"; it might also be called the poor man's emphysema, because, like emphysema, this extremely debilitating disease is environmentally induced through conditions created by man. The snails and the fluke thrive in perennial irrigation systems, where they are in close proximity to large human populations. The incidence of the disease is rising rapidly as the world's large rivers are harnessed for irrigation, and today schistosomiasis is estimated to afflict 250 million people. It now surpasses malaria, the incidence of which is declining, as the world's most prevalent infectious disease.

As a necessity for food production water is of course becoming an increasingly crucial commodity. The projected increases in population and in food requirements will call for more and more water, forcing man to consider still more massive and complex interventions in the biosphere. The desalting of seawater for irrigation purposes is only one major departure from traditional practices. Another is a Russian plan to reverse the flow of four rivers currently flowing northward and emptying into the Arctic Ocean. These rivers would be diverted southward into the semiarid lands of southern Russia, greatly enlarging the irrigated area of the U.S.S.R. Some climatologists are concerned, however, that the shutting off of the flow of relatively warm water from these four rivers would have far-reaching implications for not only the climate of the Arctic but also the climatic system of the entire earth.

The growing competition for scarce water supplies among states and among various uses in the western U.S. is also forcing consideration of heroic plans. For example, a detailed engineering proposal exists for the diversion of the Yukon River in Alaska southward across Canada into the western U.S. to meet the growing need for water for both agricultural and industrial purposes. The effort would cost an estimated $100 billion.

Representing an even greater intervention in the biosphere is the prospect that man may one day consciously alter the earth's climatic patterns, shifting some of the rain now falling on the oceans to the land. Among the steps needed for the realization of such a scheme are the construction of a comprehensive model of the earth's climatic system and the development of a computational facility capable of simulating

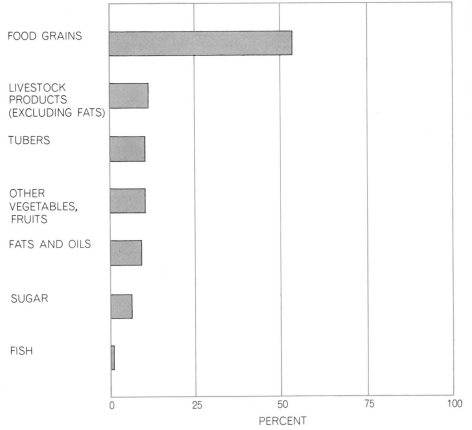

WORLDWIDE FOOD ENERGY comes in different amounts from different products. Cereals outstrip other foodstuffs; wheat and rice each supply a fifth of mankind's food energy.

and manipulating the model. The required information includes data on temperatures, humidity, precipitation, the movement of air masses, ocean currents and many other factors that enter into the weather. Earth-orbiting satellites will doubtless be able to collect much of this information, and the present generation of advanced computers appears to be capable of carrying out the necessary experiments on the model. For the implementation of the findings, that is, for the useful control of rainfall, there will of course be a further requirement: the project will have to be managed by a global and supranational agency if it is not to lead to weather wars among nations working at cross purposes. Some commercial firms are already in the business of rainmaking, and they are operating on an international basis.

The third great technology that man has introduced to increase food production is the use of chemical fertilizers. We owe the foundation for this development to Justus von Liebig of Germany, who early in the 19th century determined the specific requirements of nitrogen, phosphorus, potassium and other nutrients for plant growth. Chemical fertilizers did not come into widespread use, however, until this century, when the pressure of population and the disappearance of new frontiers compelled farmers to substitute fertilizer for the expansion of cropland to meet growing food needs. One of the first countries to intensify its agriculture, largely by the use of fertilizers, was Japan, whose output of food per acre has steadily risen (except for wartime interruptions) since the turn of the century. The output per acre of a few other countries, including the Netherlands, Denmark and Sweden, began to rise at about the same time. The U.S., richly endowed with vast farmlands, did not turn to the heavy use of fertilizer and other intensive measures until about 1940. Since then its yields per acre, assisted by new varieties of grain highly responsive to fertilizer, have also shown remarkable gains. Yields of corn, the production of which exceeds that of all other cereals combined in the U.S., have nearly tripled over the past three decades.

Experience has demonstrated that in areas of high rainfall the application of chemical fertilizers in conjunction with other inputs and practices can double, triple or even quadruple the productivity of intensively farmed soils. Such levels of productivity are achieved in Japan and the Netherlands, where farmers ap-

ply up to 300 pounds of plant nutrients per acre per year. The use of chemical fertilizers is estimated to account for at least a fourth of man's total food supply. The world's farmers are currently applying 60 million metric tons of plant nutrients per year, an average of nearly 45 pounds per acre for the three billion acres of cropland. Such application, however, is unevenly distributed. Some poor countries do not yet benefit from the use of fertilizer in any significant amounts. If global projections of population and income growth materialize, the production of fertilizer over the remaining three decades of this century must almost triple to satisfy food demands.

Can the projected demand for fertilizer be met? The key ingredient is nitrogen, and fortunately man has learned how to speed up the fixation phase of the nitrogen cycle [see "The Nitrogen Cycle," by C. C. Delwiche, page 69]. In nature the nitrogen of the air is fixed in the soil by certain microorganisms, such as those present in the root nodules of leguminous plants. Chemists have now devised various ways of incorporating nitrogen from the air into inorganic compounds and making it available in the form of nitrogen fertilizers. These chemical processes produce the fertilizer much more rapidly and economically than the growing of leguminous-plant sources such as clover, alfalfa or soy-

beans. More than 25 million tons of nitrogen fertilizer is now being synthesized and added to the earth's soil annually.

The other principal ingredients of chemical fertilizer are the minerals potassium and phosphorus. Unlike nitrogen, these elements are not replenished by comparatively fast natural cycles. Potassium presents no immediate problem; the rich potash fields of Canada alone are estimated to contain enough potassium to supply mankind's needs for centuries to come. The reserves of phosphorus, however, are not nearly so plentiful as those of potassium. Every year 3.5 million tons of phosphorus washes into the sea, where it remains as sediment on the ocean floor. Eventually it will be thrust above the ocean surface again by geologic uplift, but man cannot wait that long. Phosphorus may be one of the first necessities that will prompt man to begin to mine the ocean bed.

The great expansion of the use of fertilizers in this century has benefited mankind enormously, but the benefits are not unalloyed. The runoff of chemical fertilizers into rivers, lakes and underground waters creates two important hazards. One is the chemical pollution of drinking water. In certain areas in Illinois and California the nitrate content of well water has risen to a toxic

EXPERIMENTAL PLANTINGS at the International Rice Research Institute in the Philippine Republic are seen in an aerial photograph. IR-8, a high-yield rice, was bred here.

RUINED FARM in the "dust bowl" area of the U.S. in the 1930's is seen in an aerial photograph. The farm is near Union in Terry County, Tex. The wind has eroded the powdery, drought-parched topsoil and formed drifts among the buildings and across the fields.

level. Excessive nitrate can cause the physiological disorder methemoglobinemia, which reduces the blood's oxygen-carrying capacity and can be particularly dangerous to children under five. This hazard is of only local dimensions and can be countered by finding alternative sources of drinking water. A much more extensive hazard, profound in its effects on the biosphere, is the now well-known phenomenon called eutrophication.

Inorganic nitrates and phosphates discharged into lakes and other bodies of fresh water provide a rich medium for the growth of algae; the massive growth of the algae in turn depletes the water of oxygen and thus kills off the fish life. In the end the eutrophication, or overfertilization, of the lake slowly brings about its death as a body of fresh water, converting it into a swamp. Lake Erie is a prime example of this process now under way.

How much of the now widespread eutrophication of fresh waters is attributable to agricultural fertilization and how much to other causes remains an open question. Undoubtedly the runoff of nitrates and phosphates from farmlands plays a large part. There are also other important contributors, however. Considerable amounts of phosphate, coming mainly from detergents, are discharged into rivers and lakes from sewers carrying municipal and industrial wastes. And there is reason to believe that in some rivers and lakes most of the

nitrate may come not from fertilizers but from the internal-combustion engine. It is estimated that in the state of New Jersey, which has heavy automobile traffic, nitrous oxide products of gasoline combustion, picked up and deposited by rainfall, contribute as much as 20 pounds of nitrogen per acre per year to the land. Some of this nitrogen washes into the many rivers and lakes of New Jersey and its adjoining states. A way must be found to deal with the eutrophication problem because even in the short run it can have damaging effects, affecting as it does the supply of potable water, the cycles of aquatic life and consequently man's food supply.

Recent findings have presented us with a related problem in connection with the fourth technology supporting man's present high level of food production: the chemical control of diseases, insects and weeds. It is now clear that the use of DDT and other chlorinated hydrocarbons as pesticides and herbicides is beginning to threaten many species of animal life, possibly including man. DDT today is found in the tissues of animals over a global range of life forms and geography from penguins in Antarctica to children in the villages of Thailand. There is strong evidence that it is actually on the way to extinguishing some animal species, notably predatory birds such as the bald eagle and the peregrine falcon, whose capacity for using calcium is so impaired by DDT that the shells of their eggs are too thin

to avoid breakage in the nest before the fledglings hatch. Carnivores are particularly likely to concentrate DDT in their tissues because they feed on herbivores that have already concentrated it from large quantities of vegetation. Concentrations of DDT in mothers' milk in the U.S. now exceed the tolerance levels established for foodstuffs by the Food and Drug Administration.

It is ironic that less than a generation after 1948, when Paul Hermann Müller of Switzerland received a Nobel prize for the discovery of DDT, the use of the insecticide is being banned by law in many countries. This illustrates how little man knows about the effects of his intervening in the biosphere. Up to now he has been using the biosphere as a laboratory, sometimes with unhappy results.

Several new approaches to the problem of controlling pests are now being explored. Chemists are searching for pesticides that will be degradable, instead of long-lasting, after being deposited on vegetation or in the soil, and that will be aimed at specific pests rather than acting as broad-spectrum poisons for many forms of life. Much hope is placed in techniques of biological control, such as are exemplified in the mass sterilization (by irradiation) of male screwworm flies, a pest of cattle that used to cost U.S. livestock producers $100 million per year. The release of 125 million irradiated male screwworm flies weekly in the U.S. and in adjoining areas of Mexico (in a cooperative effort with the Mexican government) is holding the fly population to a negligible level. Efforts are now under way to get rid of the Mexican fruit fly and the pink cotton bollworm in California by the same method.

Successes are also being achieved in breeding resistance to insect pests in various crops. A strain of wheat has been developed that is resistant to the Hessian fly; resistance to the corn borer and the corn earworm has been bred into strains of corn, and work is in progress on a strain of alfalfa that resists aphids and leafhoppers. Another promising approach, which already has a considerable history, is the development of insect parasites, ranging from bacteria and viruses to wasps that lay their eggs in other insects. The fact remains, however, that the biological control of pests is still in its infancy.

I have here briefly reviewed the major agricultural technologies evolved to meet man's increasing food needs, the problems arising from them and some possible solutions. What is the present balance sheet on the satisfaction of human food needs? Although man's food supply has expanded several hundred fold since the invention of agriculture, two-thirds of mankind is still hungry and malnourished much of the time. On the credit side a third of mankind, living largely in North America, Europe, Australia and Japan, has achieved an adequate food supply, and for the remaining two-thirds the threat of large-scale famine has recently been removed, at least for the immediate future. In spite of rapid population growth in the developing countries since World War II, their peoples have been spared from massive famine (except in Biafra in 1969–1970) by huge exports of food from the developed countries. As a result of two consecutive monsoon failures in India, a fifth of the total U.S. wheat crop was shipped to India in both 1966 and 1967, feeding 60 million Indians for two years.

Although the threat of outright famine has been more or less eliminated for the time being, human nutrition on the global scale is still in a sorry state. Malnutrition, particularly protein deficiency, exacts an enormous toll from the physical and mental development of the young in the poorer countries. This was dramatically illustrated when India held tryouts in 1968 to select a team to represent it in the Olympic games that year. Not a single Indian athlete, male or female, met the minimum standards for qualifying to compete in any of the 36

track and field events in Mexico City. No doubt this was partly due to the lack of support for athletics in India, but poor nutrition was certainly also a large factor. The young people of Japan today are visible examples of what a change can be brought about by improvement in nutrition. Well-nourished from infancy, Japanese teen-agers are on the average some two inches taller than their elders.

Protein is as crucial for children's mental development as for their physical development. This was strikingly shown in a recent study extending over several years in Mexico: children who had been severely undernourished before the age of five were found to average 13 points lower in I.Q. than a carefully selected control group. Unfortunately no amount of feeding or education in later life can repair the setbacks to development caused by undernourishment in the early years. Protein shortages in the poor countries today are depreciating human resources for at least a generation to come.

Protein constitutes the main key to human health and vigor, and the key to the protein diet at present is held by grain consumed either directly or indirectly (in the form of meat, milk and eggs). Cereals, occupying more than 70 percent of the world's cropland, provide 52 percent of man's direct energy intake. Eleven percent is supplied by livestock products such as meat, milk and eggs, 10 percent by potatoes and other tubers, 10 percent by fruits and vegetables, 9 percent by animal fats and vegetable oils, 7 percent by sugar and 1 percent by fish. As in the case of the total quantity of the individual diet, however, the composition of the diet varies greatly around the world. The difference is most marked in the per capita use of grain consumed directly and indirectly.

The two billion people living in the poor countries consume an average of about 360 pounds of grain per year, or about a pound per day. With only one pound per day, nearly all must be consumed directly to meet minimal energy requirements; little remains for feeding to livestock, which may convert only a tenth of their feed intake into meat or other edible human food. The average American, in contrast, consumes more than 1,600 pounds of grain per year. He eats only about 150 pounds of this directly in the form of bread, breakfast cereal and so on; the rest is consumed indirectly in the form of meat, milk and eggs. In short, he enjoys the luxury of the highly inefficient animal conversion

of grain into tastier and somewhat more nutritious proteins.

Thus the average North American currently makes about four times as great a demand on the earth's agricultural ecosystem as someone living in one of the poor countries. As the income levels in these countries rise, so will their demand for a richer diet of animal products. For the increasing world population at the end of the century, which is expected to be twice the 3.5 billion of today, the world production of grain would have to be doubled merely to maintain present consumption levels. This increase, combined with the projected improvement in diet associated with gains in income over the next three decades, could nearly triple the demand for grain, requiring that the food supply increase more over the next three decades than it has in the 10,000 years since agriculture began.

There are ways in which this pressure can be eased somewhat. One is the breeding of higher protein content in grains and other crops, making them nutritionally more acceptable as alternatives to livestock products. Another is the development of vegetable substitutes for animal products, such as are already available in the form of oleomargarine, soybean oil, imitation meats and other replacements (about 65 percent of the whipped toppings and 35 percent of the coffee whiteners now sold in U.S. supermarkets are nondairy products). Pressures on the agricultural ecosystem would thus drive high-income man one step down in the food chain to a level of more efficient consumption of what could be produced by agriculture.

What is clearly needed today is a cooperative effort—more specifically, a world environmental agency—to monitor, investigate and regulate man's interventions in the environment, including those made in his quest for more food. Since many of his efforts to enlarge his food supply have a global impact, they can only be dealt with in the context of a global institution. The health of the biosphere can no longer be separated from our modes of political organization. Whatever measures are taken, there is growing doubt that the agricultural ecosystem will be able to accommodate both the anticipated increase of the human population to seven billion by the end of the century and the universal desire of the world's hungry for a better diet. The central question is no longer "Can we produce enough food?" but "What are the environmental consequences of attempting to do so?"

X

Human Energy Production as a Process in the Biosphere

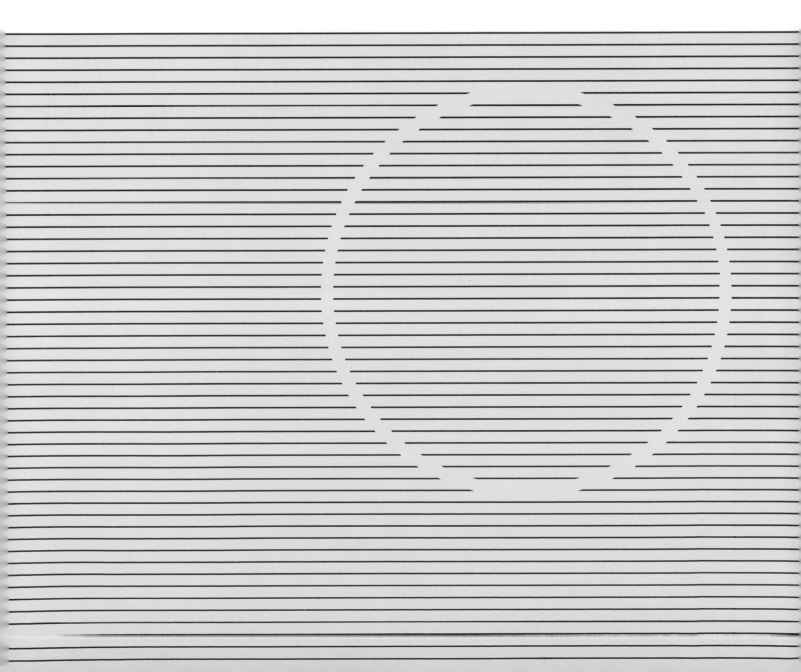

Human Energy Production as a Process in the Biosphere

by s. fred singer

In releasing the energy stored in fossil and nuclear fuels man accelerates slow cycles of nature. The waste products of power generation then interact with the fast cycles of the biosphere

As has been noted in other chapters of this book on the biosphere, the earth in general and the biosphere in particular have grand-scale pathways of energy metabolism. For example, solar energy falls on the earth, green plants utilize a tiny fraction of it to manufacture energy-rich compounds and some of these compounds are stored in the earth's crust as what we have come to call fossil fuels. The primary fission fuel uranium and the potential fusion fuel deuterium were originally "cooked" in the interior of stars. In releasing the energy of these chemical and nuclear fuels man is in effect racing the slow cycles of nature, with inevitable effects on the cycles themselves.

Before 1800 the power available to human societies was limited to solar energy that had only recently been radiated to the earth. The most direct form of such power was human or animal power; the energy came from the metabolism of food, which is to say from the biological oxidation of compounds storing solar energy. The burning of

wood or oils of animal or vegetable origin to provide light and heat also represented the conversion of recently stored solar energy. By the same token the use of moving air or falling water to drive mills or pumps constituted the use of recently arrived solar energy. Among the other limitations of such power sources was the fact that they could not be readily transported and that their energy could not be transmitted any considerable distance.

This picture has of course changed completely since 1800, and it has assumed significant new dimensions in the past two decades with the advent of nuclear power. The most striking measure of these changes is the increased per capita consumption of energy in the developed countries. Indeed, the correlation between a nation's per capita use of energy and its level of economic development is almost linear [see illustration on page 109]. The minimum per capita consumption of energy is what is required in food for a man to stay alive, namely about 2,000 kilocalories per day or 100 watts (thermal). Today the per capita use of energy in the U.S. is 10,000 watts, and the figure is rising by some 2.5 percent per year.

Hand in hand with the advance in the rate of energy consumption has gone the introduction of the new sources of energy: fossil and nuclear fuels. In contrast to the sources used before 1800, fossil and nuclear fuels represent energy that reached the earth millions and even some billions of years ago. Except occasionally for political reasons, it matters little where the new fuels are found; they can be transported readily, and the energy produced from them can be transmitted over great distances.

On first consideration it might seem that fossil and nuclear fuels are fundamentally different, in that the energy of one is released by oxidation, or burning, and the energy of the other is released by fission or fusion. In a deeper sense, however, the two kinds of fuel are closely related. Fossil fuels store the radiant energy originally produced by nuclear reactions in the interior of the sun. Nuclear fuels store energy produced by another set of nuclear reactions in the interior of certain stars. When such stars exploded, they showered into space the elements that had been synthesized within them. These elements then went into the formation of younger stars such as the sun, together with its family of planets.

The production of fossil fuels is based on the carbon cycle that has been described in the article by Bert Bolin [page 47]. In the process of photosynthesis plants use radiant energy from the sun to convert carbon dioxide and water into carbohydrates, at the same time releasing oxygen into the atmosphere. When the plant materials decompose or are eaten by animals, the process is reversed: oxygen is used to convert carbohydrates into energy plus carbon dioxide and water.

The amount of carbon dioxide involved in photosynthesis annually is about 110 billion tons, or roughly 5 percent of the carbon dioxide in the atmosphere. The consumption of carbon dioxide through photosynthesis is matched to one part in 10,000 by the annual release of carbon dioxide to the atmosphere through oxidation. Under normal conditions the amounts of carbon dioxide and oxygen in the atmosphere re-

107

main approximately in equilibrium from year to year.

There are, however, small long-term imbalances in the carbon cycle, and it is owing to them that the fossil fuels being exploited today all derive from plants and animals that lived long ago. Over a span of geologic history extending back into the Cambrian period of some 500 million years ago, a small fraction of these organisms have been buried in sediments or mud under conditions that prevented complete oxidation. Various chemical changes have transformed them into fossil fuels: coal, oil, natural gas, lignite, tar and asphalt. Although the same geological processes are still operative, they function over vast periods of time, and so the amount of new

fossil fuel that is likely to be produced during the next few thousand years is inconsequential. Therefore one can assume that the existing fossil fuels constitute a nonrenewable resource.

Coal has been burned for some eight centuries, but it was consumed in negligible amounts until early in the 19th century. Since the middle of that century the rise in the consumption of coal has been spectacular: in 1870 the world production rate of coal was about 250 million metric tons per year, whereas this year it will be about 2.8 billion tons. The rate of increase, however, is lower now than it was at the beginning of the period, having declined from an average of 4.4 percent per year to 3.6 percent, largely because of the rapid increase in

the fraction of total industrial energy contributed by oil and gas. In the U.S. that fraction rose from 7.9 percent in 1900 to 67.9 percent in 1965, whereas the contribution of coal declined from 89 percent to 27.9 percent.

World production of crude oil was negligible as recently as 1890; now it is close to 12 billion barrels per year. The rise in the rate of production has been nearly 7 percent per year, so that the amount of oil extracted has doubled every 10 years. As yet there is no sign of a deceleration in this rate.

Nonetheless, the finiteness of the earth's fossil fuel supplies gives rise to the question of how long they will last. M. King Hubbert of the U.S. Geological Survey has estimated that the earth's

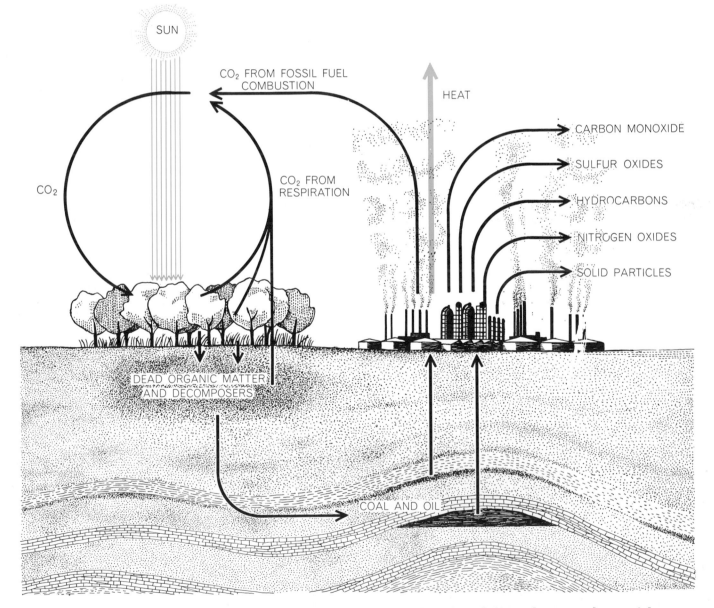

ENERGY CYCLE involved in the combustion of fossil fuels begins with solar energy employed in photosynthesis millions of years ago. A small fraction of the plants is buried under conditions that prevent complete oxidation. The material undergoes chemical changes that transform it into coal, oil and other fuels. When they are burned to release their stored energy, only part of the energy goes into useful work. Much of the energy is returned to the atmosphere as heat, together with such by-products of combustion as carbon dioxide and water vapor. Other emissions in fossil fuel combustion are listed at right in the relative order of their volume.

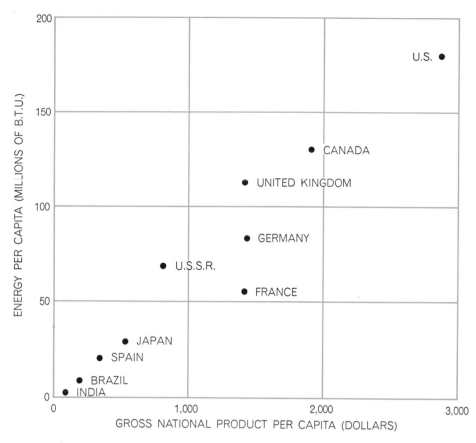

CLOSE RELATION between a nation's consumption of energy and its gross national product is depicted on the basis of a study made by the Office of Science and Technology in 1961. Most of the nations covered beyond the 10 shown would be in the lower left-hand rectangle.

coal supply can serve as a major source of industrial energy for another two or three centuries. His estimate for petroleum is 70 to 80 years. However much these periods may be stretched by unforeseen discoveries and improved technology, the end of the fossil fuel era will inevitably come. From the perspective of that time—perhaps the 23rd century—the period of exploitation of fossil fuels will be seen as only a brief episode in the span of human history.

This year the U.S. will consume some 685,000 million million B.T.U. of energy, most of it derived from fossil fuels. (One short ton of coal has a thermal value of 25.8 million B.T.U. The thermal value of one barrel of oil is 5.8 million B.T.U.) Industry takes more than 35 percent of the total energy consumption. About a third of industry's share is in the form of electricity, which, as of 1960, was generated roughly 50 percent from coal, 20 percent from water power, 20 percent from natural gas and 10 percent from oil.

The nation's homes use almost as much energy as industry does. A major consumer is space heating, which for the average home requires as much energy as the average family car: about 70 mil-lion B.T.U. per year, or the equivalent of 900 gallons of oil. The other domestic uses are for cooking, heating water, lighting and air conditioning.

Transportation accounts for 20 percent of the annual energy consumption, mainly in the form of gasoline for automobiles. Another 10 percent goes for commercial consumption in stores, offices, hotels, apartment houses and the like. Agriculture probably consumes no more than 1 percent of all the energy, chiefly for the operation of tractors and for running irrigation and drainage equipment.

Looking at the use of fossil fuels from another viewpoint, one finds that most of the coal goes into the generation of electricity. Oil and natural gas tend to be used directly, either for heating purposes or to provide motive power for vehicles. Fossil fuels are also used as the raw materials for the petrochemical industry. Notwithstanding that industry's rapid growth, however, it still accounts for less than 2 percent of the annual consumption of fossil fuels.

Clearly the production of energy from fossil fuels on the scale typical of a modern industrial nation represents an enormous amount of combustion, with attendant effects on the biosphere. By far the greatest effect is the emission of carbon dioxide. Combustion also injects a number of pollutants into the air. In the U.S. the five most common air pollutants, listed in the order of their annual tonnage, are carbon monoxide, sulfur oxides, hydrocarbons, nitrogen oxides and solid particles. The major sources are automobiles, industry, electric power plants, space heating and refuse disposal. The burning of fossil fuels also produces effects on water: chemical effects when the air pollutants are washed down by water and thermal effects arising from the dispersal of waste heat from thermal power plants.

Carbon dioxide is the only combustion product whose increase has been documented on a worldwide basis. The injection of large quantities of carbon dioxide into the atmosphere in the past few decades has been extremely sudden in relation to important natural time scales. For example, although the surface of the sea can adjust to changes in the level of carbon dioxide in the atmosphere in about five years, the deeper layers require some hundreds or thousands of years to adjust. If the oceans were perfectly mixed at all times, carbon dioxide added to the atmosphere would distribute itself about five-sixths in the water and about one-sixth in the air. In actuality the distribution is about equal.

It appears that between 1860 and the present the concentration of carbon dioxide in the atmosphere has increased from about 290 parts per million to about 320 parts per million, an increase of more than 10 percent. Precise measurements by Charles D. Keeling of the Scripps Institution of Oceanography have established that the carbon dioxide content increased by six parts per million between 1958 and 1968. Reasonable projections indicate an increase of 25 percent (over 1970) to about 400 parts per million by the turn of the century and to between 500 and 540 parts per million by 2020.

The most widely discussed matter related to these increases is the possibility that they will lead to a worldwide rise in temperature. The molecule of carbon dioxide has strong absorption bands, particularly in the infrared region of the spectrum at wavelengths of from 12 to 18 microns. This is the spectral region where most of the thermal energy radiating from the earth into space is concentrated. By increasing the absorption of this radiation and by reradiating it at a lower temperature corresponding to the temperature of the upper atmo-

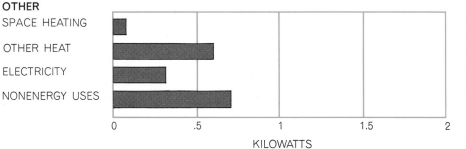

HOUSEHOLD
SPACE HEATING
OTHER HEAT
ELECTRICITY

COMMERCIAL
SPACE HEATING
OTHER HEAT
ELECTRICITY

TRANSPORT
SPACE HEATING
MOTIVE USE

INDUSTRY
SPACE HEATING
OTHER HEAT
ELECTRICITY
NONENERGY USES

OTHER
SPACE HEATING
OTHER HEAT
ELECTRICITY
NONENERGY USES

0 .5 1 1.5 2

KILOWATTS

USE OF ENERGY in the U.S. is expressed in terms of thermal kilowatts per capita per day in 1967. All together the consumption averages some 10,000 watts per person, which is 100 times the food-intake level of 100 watts that is barely exceeded in many nations.

sphere the carbon dioxide reduces the amount of heat energy lost by the earth to outer space. The phenomenon has been called the "greenhouse effect," although the analogy is inexact because a real greenhouse achieves its results less from the fact that the glass blocks reradiation in the infrared than from the fact that it cuts down the convective transfer of heat.

The possibility that additional carbon dioxide from the burning of fossil fuels could produce a worldwide increase in temperature seems to have been raised initially by the American geologist P. C. Chamberlain in 1899. In 1956 Gilbert N. Plass calculated that a doubling of the carbon dioxide content of the atmosphere would result in a rise of 6.5 de-

grees Fahrenheit at the earth's surface. In 1963 Fritz Möller calculated that a 25 percent increase in atmospheric carbon dioxide would increase the average temperature by one to seven degrees F., depending on the effects of water vapor in the atmosphere. The most extensive calculations have been made by Syukuro Manabe and R. T. Wetherald, who estimate that a rise in atmospheric carbon dioxide from 300 to 600 parts per million would increase the average surface temperature by 4.25 degrees, assuming average cloudiness, and by 5.25 degrees, assuming no clouds.

Unfortunately the problem is more complicated than these calculations imply. An increase of temperature at the surface of the earth and in the lower

levels of the atmosphere not only increases evaporation but also changes cloudiness. Changes of cloudiness alter the albedo, or average reflecting power, of the earth. The normal average albedo is about 30 percent, meaning that 30 percent of the sunlight reaching the earth is immediately reflected back into space. Changes in cloudiness, therefore, can have a pronounced effect on the atmospheric temperature and on climate.

The situation is further complicated by atmospheric turbidity. J. Murray Mitchell, Jr., of the Environmental Science Services Administration has determined that atmospheric temperatures rose generally between 1860 and 1940. Between 1940 and 1960, although warming occurred in northern Europe and North America, there was a slight lowering of temperature for the world as a whole. Mitchell finds that a cooling trend has set in; he believes it is owing partly to the dust of volcanic eruptions and partly to such human activities as agricultural burning in the Tropics. (In the future the condensation trails left by jet airplanes may contribute to this problem.)

In sum, the fact that the carbon dioxide content of the atmosphere has increased is firmly established by reliable measurements. The effect of the increase on climate is uncertain, partly because no good worldwide measurements of radiation are available and partly because of the counteractive effects of changes in cloudiness and in the turbidity of the atmosphere. An exciting technological possibility is the use of a weather satellite to keep track of the energy radiated back into space by the earth. The data would provide a basis for the first reliable and standardized measurement of the "global radiation climate."

In any event, the higher levels of carbon dioxide may not persist for long. For one thing, the oceans, which contain 60 times as much carbon dioxide as the atmosphere does, will begin to absorb the excess as the mixing of the intermediate and deeper levels of water proceeds. For another, the increased atmospheric content of carbon dioxide will stimulate a more rapid growth of plants—a phenomenon that has been utilized in greenhouses. It is true that the carbon dioxide thus removed from the atmosphere will be returned when the plants decay. Forests, however, account for about two-thirds of the photosynthesis taking place on land (and therefore for nearly half of the world total), and since forests are long-lived, they tend to spread over a

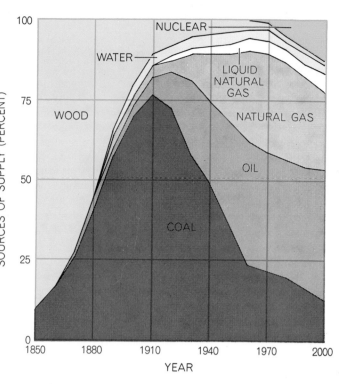

CHANGING SOURCES of energy in the U.S. since 1850 are compared (*right*) with total consumption (*left*) over the same period. At right one can see that in 1850 fuel wood was the source of 90 percent of the energy and coal accounted for 10 percent. By 2000 it is foreseen that coal will be back to almost 10 percent and that other sources will be oil, natural gas, liquid natural gas, hydroelectric power, fuel wood and nuclear energy. The estimates were made by Hans H. Landsberg of Resources for the Future, Inc.

long period of time the return of carbon dioxide to the atmosphere.

The five major air pollutants resulting from the combustion of fossil fuels also interact with the biosphere in various ways, not all of them clearly understood. One tends to think of pollutants as harmful, but the situation is not that simple, as becomes apparent in a consideration of the pollutants and their known effects.

Carbon monoxide appears to be almost entirely a man-made pollutant. The only significant source known is the imperfect combustion of fossil fuels, resulting in incomplete oxidation of the carbon. Although carbon monoxide is emitted in large amounts, it does not seem to accumulate in the atmosphere. The mechanism of removal is not known, but it is probably a biological sink, such as soil bacteria.

Sulfur, which occurs as an impurity in fossil fuels, is among the most troublesome of the air pollutants. Although there are natural sources of sulfur dioxides, such as volcanic gases, more than 80 percent is estimated to come from the combustion of fuels that contain sulfur. The sulfur dioxide may form sulfuric acid, which often becomes associated with atmospheric aerosols, or it may react further to form ammonium sulfate. A typical lifetime in the atmosphere is about a week.

When the sulfur products are removed from the atmosphere by precipitation, they increase the acidity of the rainfall. Values of pH of about 4 have been found in the Netherlands and Sweden, probably because of the extensive industrial activity in western Europe. As a result small lakes and rivers have begun to show increased acidity that endangers the stability of their ecosystems. Certain aquatic animals, such as salmon, cannot survive if the pH falls below 5.5.

Nothing is known about the global effects of sulfur emission, but they are

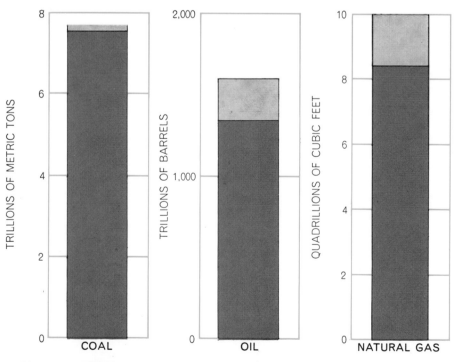

FOSSIL FUEL SUPPLIES remaining in the world are indicated by a scheme wherein the entire gray bar represents original resources, light gray portion shows how much has been extracted and dark gray area shows what remains. Figures reflect estimates by M. King Hubbert of the U.S. Geological Survey and could be changed by unforeseen discoveries.

believed to be small. In any case most of the sulfur ends up in the oceans. It is possible, however, that sulfur compounds are accumulating in a layer of sulfate particles in the stratosphere. The layer's mechanism of formation, its effects and its relation to man-made emissions are not clear. The fine particles of the layer could have an effect on radiation from the upper atmosphere, thereby affecting mean global temperatures.

Hydrocarbons are emitted naturally into the atmosphere from forests and vegetation and in the form of methane from the bacterial decomposition of organic matter. Human activities account for only about 15 percent of the emissions, but these contributions are concentrated in urban areas. The main contributor is the processing and combustion of petroleum, particularly gasoline for the internal-combustion engine.

The reactions of hydrocarbons with nitrogen oxides in the presence of ultraviolet radiation produce the photochemical smog that appears so often over Los Angeles and other cities. The biological effects of several of the products of the reactions, including ozone and complex organic molecules, can be quite severe. Some of the products are thought to be carcinogenic. Ozone has highly detrimental effects on vegetation, but fortunately they are localized. As yet no regional or worldwide effects have been discovered.

Hydrocarbon pollutants in the form of oil spills are well known to have drastic ecological effects. The spill in the Santa Barbara Channel last year, which involved some 10,000 tons, and the *Torrey Canyon* spill in 1967, involving about 100,000 tons, produced intense local concentrations of oil, which is toxic to many marine organisms. Besides these well-publicized events there is a yearly worldwide spillage from various oil operations that adds up to about a million tons, even though most of the individual spills are small. There are also natural oil seeps of unknown magnitude. Added to all of these is the dumping of waste motor oil; in the U.S. alone about a million tons of such oil is discarded annually. Up to the present time no worldwide effects of these various oil spills are detectable. It can therefore be assumed that bacteria degrade the oil rapidly.

Nitrogen oxides occur naturally in the atmosphere as nitrous oxide (N_2O), nitric oxide (NO) and nitrogen dioxide (NO_2). Nitrous oxide is the most plentiful at .25 part per million and is relatively inert. Nitrogen dioxide is a strong absorber of ultraviolet radiation and triggers photochemical reactions that produce smog. In combination with water it can form nitric acid.

The production of nitrogen oxides in combustion is highly sensitive to temperature. It is particularly likely to result from the explosive combustion taking place in the internal-combustion engine. If this engine is ever replaced by an external-combustion engine that operates at a steady and relatively low temperature rather than at high peaks, the emission of nitrogen oxides will be greatly reduced.

Solid particles are injected into the lower atmosphere from a number of sources, with the combustion of fossil fuels making a major contribution. The technology of pollution control is adequate for limiting such emissions. If it is applied, solid particles will become insignificant pollutants.

Although the fossil fuels still predominate as sources of power, the introduction of nuclear fuels into the generation of power is changing both the scale of energy conversion and the effects of that conversion on the biosphere. Nuclear energy can be considered as a heat source differing from coal or oil, but once the energy has been released in the form of heat it is used in the same way as heat from other sources. Therefore the problem of waste heat is the same. The pollution characteristics of nuclear energy, however, differ from those of the fossil fuels, being radioactive rather than chemical.

Two processes are of concern: the fission of heavy nuclei such as uranium and the fusion of light nuclei such as deuterium. The fission reaction has to start with uranium 235, because that is the only naturally occurring isotope that is fissioned by the capture of slow neu-

SOURCES OF WASTE HEAT are evident in a thermal infrared image, made at an altitude of 2,000 feet, of an industrial concentration along the Detroit River in Detroit. The whiter an object is, the hotter it was when the image was made. The complex at left

trons. On fissioning the uranium 235 supplies the neutrons needed to carry out other reactions.

Each fission event of uranium 235 releases some 200 million electron volts of energy. One gram of uranium 235 therefore corresponds to 81,900 million joules, an energy equivalent of 2.7 metric tons of coal or 13.7 barrels of crude oil. A nuclear power plant producing 1,000 electrical megawatts with a thermal efficiency of 33 percent would consume about three kilograms of uranium 235 per day.

A nuclear "burner" uses up large amounts of uranium 235, which is in short supply since it has an abundance of only .7 percent of the uranium in natural ore. If reactor development proceeds as foreseen by the Atomic Energy Commission, inexpensive reserves of uranium (costing less than $10 per pound) would be used up within about 15 years and medium-priced fuel (up to $30 per pound) would be used up by the year 2000. Hence there has been concern that present reactors will deplete these supplies of uranium before converter and breeder reactors are developed to make fissionable plutonium 239 and uranium 233. Either of these isotopes can be used as a catalyst to burn uranium 238 or thorium 232, which are relatively abundant. Thorium and uranium together have an abundance of about 15 parts per million in the earth's crust, representing therefore a source of energy

millions of times larger than all known reserves of fossil fuel.

The possibility of generating energy by nuclear fusion is more remote. Of the two processes being considered—the deuterium-deuterium reaction and the deuterium-tritium reaction—the latter is somewhat easier because it proceeds at a lower temperature. In it lithium 6 is the basic fuel, because it is needed to make tritium by nuclear bombardment. The amount of energy available in this way is limited by the abundance of lithium 6 in the earth's crust, namely about two parts per million. The deuterium-deuterium reaction, on the other hand, would represent a practically inexhaustible source of energy, since one part in 5,000 of the hydrogen in the oceans is deuterium.

One must hope, then, that breeder reactors and perhaps fusion reactors will be developed commercially before the supplies of fossil fuel and uranium 235 are exhausted. With inexhaustible (but not cheap) supplies of nuclear energy, automobiles may run on artificially produced ammonia or methane; coal and oil shale will be used as the basis for chemicals, and electricity generated in large breeder or fusion reactors will be used for such purposes as the manufacture of ammonia and methane, the reduction of ores and the production of fertilizers.

It is difficult at this stage to predict the effects of large-scale use of nuclear

energy on the biosphere. One must make certain assumptions about the disposal of radioactive wastes. A reasonable assumption is that they will be rendered harmless by techniques whereby long-lived radioactive isotopes are made into solids and buried. (They are potentially dangerous now because of the technique of storing them as liquids in underground tanks.) Short-lived radioactive wastes can presumably be stored safely until they decay.

For both nuclear energy and for processes involving fossil fuels the major problem and the major impact of human energy production is the dissipation of waste heat. The heat has direct effects on the biosphere and could have indirect effects on climate. It is useful to distinguish between local problems of thermal pollution, meaning the problems that arise in the immediate vicinity of a power plant, and the global problem of thermal balance created by the transformation of steadily rising amounts of energy.

The efficiency of a power plant is determined by the laws of thermodynamics. No matter what the fuel is, one tries to create high-temperature steam for driving the turbines and to condense the steam at the lowest possible temperature. Water is the only practical medium for carrying the heat away. Hence more than 80 percent of the cooling water used by U.S. industry is accounted for by electric power plants. For every kilowatt-hour of energy produced about 6,000 B.T.U. in heat must be dissipated from a fossil fuel plant and about 10,000 B.T.U. from a contemporary nuclear plant.

In the U.S., where the consumption of power has been doubling every eight to 10 years, the increase in the number and size of electric power plants is putting a severe strain on the supply of cooling water. By 1980 about half of the normal runoff of fresh water will be needed for this purpose. Even though some 95 percent of the water thus used is returned to the stream, it is not the same: its increased temperature has a number of harmful effects. Higher temperatures decrease the amount of dissolved oxygen and therefore the capacity of the stream to assimilate organic wastes. Bacterial decomposition is accelerated, further depressing the oxygen level. The reduction of oxygen decreases the viability of aquatic organisms while at the same time the higher temperature raises their metabolic rate and therefore their need for oxygen.

center, identifiable by a distinctly warm effluent entering the river, is a power plant. Group of hot buildings at right is a steel mill. Cool land area at the bottom is part of Grosse Ile.

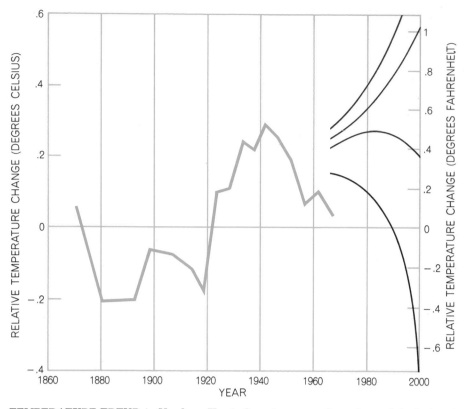

TEMPERATURE TREND in Northern Hemisphere is portrayed as observed (*color*) and as predicted under various conditions (*black*). The top black curve assumes an effect from carbon dioxide only; the other black curves also take account of dust. Second and third curves assume doubling of atmospheric dust in 20 and 10 years respectively; bottom curve, doubling in 10 years with twice the thermal effect thought most probable. Chart is based on work of J. Murray Mitchell, Jr., of the Environmental Science Services Administration.

In the face of stringent requirements being laid down by the states and the Department of the Interior, power companies are installing devices that cool water before it is returned to the stream. The devices include cooling ponds, spray ponds and cooling towers. They function by evaporating some of the cooling water, so that the excess heat is dissipated into the atmosphere rather than into the stream.

This strategy of spreading waste heat

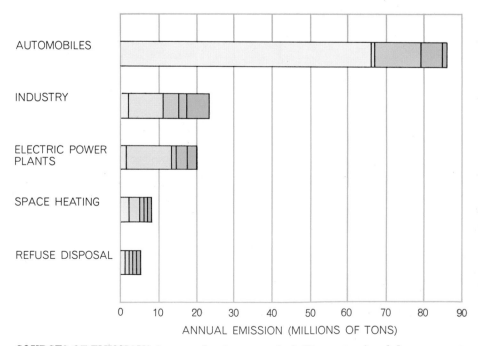

SOURCES OF EMISSIONS from combustion are ranked. Five parts of each bar represent (*from left*) carbon monoxide, sulfur oxides, hydrocarbons, nitrogen oxides and particles.

has to be reexamined as the scale of the problem increases. It is already apparent that the "heat islands" characteristic of metropolitan areas have definite meteorological effects—not necessarily all bad. The fact that a city is warmer than the surrounding countryside affects the ecology and biospheric activity in metropolitan areas in numerous ways. For example, the release of heat in a relatively small local area causes a change in the convective pattern of the atmosphere. The addition of large amounts of particulate matter from industry, space heating and refuse disposal provides nuclei for the condensation of clouds. A study in the state of Washington showed an increase of approximately 30 percent in average precipitation over long periods of time as a result of air pollution from pulp and paper mills.

The worldwide consumption of energy can be estimated from the fact that the U.S. accounts for about a third of this consumption. The U.S. consumption of 685,000 million million B.T.U. per year is equivalent to 2.2 million megawatts. World consumption is therefore some 6.6 million megawatts. Put another way, the present situation is that the per capita consumption of energy in the U.S. of 10,000 watts compares with somewhat more than 100 watts (barely above the food-intake level) in most of the rest of the world.

Projections for the future depend on the assumptions made. If one assumes that in 50 years the rest of the world will reach the present U.S. level of energy consumption and that the population will be 10 billion, the total manmade energy would be 110 million megawatts per year. The energy would of course be distributed in a patchy manner reflecting the location of population centers and the distributing effects of the atmosphere and the oceans.

That figure is numerically small compared with the amount of solar energy the earth radiates back into space. Over the entire earth the annual heat loss is about 120,000 million megawatts, or more than 1,000 times the energy that would be dissipated by human activity if the level of energy consumption projected for 2020 were reached. It would be incautious to assume, however, that the heat put into the biosphere as a result of human energy consumption can be neglected because it is so much smaller than the solar input. The atmospheric engine is subtle in its operation and delicate in its adjustments. Extra inputs of energy in particular places can have significant and far-reaching consequences.

XI

Human Materials Production as a Process in the Biosphere

Human Materials Production as a Process in the Biosphere

by HARRISON BROWN

Materials such as metals and concrete are not renewable.
Man's problem is to devise cycles that will conserve
resources of this kind and at the same time
prevent their accumulation as solid waste

The materials used by man for tools, shelter and clothing have traditionally been both organic (for example wood and natural fiber) and inorganic (stone, including glass and ceramics, and metals). To this classification we now add synthetic materials, which are mostly made from what are called in another connection fossil fuels. The organic materials are of course products of the biosphere, and assuming appropriate levels of use and sensible management they are self-renewing. The inorganic materials are the product of extremely slow processes in the lithosphere, and are hence not self-renewing in the human scheme of things. Yet the increasing need for such materials—mainly metals, stone and concrete—is one of the outstanding features of advancing societies. Moreover, the fact that inorganic materials are for the most part not recycled creates a pressing need for their disposal. These demands present men with numerous difficult choices, many of which inevitably involve the functioning of the biosphere.

For the greater part of the two million years or so of human existence man's need for materials was modest. With the adoption of each technological innovation that improved the chances of human survival, however, the need for materials increased in both absolute and per capita terms. For example, the controlled use of fire, which increased the variety of things that could be eaten and extended man's environment, created a substantial demand for firewood. Here, of course, a material was being used as fuel, but the development of tools that improved the efficiency of hunting and food gathering and protected men against predators created demands for materials in the strict sense: the right kinds of stone or of plant or animal substance.

With the invention of agriculture the need for materials increased considerably. The new technology made it possible for thousands of people to be supported by the produce of land that formerly could support only one person. Moreover, it was no longer necessary for everyone to be involved in food production. Farmers were able to grow a surplus of food to support nonfarmers. Until relatively recent times this surplus was never large, amounting to perhaps 5 percent, but it meant that some people could devote their energies to occupations other than farming. It was the surplus of food that made possible the emergence of cities and the evolution of the great civilizations of antiquity.

The oldest civilizations came into existence in regions that had ample areas of arable land and adequate supplies of water. Cities could become large only if they could draw on the agricultural surpluses of vast farmlands. Since water transport was by far the easiest way to ship foodstuffs in ancient times, the earliest civilizations and the first large cities came into being in the valleys of the great rivers such as the Tigris and the Euphrates, the Nile, the Indus and the Yellow River. With the emergence of major urban centers increasingly elaborate technologies were developed, and they in turn led to the need for larger per capita quantities of raw materials such as stone, wood, clay, fiber and skin. (The ancient urban centers also confronted a problem that continues today: the disposal of garbage and rubbish. Scavenger birds, such as the kites of modern Calcutta, were probably essential elements in the system of processing garbage, but even so life must have been unsanitary, unsightly and odoriferous, at least for the great masses of the poor. The evidence suggests the prevalence of high mortality rates. Many ancient cities appear to have been literally buried in their own rubbish.)

Until the development of metal technology men appear to have used renewable resources such as wood at rates that were small compared with the rates of renewal. The consumption of nonrenewable resources such as stone was also small, particularly in comparison with the nearly infinite availability of resources with respect to the demand.

Copper was the first metal to come into widespread use on a substantial scale. In actuality copper is not very abundant in the lithosphere, but the metal can be won easily from its ore. The reduction temperature is fairly low, so that smelting can be accomplished in a simple furnace. Once the technology of extracting copper was developed the use of the metal became widespread in the ancient civilizations and the demand for the ore grew rapidly.

COPPER IS MINED at the Twin Buttes mine of the Anaconda Company near Tucson. The conspicuous hole in the photograph on the opposite page was made by removing some 236 million tons of overburden and rock to get at the ore lying between 600 and 800 feet below the surface of the ground. The ore has a copper content of about .5 percent and is considered to be a low-grade ore. Since copper is not highly abundant in the lithosphere but is extensively used, the trend has been toward mining low-grade ores.

In this situation the high-grade deposits of ore close to the ancient urban centers were soon used up. Egypt, for example, quickly depleted her own copper reserves and had to develop an elaborate network of trade routes that enabled her to import copper from as far away as the British Isles and Scandinavia. Even so, high-grade ores of copper were uncommon enough to preclude widespread use of the metal. Copper did make possible a number of new technologies, but farmers, who were by far the greater proportion of society, were almost unaffected. Their implements continued to be made of stone, clay, wood and leather.

Gold is considerably easier to extract from its ore than copper; often the "ore" is metallic gold itself. As one might expect, therefore, the use of gold appears to predate the use of copper by a considerable span of time. Gold, however, is one of the rarest metals in nature, so that its ores are extremely scarce. Its rarity precluded its widespread use, except in small quantities for ornament.

Iron is considerably more abundant in the lithosphere than copper, but it is a much more difficult metal to win from the ore. The reduction temperature is high, and furnaces capable of attaining it were not developed until about 1100 B.C. The new high-temperature technology appeared first in the Middle East and quickly spread westward. The widespread availability of the ore made it possible for metal to be used on an unprecedented scale. New tools of iron helped to transform Europe from a land of dense forests to a fertile cropland.

One of the primary limitations to economic development in the ancient empires was the lack of ability to concentrate large quantities of energy. Insofar as it could be done at all it was usually accomplished by mobilizing gangs of men and to a lesser extent by the use of work animals. Use of the water mill and the windmill spread slowly. Only in sea transport was the wind used even with moderate effectiveness on a large scale as a prime mover. Remarkable as the Roman engineers were, they were limited by the concentration of energy they could mobilize. They went about as far as engineers could in the absence of a steam engine.

The development of a practical steam engine had to await the convergence of a series of developments in England in the late 17th century and the early 18th century. The island entered the Iron Age richly endowed with iron ore. For-

ests were also abundant, and the trees were used to produce charcoal, which in turn was used to reduce the iron oxide to the metal. These resources enabled England to become a major supplier of metallic iron for the world.

As iron production expanded English trees were consumed faster than they grew. Eventually the depletion of wood for charcoal threatened the entire iron industry. Clearly a substitute for charcoal was needed. The most likely one was coal, which existed abundantly on the island. Unfortunately, although coal can be used to reduce iron ore to the metal, the impurities in it render the metallurgical properties of the iron quite unsatisfactory.

The Darby family, which owned a substantial iron industry, spent many years attempting to transform coal into a substance suitable for the reduction of iron. Eventually a successful process was developed. It was based on the discovery that volatile impurities could be driven off by heating coal under suitable conditions. The resulting product, called coke, yielded metallic iron of satisfactory quality.

Here was a development—the linking of coal to iron—second only to agriculture in its importance to man. The new development led to a rapid expansion of the iron industry. Even more significant, it led directly to the development of the steam engine, which gave man for the first time a means of concentrating enormous quantities of inanimate energy.

Coal, iron and the steam engine gave rise to the Industrial Revolution, which spread from England to Europe and then to the U.S., the U.S.S.R. and most recently to Japan. Why did it start in the 18th century in England and not several centuries earlier in Rome? The Romans in many ways were the better engineers, and yet the harnessing of steam eluded them.

It is interesting to speculate on the role that random natural processes have played in cultural evolution. What would the course of history have been if copper had been as abundant as iron or if iron could be reduced from its ore as easily as copper? Perhaps the Iron Age would have started in the third millennium B.C. Suppose the Roman iron industry had run out of wood in the second century. Would there have been a linking of coal to iron and would the steam engine have emerged some 1,500 years earlier than it did? Such questions are diverting, but they cannot be answered with anything better than guesses.

The most important characteristics of

BLAST FURNACE for smelting iron in the 18th century was depicted in Diderot's *Encyclopédie*. The reason for the furnace's lo-

Fig . 1.

Fig . 4 .

Fig . 5

Fig 2

Fig . 3 .

cation near a wooded area was the need for charcoal, which is what the horses in the background are carrying. In England the consumption of charcoal virtually exhausted the supply of trees before the technique of making coke from coal was developed. A furnace of this type might produce some two tons of iron a day. In the foreground a freshly produced pig, No. 289, is being weighed.

120

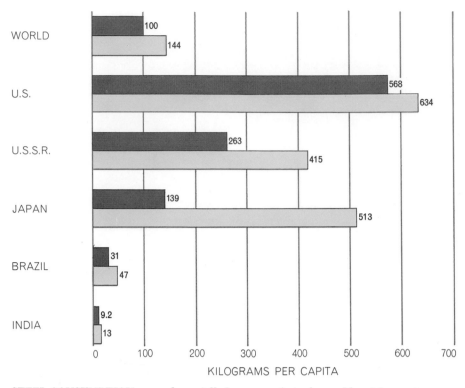

STEEL CONSUMPTION rose substantially but unevenly in the world and five major countries between 1957 (*gray*) and 1967 (*color*). The units are kilograms per person per year.

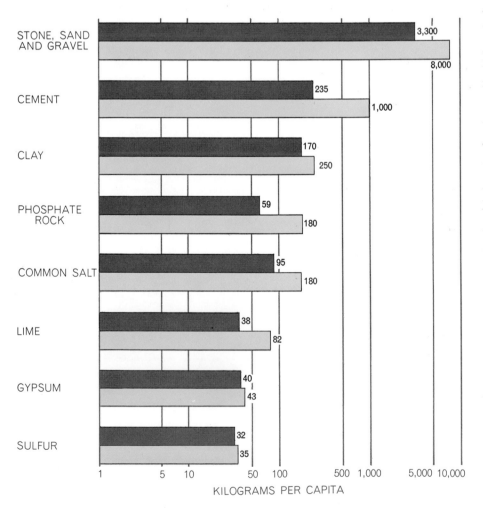

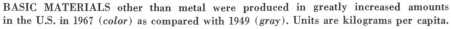

BASIC MATERIALS other than metal were produced in greatly increased amounts in the U.S. in 1967 (*color*) as compared with 1949 (*gray*). Units are kilograms per capita.

the Industrial Revolution have been rapid change and rapid increases in rates of change. Since the beginnings of the epoch mankind has seen the emergence of almost innumerable technological innovations that have competed with existing ways of doing things and have further released men from physical labor. It is now generally recognized that technological innovation has been a prime contributing factor to economic growth, perhaps equaling the combined effect of the classical factors of land, labor and capital.

Successful innovations have driven many older technologies to extinction and have resulted in higher productivity, greater consumption of energy, increased demand for raw materials, accelerated flow of materials through the economy and increased quantities of metals and other substances in use per capita. The history of industrial development abounds with examples.

In 1870 horses and mules were the prime source of power on U.S. farms. One horse or mule was required to support four human beings—a ratio that remained almost constant for many decades. Had a national commission been asked at that time to forecast the horse and mule population in 1970, its answer probably would have depended on whether its consultants were of an economic or a technological turn of mind. Had they been "economists," they would in all likelihood have estimated the 1970 horse and mule population at more than 50 million. Had they been "technologists," they would have recognized that steam had already been harnessed to industry and to ground and ocean transport. They would have recognized further that it would be only a matter of time before steam would be the prime source of power on the farm. It would have been difficult for them to avoid the conclusion that the horse and mule population would decline rapidly.

In fact, steam power appeared on the farm in about 1875 and spread rapidly. Had it not been for the introduction of the internal-combustion engine shortly after the turn of the century, steam power alone would have driven the horse off the farm. The internal-combustion engine, which was unforeseen in 1875, succeeded in driving off both the horse and the steam combine. Today the horse population is little more than 1.5 million, and most of the horses cannot in any real sense be regarded as work animals.

A second example of technological competition was the introduction of the steam-powered iron ship. In a period of only 30 years (1870 to 1900) the composition of the United Kingdom's merchant marine was transformed from 90 percent wooden sailing ships to 90 percent iron ships powered by steam. This technological transformation resulted in a greatly enhanced ability to transport goods rapidly and inexpensively over long distances. It also resulted in a greatly increased demand for iron and coal.

In the modes of intercity transportation in the U.S. one can see a dramatic sequence of competitions. In the first years of this century nearly all passenger traffic between cities was carried by the railroads. By 1910 the private car was competing seriously, and by 1920 the automobile was accounting for more passenger-miles between cities than the railroads were. Since World War II the airplane has competed with both the railroad and the automobile for intercity traffic. The combined impact of the automobile and the airplane has come close to putting railroads out of the passenger business. In the decade of the 1970's the airplane will probably make serious inroads on intercity automobile traffic as well. The net result of these changes, as with others, has been increased expenditure of energy and increased demand for materials in both absolute and per capita terms.

Levels of steel production and consumption are among the most useful indicators of worldwide technological and economic change. In the 19th century England became the dominant producer and consumer of steel, later being replaced by Germany. After World War I the U.S. became the largest industrial power, and steel production rose rapidly. In 1900 per capita steel production in the U.S. reached 140 kilograms, and by 1910 it was up to 300 kilograms. The level exceeded 400 kilograms during World War I, and during World War II it rose to 600 kilograms. Since World War II the picture has changed: although total steel production has continued to rise, the annual per capita level has changed little, averaging about 550 kilograms.

Per capita steel consumption has risen since World War II, but the rise has been slow. The difference between production and consumption has been made up by an increase in imports. In 1967 U.S. steel consumption was 634 kilograms per capita.

Although this is at present the highest per capita level of steel consumption in the world, the U.S. is being overtaken rapidly by other countries. Levels of consumption in much of western Europe and in Japan, Czechoslovakia, East Germany, the U.S.S.R. and Australia are now close to the U.S. level, and the rates of growth are such that Japan will overtake the U.S. quite soon. The per capita level of steel consumption in the U.S.S.R. will probably equal that of the U.S. within another decade. The worldwide rate of increase in per capita steel consumption from 1957 to 1967 was 44 percent, compared with the U.S. rate of 12 percent and the Japanese rate of 270 percent [*see top illustration on page 120*]. In view of the fact that virtually all elements of economic growth correlate reasonably well with per capita steel consumption, it is useful to inquire into the future levels of consumption in the U.S. and the rest of the world.

Consumption of metals other than iron can conveniently be stated in terms of steel consumption. When this is done, it becomes apparent that the consumption levels of certain metals, such as copper, zinc and lead, have remained remarkably constant over the past 50 years in spite of rapidly changing technologies. Consumption of certain other metals, such as tin, has been decreasing with respect to steel as a result of decreasing availability of ore and the development of substitutes. Consumption levels of the light metals, such as aluminum, are rising. Although these metals are still much less used than steel is, they will increasingly supplant steel for certain purposes.

If all the metallic iron that has been produced in the U.S. were still in ex-

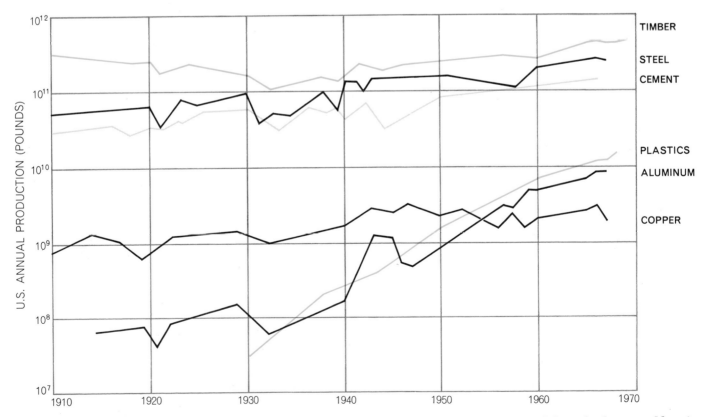

TREND IN CONSUMPTION of key materials is traced. The production of timber is usually reckoned in terms of board feet or cubic feet. For purposes of comparability it has been stated here in pounds, assuming an average density of 35 pounds per cubic foot.

istence, there would now be in use some 15 tons of steel per capita. In actuality a great deal of the steel produced has disappeared as a result of junking, production losses, corrosion and other causes. Analysis of production figures and losses suggests that the amount of steel now in use is some 9.4 metric tons of steel per capita. The greater part of it is in the form of structural materials such as heavy structural shapes and pilings, nails and staples, galvanized sheet metal and wire fence. About 8 percent of the steel, or 750 kilograms per person, is in the form of private automobiles, trucks and buses.

Of the roughly 600 kilograms of new steel consumed annually per capita in the U.S. about a third is returned to the furnaces as plant scrap, which is created as a result of the production of standard shapes and forms such as beams, sheet, pipe and wire. Therefore about 410 kilograms of the new steel enters the inventory of steel in use. At the same time about 350 kilograms of steel becomes obsolete or is lost as a result of corrosion and other processes. Of this some 140 kilograms (about 40 percent) is recovered and returned to the steel furnaces in the form of junked automobiles and other worn-out iron and steel products. The balance, corresponding to some 210 kilograms, is lost, probably never to be recovered. Some of it is dissipated widely; much of it is buried in dumps. During the course of the year the steel inventory increases by about 80 kilograms per capita, or somewhat less than 1 percent.

The mean lifetime of steel products varies enormously. Whereas an item such as a can may be in use for only a few weeks or months, steel in motor vehicles is in use on the average for about 10 years. Steel in ships may be in use for about 25 years. Steel structural shapes such as girders and concrete reinforcement may be in use for 50 years or more. The mean lifetime of all steel in use appears to be some 25 to 30 years.

Similar considerations apply to other metals. They are extracted, introduced into the national inventory and eventually lost or recycled as scrap. The mean lifetime of most of them appears to be shorter than that of steel.

Although the quantities of metal in use and the volumes of metalliferous ore that must be dug up and processed to support a human being in our society are large, the quantities of nonmetals consumed each year loom even larger and are increasing extremely rapidly [see bottom illustration on page 120].

Between 1949 and 1967 the per capita consumption of stone, sand and gravel in the U.S. rose some 2.5 times to about eight tons per capita. For cement the rise was by a factor of four to one ton per capita. In the same period the per capita consumption of phosphate rock rose by a factor of three and that of ordinary salt by a factor of two. All together, in order to support one individual in our society, something like 25 tons of materials of all kinds must be extracted from the earth and processed each year. This quantity seems certain to increase considerably in the years ahead.

The use of synthetic plastics is now increasing with impressive speed. Total world production of these materials now exceeds in both volume and weight the production of copper and aluminum combined. The production of synthetic fibers is now about half the combined production of cotton and wool. The relative rates of growth suggest that the output of such fibers will exceed that of cotton and wool within a short time.

Between 1945 and 1965 the price of polyethylene dropped by about 75 percent while the price of steel tripled. Already polyethylene is less expensive than steel on a volume basis, although per unit of strength it remains some 15 times more expensive than steel. It is quite possible, however, that before long fiber-glass laminates will compete seriously with steel for structural purposes.

The overall figures suggest that the U.S. now has in use for every person about 150 kilograms each of copper and lead, well over 100 kilograms of aluminum, some 100 kilograms of zinc and perhaps 20 kilograms of tin. To meet the need for raw materials and the products derived from them the nation transports almost 15,000 ton-kilometers of freight per capita per year. Each person travels on the average each year some 8,500 kilometers between cities, makes more than 700 telephone calls and receives nearly 400 pieces of mail. There is now a ratio of almost one private automobile for every two people. In order to accomplish all the mining, production and distribution the American people spend energy at a rate equivalent to the burning

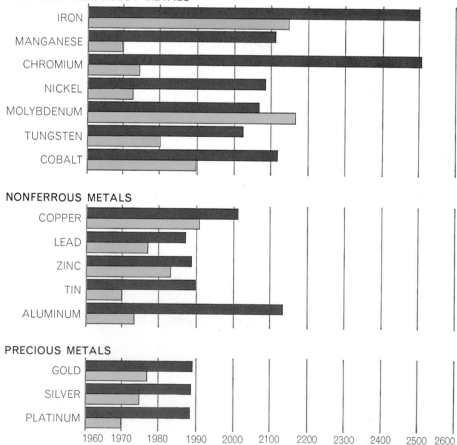

LIFETIMES OF METAL RESERVES are indicated for the world (gray) and the U.S. (color). These rough estimates are based on the assumption that the utilization of metals will continue to increase with population growth and rising per capita demand. They take into account, however, that new reserves will be discovered by exploration or created by innovation. It is estimated U.S. demands will increase four and a half times by the year 2000.

of about 10 tons of coal annually per person or about 16 tons of coal per ton of steel consumed or about one ton of coal per ton of steel in use. A convenient rule of thumb is that we must burn about one ton of coal each year, or its equivalent in some other source of energy, to keep one ton of steel in use.

Clearly man has become a major geologic force. The amount of rock and earth he moves each year in the present industrialized regions of the world is already prodigious and will continue to grow because of rising population levels, increasing demand from the industrialized nations and the gradual decline in grades of raw materials. If one adds to these requirements the fantastically high demand that would arise if the development process were to be accelerated in the poor countries, the total potential demand staggers the imagination. If the entire human population were to possess the average per capita level of metal characteristic of the 10 richest nations, all the present mines and factories in the world would have to be operated for more than 60 years just to produce the capital, assuming no losses.

Given an eventual world population of 10 billion, which is probably a conservative estimate, and a per capita steel inventory of 20 tons, some 200 billion tons of iron would have to be extracted from the earth. The task would require 400 years at current rates of extraction. Anything approaching such a demand would clearly place enormous strains on the earth's resources and would greatly accentuate rivalries between nations for

the earth's remaining deposits of relatively high-grade ores. Most of the industrialized nations already import a substantial fraction of their raw materials. Japan is almost completely dependent on imports. Whereas the U.S. imported in 1950 only 8 percent of the iron ore that it consumed, the figure today is more than 35 percent.

At present the world can be divided into two major groups of steel consumers. The first group consists of about 680 million people, living in 18 nations, who consume steel at rates varying between 300 and 700 kilograms annually per capita. The total consumption of this group comes to about 420 million tons of steel per year. The second group consists of 1,400 million people, living in 13 nations, who consume steel at rates varying between 10 and 25 kilograms annually per capita. The total consumption of this group comes to 27 million tons of steel per year. An additional 400 million people live under circumstances that are still poorer, and 440 million more live under circumstances intermediate between those of the rich and the poor. The distribution of per capita energy consumption follows a similar pattern, as does the distribution of per capita income.

The slowness of the development process and the magnitude of the task the poor countries face can be gauged by the fact that with existing production facilities the poorer group (not the poorest one) would need about 500 years to produce the per capita quantity of steel in use now characteristic of the

U.S. Although production levels in the poorer group are increasing fairly rapidly (close to 50 percent per decade on a per capita basis), many decades will be required, even in the absence of any major upheaval, before the amounts of steel in use can enable those nations to feed, clothe and house their populations adequately.

What goes into a system must eventually come out. As I have noted, somewhat less than 4 percent of the steel inventory in the U.S. is exuded annually into the environment, and only about 40 percent of this amount is recovered. As the grades of resources dwindle and locations for dumping solid wastes become more difficult to find, the economic and social pressure for more substitution, more attention to priorities of use of scarce materials and more efficient cycling will increase.

It is clear that various metals can substitute for one another, and that plastics can substitute for a number of metals. Aluminum already substitutes for copper in many roles, as copper and nickel now replace silver in coinage. Synthetic crystals come increasingly into use. All these techniques can be pushed a good deal farther than they have been up to now.

Improved efficiency of cycling is desirable for all solid wastes not only to lower the rate of depletion of high-grade resources but also to reduce the injurious effects of such wastes on the biosphere. The quantities of wastes are becoming substantial. They now amount to nearly one ton per year per person, of which

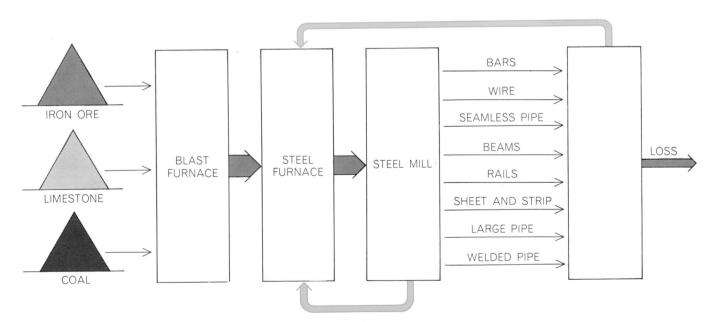

FLOW OF MATERIALS through the biosphere is depicted using steel as an example. Of the steel produced from iron ore, about a third is recycled immediately in the form of scrap left over from the production of beams, wire and other shapes. Two-thirds enters the national inventory. During each year, however, a somewhat smaller amount of steel becomes obsolete. About 40 percent of it is recycled in the form of scrap. The remainder is lost as a result of such factors as wear, corrosion and disposal through junking.

about a third consists of packaging materials. In 1968, for example, the average American threw away almost 300 cans, 150 bottles and about 140 kilograms of paper. The quantities are increasing rapidly on both an absolute and a per capita basis. Properly cycled, they could provide raw materials for the glass, steel, aluminum and plastics industries.

From a purely technological point of view man could in principle live comfortably on a combination of his own trash and the leanest of earth substances. Already, for example, copper ore containing only .4 percent copper is being processed. If the need arose, copper could be extracted from ore that is considerably leaner than .4 percent. Eventually man could, if need be, extract his metals from ordinary rock. A ton of granite contains easily extractable uranium and thorium equivalent to about 15 tons of coal, plus all the elements necessary to perpetuate a highly technological civilization. Such a way of life would create new problems, because under those circumstances man would become a geologic force transcending by orders of magnitude his present effect on the earth. Per capita energy consumption would come to the equivalent of perhaps 100 tons of coal per year, and there might be some 100 tons of steel in use per person. The world would be quite different from the present one, but there is no reason a priori why it would necessarily be unpleasant.

Man has it in his power technologically to maintain a high level of industrial civilization, to eliminate deprivation and hunger and to control his environment for many millenniums. His main danger is that he will not learn enough quickly enough and that he will not take adequate measures in time to forestall situations that will be very unpleasant indeed.

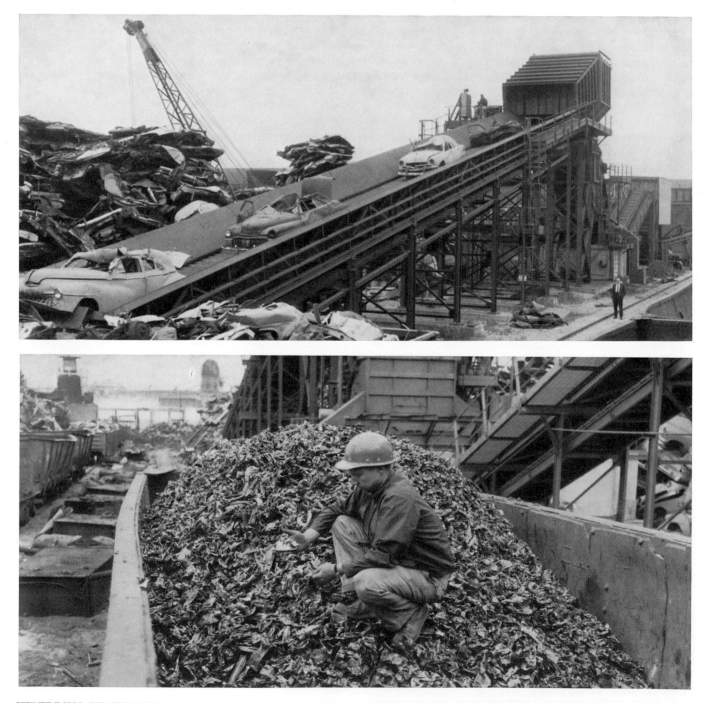

SHREDDING TECHNIQUE was recently developed for turning worn-out or wrecked automobiles into scrap that can be recycled to steel furnaces. At top stripped automobile bodies are being fed into the shredder; the product that emerges is shown at bottom.

Index